LESSONS FOR
INTRODUCING
MULTIPLICATION

GRADE 3

THE TEACHING ARITHMETIC SERIES

Fall 2001

Lessons for First Grade
Lessons for Addition and Subtraction, Grades 2–3
Lessons for Introducing Multiplication, Grade 3
Lessons for Extending Multiplication, Grades 4–5
Lessons for Introducing Fractions, Grades 4–5

Fall 2002

Lessons for Place Value, Grades 1–2
Lessons for Introducing Division, Grades 3–4
Lessons for Decimals and Percents, Grades 5–6

Fall 2003

Lessons for Extending Division, Grades 4–5
Lessons for Extending Fractions, Grades 5–6

Teaching
ARITHMETIC

LESSONS FOR
INTRODUCING
MULTIPLICATION

▲▲▲▲▲

GRADE 3

MARILYN BURNS

MATH SOLUTIONS PUBLICATIONS
SAUSALITO, CA

Math Solutions Publications
A division of
Marilyn Burns Education Associates
150 Gate 5 Road, Suite 101
Sausalito, CA 94965
www.mathsolutions.com

Library of Congress Cataloging-in-Publication Data
Burns, Marilyn, 1941–
    Lessons for introducing multiplication : grade 3 / Marilyn Burns.
        p. cm. — (Teaching arithmetic)
Includes index.
    ISBN 0-941355-41-1 (alk. paper)
 1. Multiplication—Study and teaching (Primary) I. Title. II. Series.
    QA115 .B955 2001
      372.7'2—dc21
                                             2001003872

Editor: Toby Gordon
Production: Melissa L. Inglis
Cover & interior design: Leslie Bauman
Composition: Argosy Publishing

Printed in the United States of America on acid-free paper
05 04 03 02 01   ML   1 2 3 4 5

A Message from Marilyn Burns

We at Marilyn Burns Education Associates believe that teaching mathematics well calls for continually reflecting on and improving one's instructional practice. Our Math Solutions Publications include a wide range of choices, from books in our new Teaching Arithmetic series—which address beginning number concepts, place value, addition, subtraction, multiplication, division, fractions, decimals, and percents—to resources that help link math with writing and literature; from books that help teachers more deeply understand the mathematics behind the math they teach to children's books that help students develop an appreciation for math while learning basic concepts.

Along with our large collection of teacher resource books, we have a more general collection of books, videotapes, and audiotapes that can help teachers and parents bridge the gap between home and school. All of our materials are available at education stores, from distributors, and through major teacher catalogs.

In addition, Math Solutions Inservice offers five-day courses and one-day workshops throughout the country. We also work in partnership with school districts to help implement and sustain long-term improvement in mathematics instruction in all classrooms.

To find a complete listing of our publications and workshops, please visit our Web site at *www.mathsolutions.com*. Or contact us by calling (800) 868-9092 or sending an e-mail to *info@mathsolutions.com*.

We're eager for your feedback and interested in learning about your particular needs. We look forward to hearing from you.

A DIVISION OF MARILYN BURNS EDUCATION ASSOCIATES

CONTENTS

ACKNOWLEDGMENTS

I am deeply appreciative to Dee Uyeda, third-grade teacher at Park School in Mill Valley, California, for making her class available to me, for learning with me how to teach her students better, and for sharing in the excitement of the children's learning.

INTRODUCTION

For more than a dozen years, I've explored ways to teach multiplication so that children develop the understanding and skills they need. In 1991, I wrote *Math By All Means: Multiplication, Grade 3,* a unit of instruction for introducing multiplication to third graders that has been used by more than eighty-five thousand teachers. Since then, I've tried new lessons in many classrooms, pored over a great deal of student work, and had many conversations with other teachers. It's been a joy to teach classes and watch learning occur, understanding blossom, and skills develop. While many of the lessons I still teach are from the book I wrote in 1991, I've incorporated many new lessons into my repertoire and have made changes and adjustments to many of my old favorites. This book replaces the original unit. It is a result of what I've learned since writing the original unit, offering a collection of multiplication lessons that will enhance any third-grade mathematics program.

The original book began with a description of a conversation I had with a class of third graders on January 2, the first day back in school after the holiday, when I was about to begin instruction on multiplication. "What do you know about multiplication?" I asked the children.

Several hands went up. I waited, giving more children a chance to collect their thoughts, and then called on Rebecca. "It's times," she said.

I nodded and called on Roberto. "It has an X," he said.

I called on Tanya next. "I think it's kind of like addition, but different," she said.

"How is multiplication like addition?" I asked. Tanya thought for a moment and then shrugged.

I called on Alex. "You can do it for hard problems," he said. "My sister does multiplication." Alex's sister was in the sixth grade.

Josh offered different information. "You get big answers," he said. "Multiplication makes numbers get big faster." Josh was numerically comfortable and adept.

Maria was tentative but wanted to give her idea. "Sometimes you have to carry, I think," she said.

Emily had another perspective. "You have to learn times tables," she said, "and then you know it."

"Oh, yeah," Kristina added, "some are easy to say, like the fives, and some are hard, like the sevens, because they're not regular."

Michael gave an example. "Maybe you were going shopping and you said to yourself, I'm only going to get fifteen things, so you get five things three times, so you multiply to get the answer."

The children's responses gave me some information about the range of their previous experiences with multiplication and their current knowledge about it. I've had similar conversations with many classes of third graders since then, and while children's specific responses have differed, the essence of the discussions has been remarkably similar. In all classes, some of the students already have begun to grasp the meaning and the use of multiplication. Others have disconnected bits of information. And typically, about half of the children in third-grade classes either don't have any ideas to share or don't feel comfortable offering them.

Goals for Multiplication Instruction

Multiplication is a major focus of third-grade mathematics instruction. Instruction continues in the fourth and fifth grades, but third grade is key for establishing a firm foundation of understanding and skills. At the end of third grade, students should be able to

▲ explain how multiplication relates to repeated addition;

▲ explain how multiplication relates to rectangular arrays;

▲ interpret multiplication in real-world situations;

▲ calculate products up to 12 × 12;

▲ solve problems that involve multiplication.

Traditionally, instruction in multiplication has focused on two objectives: learning the multiplication facts and developing computational facility. After memorizing the times tables, children often focus on learning procedures for multiplying with paper and pencil, first practicing with one-digit multipliers and then progressing through the grades to two-digit and three-digit multipliers.

Knowing the multiplication tables and being able to compute efficiently are important goals, but a broader view of multiplication instruction is essential. Equally important goals for students include learning what multiplication is, how multiplication relates to addition, and how multiplication can be interpreted geometrically. Students should learn to make reasonable estimates for multiplication problems and develop strategies for computing mentally as well as with paper and pencil. The lessons in this book address these broader goals and are aimed at building a strong foundation of multiplication understanding. Further instruction is needed beyond the lessons in this book, and the companion resource in this series, *Extending Multiplication,* provides instructional ideas for students in the fourth and fifth grades.

What's in This Book?

Over the ten years since I wrote the initial unit, I've learned a good deal more about teaching multiplication to third graders, both from my own teaching experience and from feedback from teachers who have been using the unit in their classes. The changes in this book reflect what I've learned.

The book includes practically all of the lessons and assessments from the initial unit, some reorganized and others with additions and edits. Five completely new lessons are included in this book, and five of the seven lessons in the Additional Activities section are also new. In addition, four children's books, none of which appeared in the earlier book, are incorporated into lessons here.

The Structure of the Lessons

In order to help you with planning and teaching the lessons in this book, each is organized into the following sections:

Overview   To help you decide if the lesson is appropriate for your students, this is a nutshell description of the mathematical goal of the lesson and what the students will be doing.

Materials   This section lists the special materials needed along with quantities. Not included in the list are regular classroom supplies such as pencils and paper. Worksheets that need to be duplicated are included in the Blackline Masters section at the back of the book.

Time   Generally, the number of class periods is provided, sometimes with a range allowing for different-length periods. It is also indicated for some activities that they are meant to be repeated from time to time.

Teaching Directions   The directions are presented in a step-by-step lesson plan.

Teaching Notes   This section addresses the mathematics underlying the lesson and at times provides information about the prior experiences or knowledge students need.

The Lesson   This is a vignette that describes what actually occurred when the lesson was taught to one or more classes. While the vignette mirrors the plan described in the teaching directions, it elaborates with details that are valuable for preparing and teaching the lesson. Samples of student work are included.

Extensions   This section is included for some of the lessons and offers follow-up suggestions.

Questions and Discussion   Presented in a question-and-answer format, this section addresses issues that came up during the lesson and/or have been posed by other teachers.

While organized similarly, the lessons here vary in several ways. Some span one class period, others take longer, and some are suitable to repeat over and over, giving students a chance to revisit ideas and extend their learning. Some use manipulative materials, others ask students to draw pictures, and others ask students to rely on reasoning mentally. And while some lessons seem to be more suited for beginning experiences, at times it's beneficial for more experienced students to engage with them as well. An activity that seems simple can reinforce students' understanding or give them a fresh way to look at a familiar concept. Also, a lesson that initially seems too difficult or advanced can be ideal for introducing students to thinking in a new way.

About Representing Multiplication Symbolically

It's important for students to learn to use the standard symbolism for multiplication. However, there isn't a definitive consensus in the mathematical community about interpreting a multiplication fact such as 4×3. One valid interpretation is that 4×3 represents "four groups of three" or "four threes." Another interpretation, equally valid, is that 4×3 represents "four three times." Using addition, the first interpretation can be represented as $3 + 3 + 3 + 3$ and the second as $4 + 4 + 4$. Since multiplication is commutative, and both interpretations produce the same correct answer, arguing for one way over the other is a debate of mathematical semantics. When you think about 4×3 abstractly, out of any context, preferring one convention over the other is an arbitrary choice. Your instructional program, however, may choose one interpretation over the other when presenting multiplication to children. I've seen both used.

That said, in this book, I've chosen to use the first interpretation. It seems natural to refer to the $\times$ sign as "groups of," and it seems to help emphasize the important idea that combining equal groups is essential to multiplication. However, most of the multiplication experiences presented in this book are contextual. When dealing with multiplication in contexts, what's important is that children can both represent situations symbolically and, no matter which way they order the factors, explain how the symbolism relates to the situation at hand. It's also important for children to learn about the commutativity of multiplication and to develop multiple strategies for computing.

When students interpret multiplication geometrically as rectangular arrays, I don't make any particular demand in these lessons about how the order of the factors should relate to the orientation of the rectangle. There isn't a general consensus in the mathematical community about which way to order the factors for a 3-by-4 array, for example, if it's oriented horizontally or vertically. What's important in these instances is that children can describe how the symbolic representation they choose relates to the geometric representation of the rectangle. A 3-by-4 array oriented vertically can be looked at as four rows of three or three columns of four. It doesn't matter how you compute the answer—by adding three fours, by adding four threes, or just by knowing the product—and both 3×4 and 4×3 are correct representations.

Whenever referring to standard multiplication symbolism, keep the emphasis on interpreting and making sense of what the symbolism represents.

How to Use This Book

Teaching the lessons as described in the twelve chapters requires a minimum of thirty days of instruction, not including time for repeat experiences as recommended for some lessons or for the seven additional assignments and seven assessments suggested. While it is possible to spend a continuous stretch of weeks on these lessons, I don't think that is the best decision. In my experience, time is required for children to absorb concepts, and I would rather spend a three-week period and then wait two months or so before returning for another three-week period, or arrange for three chunks of time, each two weeks or so, spaced throughout the year. When students return to ideas after a break, they bring not only the learning they've done in other areas but also a fresh look that some distance can provide.

The three introductory lessons in the book build the foundation for developing understanding, and I suggest that you not skip these lessons. The other lessons are categorized to identify different aspects of multiplication. Experiences in each of the categories are beneficial for students, but there is no particular sequence of categories that is best. However, the chapters within each category are placed in an order that reflects my experience teaching these lessons in several classes. A section of additional activities offers further instructional ideas. And a section on assessments will help you think about making assessment an integral part of multiplication instruction.

You may choose to use these lessons as your primary source for helping children learn about multiplication or use them along with other instructional materials or learning activities. It's important, however, to be consistent so that all lessons you teach encourage students to make sense of ideas, communicate about their reasoning both orally and in writing, and apply their learning to problem-solving situations.

CHAPTER ONE
THINGS THAT COME IN GROUPS

Overview

By grouping objects in real-world contexts, children learn to link the idea of multiplication to the world around them. After figuring out how many chopsticks are needed for everyone in the class, the children brainstorm other things that come in groups of two. Then they collaborate in small groups to identify things that occur in sets of threes, fours, fives, and so on, up to twelves. The groups' findings are compiled into class lists that are used later for solving problems and investigating multiples.

Materials

▲ 12-by-18-inch newsprint, 1 sheet per group of four
▲ 9-by-12-inch drawing paper, 11 sheets, or a large sheet of chart paper for the class lists

Time

▲ at least two class periods

Teaching Directions

1. Use chopsticks as an example to introduce this exploration. First make sure children know that a person needs two chopsticks for eating. Then pose a problem for class discussion: *How many chopsticks are needed for four people?* Hear from all volunteers, asking them to explain how they arrived at their answers.

2. Pose another problem: *How many chopsticks do we need if everyone in our class eats together?* Ask the class to discuss and solve this problem in small groups. Then have individuals tell their answers, again asking that they explain their reasoning. Record on the chalkboard the methods they report, modeling how to use mathematical notation to represent their ideas.

3. Have the class brainstorm other things that come in twos. List their suggestions. It's common for children to think of examples from their bodies—eyes, ears, hands, feet, thumbs, and so forth. If the students are limited by a particular category, offer a few suggestions to broaden their thinking—wheels on a bicycle, wings on a bird, slices of bread in a sandwich.

4. Present the problem of making lists for other numbers. Have children work in small groups and think of objects that come in threes, fours, fives, and so on, up to twelves. Give each group a sheet of 12-by-18-inch newsprint on which to organize its lists.

5. Post a sheet of 9-by-12-inch drawing paper for each list or one large sheet of chart paper for recording all the lists.

6. Have groups take turns reading an item from their charts. After a group reads an item, others guess the list on which it belongs. Record each item on the correct list. Should uncertainty or a dispute arise about some items, start a separate "research" list and resolve these questions at a later time. Continue until groups have reported all of their findings.

7. Encourage students to suggest other items that could be added to the lists. You may choose to give them the homework assignment of asking their parents to help them think of additional items.

Teaching Notes

Having children relate their math learning to real-world situations helps them avoid the pitfall of seeing math as abstract and unrelated to their lives. Too often, mathematics exists for children only on the pages of textbooks and worksheets. They need opportunities to see mathematics as an integral part of their daily experiences. While chopsticks aren't a part of all children's lives, the context worked well with the third graders in the following vignette, who lived near San Francisco, California. If you feel the context is too remote for your class, you can substitute another situation for your class that involves things that come in groups of two. For example, if the class were going out to play during a snowstorm, how many boots or mittens would you need? Or, if you were making a sandwich for each child in the class, how many slices of bread would you need?

You may want to have children write about their solutions to the chopstick problem. This gives them a chance to reflect on their thinking. It also gives you additional information about the reasoning of individual students. The writing need not be done immediately following the class discussion; waiting a day or so is fine. Samples of children's written responses are included in the classroom lesson that follows.

I used two full math periods for this lesson and a bit more time on the third day. During the first period, the children solved the chopstick problem, brainstormed other things that come in twos, and worked in groups to identify things that come in threes, fours, fives, and so on, up to twelves. I began the second day by having the students write about the methods they used the previous day to solve the chopstick problem. Then I used a class discussion to compile the findings on their lists.

The Lesson

▲▲▲

DAY 1

To begin the lesson, I asked the children, "If I were eating a Chinese or Japanese meal and using chopsticks, how many chopsticks would I need?" They all knew that I would need two chopsticks.

I continued. "Suppose I invited three friends to dinner and all four of us were going to eat with chopsticks. How many chopsticks would we need?" More than half the students raised their hands.

Before accepting any responses, I added a direction. "When I call on you," I said, "along with giving the answer, I'd like you to explain how you figured it out." I called on Brian.

"You could add up the chopsticks, two plus two plus two plus two, and that gives you eight," he said.

Tanya agreed with Brian's answer but offered a different explanation. She said, "It's eight because you go two, four, six, eight for the four people." She used her fingers to show the four people.

"Here's another question," I continued. "Suppose I plan a Chinese or Japanese meal for everyone in our class. How many chopsticks would I need to bring?"

"There are twenty-six of us," Angie said.

"You'd have to bring some for Mrs. Uyeda and for you, too," Libby added.

"So there are twenty-eight of us altogether," I said. "How many chopsticks would we need? Talk about this in your groups. In a few minutes, you'll have a chance to report the answer and explain how you got it."

The children's discussions were animated. Some used paper and pencil; others figured mentally. After a few minutes, some students raised their hands to indicate they were ready. When I could see that most had arrived at a solution, I brought the class to attention.

"I'm interested in hearing all the different ways you solved the problem," I told the class. "Please listen to one another's explanations so you can tell if you used a different method." I called on Brandon to report for his group.

He said, "We got fifty-six." There were murmurs of agreement.

"Explain how you got that," I prompted.

"You give everyone one chopstick—that's twenty-eight—and then you give another twenty-eight," Brandon answered.

I think it's valuable to relate numerical symbols to children's thinking as often as possible. In this way, they become more comfortable with using numbers to describe their ideas. To record Brandon's method, I wrote on the chalkboard:

$28 + 28 = 56$

"How did you figure out that twenty-eight plus twenty-eight is fifty-six?" I asked.

"I used paper and pencil," Brandon answered. He held up his paper to show how he lined up the numbers and added.

I then asked, "Did anyone do it a different way?" I called on Lisa.

"I wrote down two plus two plus two," she said, continuing for twenty-eight twos. I recorded the twos as she said them:

$2 + 2 + 2 + 2 + 2 + 2 + 2 + 2 + 2 + 2 + 2 + 2 +$
$2 + 2 + 2 + 2 + 2 + 2 + 2 + 2 + 2 + 2 + 2 + 2 +$
$2 + 2 + 2 + 2 = 56$

"Then I counted by twos," she continued, "and got fifty-six."

"Writing all of these twos helps me understand why mathematicians are always looking for shortcuts," I commented. "Let's quietly count by twos aloud together," I then said to the class. I pointed to each of the 2s I had written as we counted.

Maria raised her hand. "You could count by ones," she said.

"I agree," I said, "but I'm not going to write all of those ones." Some of the children giggled. I called on Rebecca next.

She said, "I did it sort of like Brandon, but I added another way. I did twenty plus twenty and then eight plus eight, and that gave me forty plus sixteen. So I went forty plus ten makes fifty and six more is fifty-six." Rebecca's strategy showed her comfort with taking numbers apart and regrouping them to make the calculations more manageable. I recorded Rebecca's method on the board:

$20 + 20 = 40$

$8 + 8 = 16$

$40 + 10 = 50$

$50 + 6 = 56$

Josh had a different idea. When doing numerical calculations, Josh often used the strategy of working with "friendly" numbers. "I did sixty minus four," he said, "and I got fifty-six." I recorded Josh's idea on the board:

$60 - 4 = 56$

Instead of having Josh explain more, I asked the class, "Can anyone explain why Josh's method makes sense?"

Tony volunteered, "Sixty would be for thirty people, and that's two too many, so you have to subtract four at the end."

Again, I asked if anyone had another way to figure the total number of chopsticks. James raised his hand. I recorded as he read from his paper:

$8 + 8 + 8 + 8 + 8 + 8 + 4 + 4 = 56$

James then explained how he used the groups in the class to organize his thinking. He said, "Well, there are six tables with four children so I did six eights, and there's just me and Elena at my table so that's four, and two grown-ups and that's four more. Then I added on the calculator and I got fifty-six."

Brian had another method. "I did twenty-six plus twenty-six plus four," he said. I recorded:

$26 + 26 + 4 = 56$

"Why did you choose those numbers to add?" I asked.

Brian explained, "It was easier for me to add twenty-six and twenty-six than twenty-eight and twenty-eight, because six plus six is easier, so I added four extra on at the end."

Alex raised his hand. "I think you could write down twenty-eight times two," he said. I recorded on the board:

$28 \times 2 = 56$

"No, write them the other way, up and down," Alex directed. I wrote:

$$28$$
$$\underline{\times 2}$$

Alex continued, "Then you do two times eight. You put down the six and carry the one. Then you do two times the twenty." He stumbled. "Nope, two times two," he said. "Oh, I don't know, but I think I could do it with paper and pencil."

"Yes, paper and pencil can help when we figure," I agreed. "What's also important, I think, is that you know different ways to solve a problem, so if you get stuck in one way, you can use another method."

I then switched the focus of the lesson. "Multiplication is a way to find out how many you have altogether when things come in equal-size groups," I told the children. "What other things can you think of that come in twos as chopsticks do? I'll make a list and then we'll use these for problems later."

I posted a 9-by-12-inch piece of drawing paper and wrote at the top: These things come in 2s.

The children had many suggestions: "Eyes." "Ears." "Hands." "Feet." "Arms." "Legs." "Eyebrows." "Lips." "Nostrils." "Thumbs." I recorded each of these suggestions and then interjected, "Can you think of things that come in twos that aren't on our bodies?"

Students quickly switched to make other suggestions. "Bicycle wheels." "Pedals on bicycles." "Bicycle handlebars." "Shoes." "Socks." "Gloves." "Twins." "Opposites."

The children raised questions about some of the suggestions offered. For "hands on a clock," Emily pointed out that some watches don't have hands, showing the digital watch that she was wearing.

Michael added that some clocks have three hands. "My Dad's watch has a second hand," he said.

"Hands on a clock only come in twos sometimes," I said. "Let's include on our list only things that always come in twos, not that sometimes come in twos. So I'm not going to put 'hands on a clock' on our list."

The same sort of discussion arose when "earrings" was suggested, since they aren't always worn in pairs.

The students continued with other suggestions: "Lenses in glasses." "Slices of bread in a sandwich." "Contact lenses." "Pairs of anything." "Wings on a bird."

Extending the Investigation

When it seemed that the children had exhausted their ideas about things that came in twos, at least for the moment, I shifted the conversation. "Could I write 'tricycle wheels' on our list?" I asked.

I received a chorus of nos. "On what list would it belong?" I asked. The answer was obvious to the class. I gave a few other examples of things that would belong on different lists. "Where would I have to write 'legs on a spider'? What about 'eggs in a dozen'?"

I then presented a problem for students to work on collaboratively at their tables. I said, "Think about things that come in groups other than twos, such as the examples I just gave about tricycle wheels, legs on spiders, and eggs in a dozen. Think about things that come in threes, fours, fives, sixes, sevens, eights, nines, tens, elevens, and twelves." I wrote these numbers

on the board as I said them. We counted to determine that there were ten different lists they needed to investigate.

I continued with the directions. "Work together at your tables. I'll give each table a large piece of newsprint." I had sheets of 12-by-18-inch newsprint ready. "Decide together how to organize all ten lists on this one sheet of paper. Then think of as many things as you can that fit on each list. Later, we'll compare the different groups you came up with."

After answering the questions a few students had, I gave each group a sheet of paper and the children got busy. I circulated and observed.

It was fascinating to watch the groups grapple with the problem of organizing their papers to accommodate the ten lists. Most of them found it complicated. Groups solved the problem in different ways. Several groups folded the paper in half, folded it again, and folded it again, each time opening it to count how many spaces they had. One of these groups put eight lists on one side and then turned the paper over for the last two lists. Another group folded the paper once again and opened it. The children counted and realized they now had sixteen sections. They resolved this by labeling ten of the sections for their lists and ignoring the other six.

Determined to find a way to get exactly ten sections, another group continued folding the paper this way and that until it was a mass of folds. The group was discouraged and frustrated. Finally, Brian drew lines by eyeballing and divided the paper into ten sections, each somewhat the same size.

The children in one group were hesitant to fold or mark their paper until they had a plan. They got some smaller sheets of newsprint and experimented with folding them. They came up with all sorts of alternatives, dividing sheets of paper into six, eight, nine, twelve, and sixteen sections, but not ten. They were stymied and frustrated, and I finally intervened. "Would you like some help organizing your paper so you can get started making your lists?" I asked. With grateful sighs, they agreed. I penciled their large sheet into ten sections and refocused them on finding entries for the ten lists.

Once the groups had organized their papers, they eagerly concentrated on finding entries for their lists. As they had when they were organizing their papers, groups worked differently on this part of the task. The children in some groups worked together, first thinking about things to write on the threes list, then the fours list, and so on. Students in other groups brainstormed things that could be written on any list, their ideas sparking one another to think of more ideas. The members of one group worked independently, writing what they found on the appropriate list with little group discussion.

Groups also differed in how they handled the recording. In some groups, one child recorded. In others, children took turns.

When it was time for lunch, I called the class to attention. I said, "Be sure that your names are on your chart. I'll collect them and return them to you tomorrow for a class discussion."

DAY 2

I began the lesson on the second day by asking the children to explain in writing how to solve the chopstick problem we had discussed the day before. "You can either describe the method you used yesterday," I said, "or explain a different way, or present several ways. I'm interested in learning how you think about the problem."

I was curious to hear from the children who hadn't volunteered explanations. Also, I was interested to see if the students who had given verbal explanations would change their methods. The children got to work more quickly than they usually did on writing assignments of this kind, because, I think, of the thinking and sharing of ideas from the previous day.

Some children explained the methods they had presented earlier. Josh, for example, wrote: *Well first I added Mrs. Uyeda and Mrs. Burns to our class so now we have 28 kids in are class. Then I pretended we had 30 kids in our class and cince each kid needs 2 chopsticks that would make 60 but cince I added 2 kids and they each used 2 chopsticks we have to take away 4 chopsticks. So the answer is 56.*

Lisa also recorded the same method she had reported. She wrote: *We need fifty six chopsticks. The way I figured it out was: 2 + 2 + 2 + 2 + 2 + 2 + 2 + 2 + 2 + 2 + 2 + 2 + 2 + 2 + 2 + 2 + 2 + 2 + 2 + 2 + 2 + 2 + 2 + 2 + 2 + 2 + 2 + 2 = 56*

Elena counted by twos. She wrote: *How many chopsticks do we need? 56. 2. 4. 6. 8. 10. 12. 14. 16. 18. 20. 22. 24. 26. 28. 30. 32. 34. 36. 38. 40. 42. 44. 46. 48. 50. 52. 54. 56.*

Angie presented several methods. She wrote: *We need 56 chopsticks. The first problem I thought of was 28 + 28. The second problem was counting by twos. The third problem was counting by ones.*

Five of the twenty-six students mentioned multiplication in their explanations. Similar to the understanding she revealed in the assessment a few days earlier, Tanya showed how multiplication relates to addition. She wrote: *We need 56 chopsticks. I figured that out by using multiplication. I did 2 × 28 = 56, or 28 + 28 = 56. (That includes Mrs. Uyeda and Ms. Burns.) I'm not sure about this answer, but it's just what I think.*

Rebecca also mentioned multiplication. Her written description differed slightly from what she had presented verbally. She wrote: *We need 56 chopsticks so that everybody could have a pair. I figured that out by doing multiplication. I took 26 × 2 and then I added 4 more. I did 20 + 20 equals 40 and then I took 6 + 6 which equals 12. Then I added 4 more and then it equaled 56.* Figures 1–1, 1–2, and 1–3 show how other students responded to this problem.

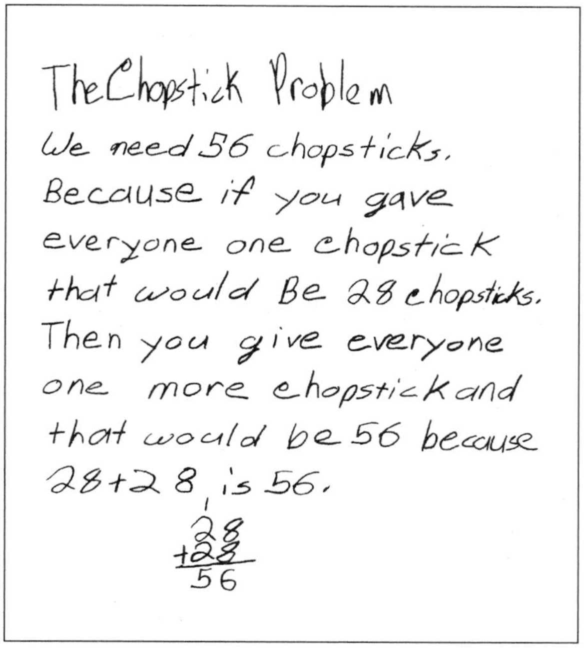

The Chopstick Problem
We need 56 chopsticks.
Because if you gave
everyone one chopstick
that would Be 28 chopsticks.
Then you give everyone
one more chopstick and
that would be 56 because
28+28 is 56.

$$\begin{array}{r} 28 \\ +28 \\ \hline 56 \end{array}$$

▲▲▲▲▲▲Figure 1–1   *Kim wrote a clear explanation about why adding 28 and 28 made sense.*

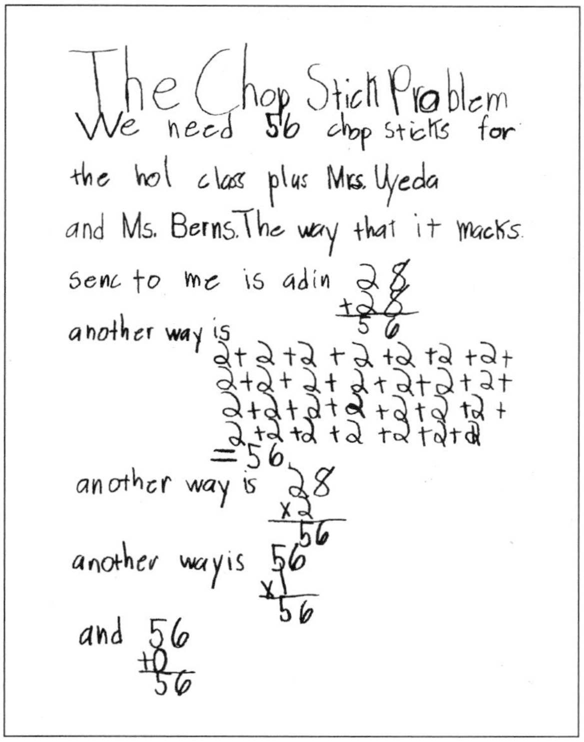

The Chop Stick Problem
We need 56 chop sticks for
the hol class plus Mrs. Uyeda
and Ms. Berns. The way that it macks
senc to me is adin $\begin{array}{r} 28 \\ +28 \\ \hline 56 \end{array}$
another way is
2+2 + 2 + 2 +2 +2 +2+
2+2+ 2+ 2 +2+2+2+
2+2+2+2 + 2+2+ 2+ +
2+2+2+2 +2 +2+2+2
=56
another way is $\begin{array}{r} 28 \\ \times 2 \\ \hline 56 \end{array}$
another way is $\begin{array}{r} 56 \\ \times 56 \\ \hline 56 \end{array}$
and $\begin{array}{r} 56 \\ +0 \\ \hline 56 \end{array}$

▲▲▲▲▲▲Figure 1–2   *The five methods Edna offered all gave the correct answer. However, the last two did not relate to the situation.*

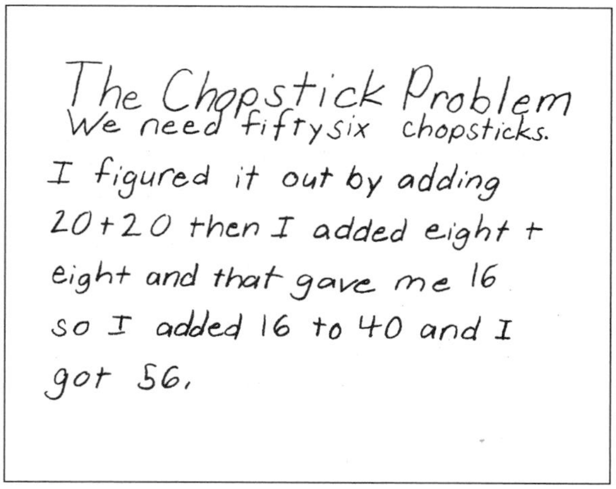

The Chopstick Problem
We need fiftysix chopsticks.
I figured it out by adding
20+20 then I added eight +
eight and that gave me 16
so I added 16 to 40 and I
got 56.

▲▲▲▲▲▲Figure 1–3   *Michael described the method that Rebecca had presented the day before.*

When the children had finished writing, I returned the lists they had made the previous day. I explained the procedure we would use to report their entries. I wanted them to listen to and think about one another's ideas.

"We'll go around the room, group by group," I said. "Each group will report one thing from any list, without telling which list it's on. Then the others in the class will have the chance to decide where it belongs. Once we agree, I'll write it on the board under the correct number.

"Also," I continued, "I want you to read something that hasn't already been suggested. Take a moment and choose several items you'd like to report so you'll have alternatives if some of your choices have already been mentioned."

The discussion did not go as I had expected or hoped. In previous years with other classes, there were always a few offerings that caused disagreement or uncertainty, such as sides on a stop sign or eyes on a spider. Sometimes there were suggestions that could be placed on more than one list, such as legs on a stool or sails on a sailboat. But there was easy agreement for most items—children in quintuplets, players on a baseball team, wings on a butterfly, cans in a six-pack of Coke, red stripes on the U.S. flag, pennies in a nickel, balls in a can of tennis balls, legs on an octopus.

In this class, however, children disputed most items in spirited discussions. I think this was because children were trying to suggest things they thought other groups hadn't thought of. In most cases they were right.

Libby contributed first. "Toilet paper," she said.

There were various opinions. "They come in twos." "There's six in a pack." "No, there's four." I finally ruled it out, telling the class that things needed to fit on just one list.

Brandon offered the next item. "Lights on a traffic light," he said.

Again, there were different opinions. "There are three." "Sometimes there's an extra arrow." "Sometimes there is just one blinking light." I didn't record Brandon's suggestion either.

Maria went next. "Innings in a baseball game," she read.

"Nine." "Not if it goes into overtime." "Not if it's rained out." "What if it's a double-header?" Another washout.

The discussion continued in this way. The children argued about the number of top teeth they had (Should molars be counted?), how many wheels there are on a pair of roller skates (What about in-line skates?), how many numbers are in a telephone number (What about faraway numbers? Should you count the one in front for long-distance numbers?).

The goal of the discussion seemed to have shifted from finding items to add to our lists to finding ways to keep items off the lists. The children were enjoying the exchange and entered into their arguments with a passion that would be gratifying in many class situations. Imagine third graders arguing for precision in language! But I had a different goal. I was trying to get things on lists that would then be available for our continued study of multiplication.

This experience was a good reminder for me to expect surprises in the classroom and to realize that the children aren't always aware of my goals. I took a moment to restate for the class the purpose of the lists. "Our job is to see how many items we can put on the lists," I said. "We'll be using them for more investigations as you continue to learn about multiplication."

Finally we had success with an item, but not without discussion. "Points on a star," Angie suggested.

"There are five." "There are six points on a Star of David."

Angie resolved the conflict. "We mean points on the stars on the American flag," she said primly. The class agreed it belonged on the fives list.

Then Brandon returned to his "traffic lights" suggestion. "Can't we put 'regular traffic lights' on the threes list?" he asked. The class agreed.

Success continued with other suggestions—candies in a package of M&M's, sides on a pentagon, sides on a square, months in a year, days in a week, legs on a dog, players on a football team out on the field at one time, outfielders on a baseball team, fingers on two hands.

It was time for lunch. I told the class that we would spend a little time the next day adding more items to our class lists. "We'll use the lists to solve multiplication problems a little later on," I added.

EXTENSIONS

For a homework assignment, have children ask others at home to help them think of things to add to the class lists. Have them prepare in class beforehand by organizing a sheet of paper for the lists. They'll need space for things that come in twos, threes, fours, fives, and so on, up to twelves. Ask them to write an item or two on each list as examples for those at home.

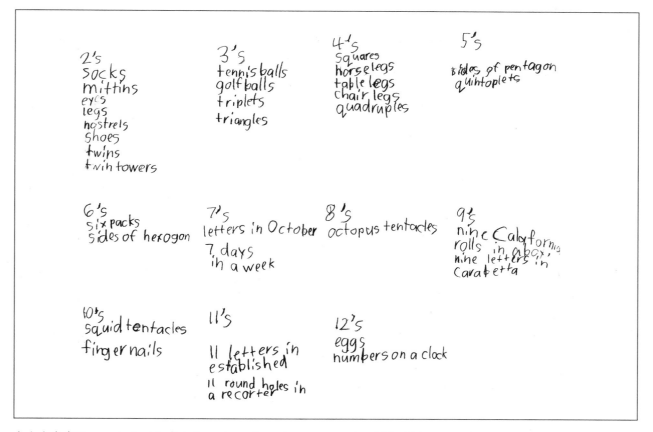

2's
socks
mittins
eyes
legs
nostrels
shoes
twins
twin towers

3's
tennis balls
golf balls
triplets
triangles

4's
squares
horse legs
table legs
chair legs
quadruples

5's
sides of pentagon
quintoplets

6's
six packs
sides of hexogon

7's
letters in October
7 days
in a week

8's
octopus tentacles

9's
nine Caloforni
rolls in a box
nine letters in
Carabetta

10's
squid tentacles
finger nails

11's
11 letters in
established
11 round holes in
a recorter

12's
eggs
numbers on a clock

▲▲▲▲▲▲**Figure 1–4** *For his homework assignment, Tony folded his paper into eight sections and used three sections on the reverse side for things that come in 10s, 11s, and 12s.*

The next day, children in groups compare the items on their lists and look for new items to add to the class lists. Then have a discussion in which groups report their findings to the class. Record any new items on the class lists. Figure 1–4 shows one student's list.

If you think it would be useful, send home a short letter to parents informing them about the purpose of this assignment. For example:

Dear Parent,

Part of studying multiplication involves learning to think about combining equal groups. To provide experience with this idea, and also to help students think about how multiplication relates to the world around us, the children have been thinking of things that come in groups of 2, 3, 4, 5, and so on, up to 12. Please help your child think of things in each category. We are interested in adding new items to our class lists.

Questions and Discussion

▲▲▲

▲ *When children answer, is it important for them always to explain their reasoning?*

I think so. If you accept answers without explanations, you run the risk of conveying that quick right answers are the goal or are most important when learning math. Asking children to explain their reasoning keeps the emphasis on thinking about and communicating their ideas. Also, children's explanations provide valuable information for assessing what they understand.

▲ *Why did you have the students count by twos aloud to get to fifty-six?*

Whenever opportunities arise, I reinforce the skill of counting by twos with the class. Practice helps children learn the pattern and become adept at using it. I gained insight into why children can have difficulty when I practiced counting by twos in Spanish, which isn't my first language. I had neither the rhythm of English nor the rhyme "Two, four, six, eight, who do we appreciate" to help me learn *dos, cuatro, seis, ocho.* When we count aloud as a class, some children stumble from time to time, particularly when starting a new decade after twenty-eight, thirty-eight, and so on. By carrying the sequence along correctly, I give everyone the chance to participate and practice.

▲ *When Alex suggested writing 28 × 2 vertically, he was trying to multiply the standard way. Wasn't this a good opportunity to try teaching this method to the class?*

Deciding when to follow the lead of a student is one of the challenges of teaching. In this lesson, my focus was on having children reason to solve a problem and communicate why their reasoning made sense to them, and modeling how to connect their ideas to standard mathematical representations by recording on the board. If Alex had been able to explain his method, I would have continued and pursued it, recording his thinking in another way and perhaps showing how what he was trying to do related to Rebecca's strategy. However, at this time, I chose not to do so and instead to continue with the lesson in the direction I had planned.

▲ *Why did you have children spend time figuring out how to get the ten lists onto a sheet of paper? Wouldn't it have been more efficient to organize this for them so that they could spend their time thinking about the problem at hand?*

Although giving the students photocopied forms or telling them how to set up their papers might have saved ten minutes or so, the children would have been robbed of the experience of having to figure out for themselves how to present the information. Watching their efforts reminded me of the problem-solving benefit students derive from being responsible for organizing their own work. It also reminded me of the creativity and uniqueness of children's thinking.

▲ *Why did you wait until the next day to have the children write about their solutions to the chopstick problem?*

I had two reasons for waiting. One was that I wanted to generate the lists of things that came in groups so that the chopstick problem fit into a context larger than just one isolated problem. Also, I've found that giving students a chance to think about a problem overnight before reflecting on it helps them come to the task of writing with some distance and new clarity.

CHAPTER TWO
CIRCLES AND STARS

Overview

Circles and Stars is a two-person game that gives children a visual interpretation of multiplication as repeated addition. To play, children take turns rolling a die to find out how many circles to draw and then rolling the die again to find out how many stars to draw in each circle. The winner is the child who draws the most stars after seven rounds. After playing the game, students learn to use the standard notation of multiplication to describe each round. In this way, they connect their drawings of circles and stars to the correct mathematical representations. By gathering data about their scores and investigating which products are more likely, children also have experience with multiples and ideas from the areas of statistics and probability.

Materials

▲ dice, 1 per pair of students
▲ scissors, 1 per student or pair of students
▲ staplers, 2 or 3 for the class
▲ class chart listing the numbers from 1 to 36 (see Blackline Masters)

Time

▲ four class periods

Teaching Directions

1. Tell the children that you're going to teach them how to play a partner game called *Circles and Stars.* To model how to play, invite a child to join you at the chalkboard.

2. Begin by rolling a die and reporting to the class the number that comes up. Draw that number of circles on the board, pointing out to the class that you're making the circles large enough to be able to draw up to six stars inside them. Roll the die again, report the number to the class, and draw that number of stars in each of your circles. Then have the child at the chalkboard roll the die and draw the correct number of circles. Have the child roll the die again and draw the correct number of stars.

3. Ask the class to figure out how many stars each of you drew. Write the total number of stars underneath each drawing. Play another round or two to be sure students know what to do. Then ask the volunteer to be seated.

4. Demonstrate how to make a booklet by folding a piece of paper into fourths, cutting it apart, and stapling it.

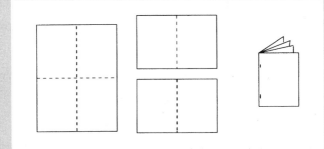

5. Write *Circles and Stars* and your name on the front of the booklet. Have the children count as you show that seven pages remain for playing. Tell them they can see who wins each round by comparing how many stars each player drew, but the winner of the game is the person who has more stars altogether after seven rounds. Tell them each child must figure out his or her total and record it on the booklet cover.

6. Tell the class: "For the rest of the period, you'll make a booklet and play the game. If you finish before the end of class, make a second booklet and play again."

7. The next day, show the students how to record a multiplication sentence on each page of their booklets. On the board, draw a sample page of three circles with two stars in each. Underneath, write: 3 × 2. Explain to the class that this is a way to use math symbols to write "three sets of two" or "three groups of two." Tell them you could also read the sentence as "three times two" or "three twos."

8. Show how adding = 6 tells how many stars there are in all. Write on the board four ways to read 3 × 2 = 6:

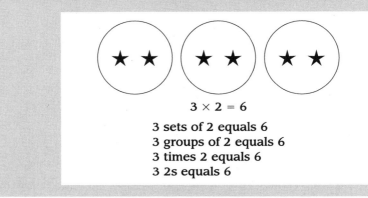

3 × 2 = 6
3 sets of 2 equals 6
3 groups of 2 equals 6
3 times 2 equals 6
3 2s equals 6

9. Ask the children to work with their partners and agree on the math sentence to write on each page of their booklets. Tell them: "As you write the math sentences, read them aloud to each other. Read each sentence in two different ways."

10. After children have recorded multiplication sentences, have them work in small groups to compare the number of stars on each page of their booklets. Ask them to notice the different numbers of stars that came up, which numbers occurred frequently, and the different ways they got the numbers. Have students present their findings in a class discussion.

11. At the beginning of the next math period, post the class chart and explain to the students that they will record their *Circles and Stars* scores on it. To model, ask a child to come up to the chart with a completed booklet and read the number of stars on each page while you mark tallies on the class chart. Repeat for another student or two or until you're sure that the children understand how to record the scores from each round.

12. For the rest of the period, and also for the beginning of class the next day, have children play and record on the class chart. It's OK for children to record the results from previous games they've played or from games they might play at home; the more data, the better the chart will be for drawing inferences.

Circles and Stars Class Chart	
1	19
2	20
3	21
4	22
5	23
6	24
7	25
8	26
9	27
10	28
11	29
12	30
13	31
14	32
15	33
16	34
17	35
18	36

13. Interrupt the children when about thirty minutes are left on the fourth day to discuss the data on the chart. Begin by asking the children how they might get a score of 3 on a page (1×3 or 3×1). Repeat for another number that has several possibilities, such as a score of 12 (2 × 6, 6 × 2, 3 × 4, 4 × 3). Then discuss as many of the following questions as possible in the time remaining:

Why do the numbers on the chart only go up to thirty-six?

Which numbers have no tally marks? Only a few tallies?

Which numbers have the most tally marks?

Which numbers are impossible to make playing *Circles and Stars?*

Why do you think that some numbers have more tallies than others?

14. If you'd like, on subsequent days have children play again and add tally marks to the class chart. Then on another day, continue discussing the questions in Step 13.

Teaching Notes

This lesson supports children's learning in several ways. Drawing circles and stars gives children experience representing multiplication pictorially. Children then connect their pictorial representations to the correct mathematical symbolism by writing multiplication sentences. And they verbally reinforce their learning by reading aloud to their partners the multiplication sentences they write.

From comparing the number of stars on the pages of their booklets, children learn that it's possible to get the same number of stars in different ways. For example, there are three ways to draw four stars on a page: one circle with four stars in it, four circles with one star in each, or two circles with two stars in each. These comparisons help illustrate the commutative property of multiplication.

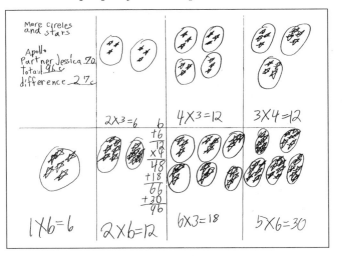

▲▲▲▲▲▲Figure 2–1   *Instead of making a booklet to play* Circles and Stars, *Apollo recorded on a sheet of paper folded into eight sections.*

Lynne Zolli has been teaching *Circles and Stars* to her third-grade classes in San Francisco, California, since 1991. She no longer asks her students to make booklets but rather has them play on a sheet of paper folded into eighths. The children play two games on each sheet, one on the front and one on the back. Lynne finds it easier to check children's papers for errors this way, both when they are playing in class and when she is looking them over later (see Figure 2–1).

Recording tally marks on the class chart for the scores from individual pages helps children analyze which products are possible with factors from 1 to 6. Also, the results on the chart give children the opportunity to think about why some numbers of stars are more likely than others. On the class chart, children should have made tally marks next to the numbers 1, 2, 3, 4, 5, 6, 8, 9, 10, 12, 15, 16, 18, 20, 24, 25, 30, and 36. If you make a multiplication table only for the factors from 1 to 6, these are the products that appear; the other numbers on the class chart are impossible. The only way to draw seven stars, for example, is to have one circle with seven stars in it or seven circles with one star in each, but neither is possible using dice with only the numbers from 1 to 6 on them. If tallies appear next to other numbers, a child has made a calculating error.

×	1	2	3	4	5	6
1	1	2	3	4	5	6
2	2	4	6	8	10	12
3	3	6	9	12	15	18
4	4	8	12	16	20	24
5	5	10	15	20	25	30
6	6	12	18	24	30	36

You may want to lead the class through an analysis of the scores. Begin by asking the children to look in their booklets to see if they got a score of 1. Have a child report what he or she drew, and record it on the board. Then ask children to look in their booklets to see if they got a score of 2, and again have students report what they drew. Record. Continue as long as the class is interested and at least as far as 8 or 10 so that children can discover one number that wasn't possible and also can see that different numbers have different numbers of possibilities.

1	*1 × 1*
2	*2 × 1*
	1 × 2
3	*3 × 1*
	1 × 3
4	*4 × 1*
	1 × 4
	2 × 2
5	*5 × 1*
	1 × 5
6	*6 × 1*
	1 × 6

	3×2
	2×3
7	impossible
8	4×2
	2×4
9	3×3
10	2×5
	5×2

It's most likely for scores with more possibilities to have more tally marks next to them on the class chart. Sometimes, however, the results on the chart don't reflect this mathematical theory. Larger sample sizes of data should give more reliable information. Having children play additional games and add to the chart over a period of time will illustrate this idea.

The Lesson

▲▲

DAY 1

To introduce the game, I wrote *Circles and Stars* on the board and asked Angie to come to the front of the room and be my partner. "I'll go first," I said. I explained the rules as I rolled the die, reported that a 2 came up, and drew two circles on the board. I rolled again, got a 3, and drew three stars in each circle. Then Angie took a turn. She rolled the die and drew four circles underneath mine. She rolled again and drew two stars in each.

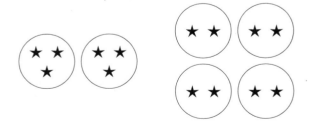

"How many stars did we each draw?" I asked the class. After a moment, most hands were raised. I called on Tony.

"Angie has more," he said, not answering my question, but getting to the heart of the game.

"How did you figure that?" I asked.

"'Cause she has eight and you only have six," he answered.

"So Angie wins by two," Josh added.

"Just on that round," I said. "Watch as we play again."

On the second round, I wound up with one circle with six stars in it and Angie had five circles with one star in each.

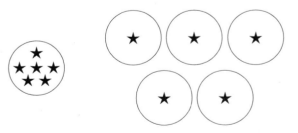

"Ms. Burns wins this time," Sara said.

"I thought she would lose when she rolled a one," Rebecca added.

"Angie still wins," Josh said, "but only by one." Josh was fascinated by and facile with numbers and often made contributions such as this to class discussions. I used his observation to present a problem to the class.

"Talk in your groups about what Josh said," I told the class, "and see if you can explain how to figure out that Angie is winning by one after two rounds." I had Angie return to her seat and join her group's discussion.

Although this problem wasn't directly related to playing *Circles and Stars,* it was a chance to engage the students in calculating mentally. Children benefit from having experiences such as this on a regular basis, and I capitalize on such opportunities whenever they appear.

In a few moments, I called the class back to attention and had children explain their reasoning.

I called on Lisa first. "Angie won by two the first round," she said, "and then you won by one, so Angie is ahead by one."

Brian had a different way to explain it. "You've got twelve stars altogether and Angie has thirteen, so she's ahead by one."

I then said, "In a moment, you'll play *Circles and Stars* with your partners. Let me show you how to record."

I took a plain sheet of duplicating paper and demonstrated how to fold it in half one way and then in half the other way. I cut it into fourths along the folds and stapled the pieces twice to make a booklet. On the front, I wrote *Circles and Stars* and my name.

I explained, "You'll each make a booklet like this one, cutting the paper apart and using just two staples." I was specific about the number of staples because some children have demonstrated too often that, when it comes to stapling, they think more is better.

"Record your circles and stars for each round on a separate page," I continued. "Your circles for each round have to fit on one page, so plan ahead. Also, be sure to draw the circles large enough to be able to draw stars inside."

I then posed a question. "How many rounds will you play to fill the book, using every page, even the back?" I asked.

The children made several guesses. I then had them count aloud as I turned the pages of my booklet, showing them that seven rounds filled the book. "So a game takes seven rounds," I said. "Although you can keep track of who wins each round, the winner of the game is the player who has the most stars after the booklets are full."

Observing the Children

The students made their booklets. I had two staplers and was busy keeping them in circulation. As the children started to play, there was a lot of talking about the game.

"This is all luck," I overheard Josh say with a condescending tone. However, it didn't seem to stop him from getting involved and staying interested.

His partner, Tony, drew six circles with two stars in each. "That's two, four, six, and six is twelve," he said.

After Michael drew two circles with five stars in each, he said, "I know I have ten because it's five plus five."

Kristina, seated at his table, said, "You could do two times five."

Rebecca rolled a 5 and then a 6. "This is a lot of stars to draw," she said.

Lisa and Kim were delighted when they had a tie for one round although they had each drawn different numbers of circles and stars—Lisa had one circle with five stars and Kim had five circles with one star in each.

Karin drew two circles with three stars in each. Her partner, Brandon, drew three circles and was about to roll the die again. He mused, "I can only win this round if I roll a three, four, five, or six." Overhearing incidental comments such as these gives me valuable feedback about the students. During this lesson, the class was noisy, but the children were all engaged and enjoying the game. I was pleased with their computing strategies and the numerical reasoning that I heard.

Most children finished a game during math time. Two pairs started to make booklets for a second game.

DAY 2

I continued with *Circles and Stars* the next day. I began by reviewing the game so Jennifer and Jason, who had been absent the day before, could learn to play. Then I taught the class how to write multiplication sentences on each page. In this way, children connect the game to the standard multiplication symbolism. I drew three circles on the board and then drew two stars in each.

"That makes six," Maria said.

"Yes," I said. "Watch as I show you how to record mathematically what I drew." I wrote on the board: *3 × 2.*

"This tells that I drew three sets of two, or three groups of two," I said, pointing to the circles and stars. "You can read it as 'three sets of two' or 'three groups of two' or 'three times two' or 'three twos,'" I said. "It's a way of mathematically recording that I've drawn three circles with two stars in each. Also, writing 'equals six' tells how many stars I drew altogether." I recorded on the board:

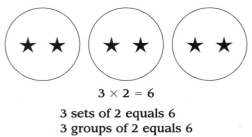

3 × 2 = 6

3 sets of 2 equals 6
3 groups of 2 equals 6
3 times 2 equals 6
3 2s equals 6

I did another example on the board, this time drawing five circles with two stars in

each. I asked the children how many sets I had, how many stars in each, and how many altogether. I then wrote: *5 × 2 = 10.*

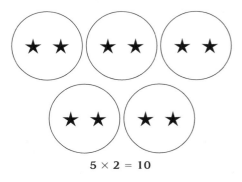

5 × 2 = 10

"Listen as I read this four different ways," I said. "You could say 'five sets of two equals ten' or 'five groups of two equals ten' or 'five times two equals ten' or 'five twos equals ten.'"

I left what I had recorded on the board and said to the class, "Before you return to playing *Circle and Stars,* write the mathematical sentence on each page you've already done. Work together to check each other. When you write a sentence, practice reading it aloud to your partner in at least two different ways."

The children went to work, recording multiplication sentences on each of their pages and then continuing to play. Figures 2–2 and 2–3 show how two students recorded their scores.

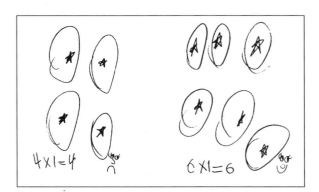

▲▲▲▲▲▲**Figure 2–2** *Karin indicated if she won or lost each round with a smiling or frowning face.*

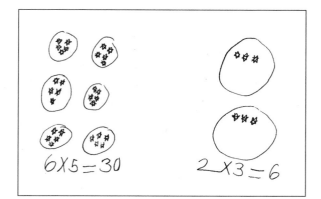

▲▲▲▲▲▲Figure 2–3 *As with all assignments, Michael recorded carefully. He was the only child in the class to draw six-pointed stars.*

Discussing the Game

About twenty minutes before the end of the period, I brought the class to attention for a class discussion.

"What's the fewest number of stars you can get on one round?" I asked. "Let's answer together." I received a chorus of "ones."

"What's the greatest number?" I asked. "Raise your hand when you think you know." Josh's, Brian's, and Angie's hands shot up immediately. I waited until more children volunteered.

"Let's say the answer together," I said. I heard a quieter chorus of "thirty-sixes." Having the children answer in unison gives everyone who wants to respond a chance to do so, while the others can just listen.

"So we know that it's possible to score one and thirty-six on a round," I said. "In your groups, compare your books. See if any of you got the same number of stars on a page and see if you got it the same way or a different way."

I gave the children a few minutes to compare their booklets. Then I asked them to report what they had noticed.

"We found two different ways to get four," Libby said. "I got it with one circle and four stars, and Brian got it with four circles and one star."

"I got four another way," Maria chimed in. "I had two circles and two stars."

"So there are three ways to get four," I said. I recorded:

$4 \times 1 = 4$

$1 \times 4 = 4$

$2 \times 2 = 4$

"Nobody got thirty-six at our table," Michael said.

"I did," Alex said.

"We got a lot of sixes," Brian said.

"Did you get it the same way each time?" I asked.

"No," Brian reported, "I got it twice, with six circles and one star and with two circles and three stars." I recorded:

$6 \times 1 = 6$

$2 \times 3 = 6$

"Did anyone get six stars in a different way?" I asked.

"I had one circle and six stars," Rebecca volunteered. I recorded:

$1 \times 6 = 6$

The children were still rummaging through their books.

"Oh yeah," Tony said, "I got six stars with three circles."

"How many stars in each?" I asked. Tony answered "Two," and I wrote:

$3 \times 2 = 6$

"Did anyone get six another way?" I asked.

Brandon raised his hand. "I got two circles and three stars," he said.

"That's already up there," Lisa said. The children couldn't find any other ways.

"So you found three ways to get four and four ways to get six," I said. "What about seven?" The children went back to looking.

Finally, Josh said, "You can't get seven." The others looked surprised.

"Why do you say that, Josh?" I asked.

"Because there's no seven on dice," he said. This was perfectly clear to Josh but not so obvious to all the others. I gave them a moment to chat about this among themselves.

I then gave the class the homework assignment of playing *Circles and Stars.* I had them prepare two booklets to take home.

DAYS 3 AND 4

To begin class, I posted the *Circles and Stars* class chart and explained to the students that they were to record the number of stars from each round by marking tallies. "Why do you think I wrote the numbers from one to thirty-six on the chart?" I asked.

About half a dozen students raised their hands. I waited a few moments, but no one else volunteered. Instead of calling on someone, I asked the children to talk about my question among themselves. I've found that small-group discussions give more children the opportunity to talk and that they often spark ideas. "Discuss in your groups why you think the numbers on the chart go from one to thirty-six," I said. "Then you'll have a chance to report to the class."

After a few moments, I brought the class back to attention and asked the question again. A few more children than before raised their hands. I called on Angie.

"Because one is the smallest number you can get and you can't go higher than thirty-six," she said.

"That's exactly why," I said. "To be sure you understand how to record on the class chart, I'll mark the tallies for someone's book." I asked Brian to come up with a finished book. As he read the scores from each page, I made the appropriate tally marks on the chart. Then I asked Emily and Roberto to report their scores and I recorded tallies for each.

I then said, "We'll have lots more data after all of you add to the chart. Then we'll look at the number of tally marks there are for different numbers and talk about what we notice."

For the rest of class and the beginning of the next day's class, children continued playing the game, writing multiplication sentences, and marking tallies on the class chart. With about half an hour remaining in the second class period, I initiated a class discussion.

"What do you notice about the tallies on the chart?" I asked.

"Sixes have a lot of them," Libby said.

"There's almost as many on eight and twelve," Michael added.

"Only two people got thirty-six," Alex said.

"One is me," Maria said.

"You've noticed some of the numbers have more tallies than others," I said. "Some numbers, like seven and eleven, don't have any tally marks at all. Can you think of any reason that this has happened?"

"It could be just luck," Jennifer said.

"I know," Tony said. "They're odd."

"But three and five are also odd," I said, "and they have tallies."

"You can't get seven," Josh said, remembering our discussion from before. "There's no way with the dice."

"Let's look at the ways to get different numbers," I said. I wrote a *1* on the board. "Did anyone get a score of one on any page?" I asked. Several children raised their hands. "Maria, what's on your page with a score of one?" I asked.

"One circle and one star," she replied. I recorded:

$$1 \qquad 1 \times 1$$

"Did anyone get one in a different way?" I asked. No one did. "What about two?" I asked, writing the number *2* on the board. "Did anyone get a score of two on a page?" I gave the children a moment to look through their books. Several hands went up. I called on Alex.

"I have two circles with a star in each," he reported.

"And I've got one circle with two stars," Roberto said. I recorded both of their ideas.

$2 \quad\quad 2 \times 1$

$\quad\quad\quad 1 \times 2$

I continued in this way, listing the different ways to get each number. When I got to the number 7, no hands were raised.

"I agree with Josh," I said. "There's no way to get a seven from a die with one to six on it. It's not possible." I circled the 7 and wrote *impossible* next to it.

"What about eight?" I continued. The children responded with the two ways to make eight.

I continued for nine and ten and then stopped. Searching through their booklets for the scores was time-consuming for the children, and while some children were fascinated, others were losing interest. Also, it was just about the end of class. I used the last few minutes to point out to the children how we might think about the information we had already gathered. I said, "It makes sense to me that our chart shows that six came up more often than the other numbers. That's because there are four different ways to make six and fewer ways to get the other numbers. So six should come up more often."

"There's a tie for second place," Brian said. "They both have three ways."

"I know why twenty-nine won't have any ways," Lisa said.

I responded to Lisa, "Maybe you'd like to write about your idea. Then we can talk about it when we look at the rest of the chart." Lisa nodded, and I ended the class. (See Figure 2–4 for Lisa's thinking.) I returned to the chart a few days later to continue investigating with the class which other numbers were impossible and which were more likely to occur than others.

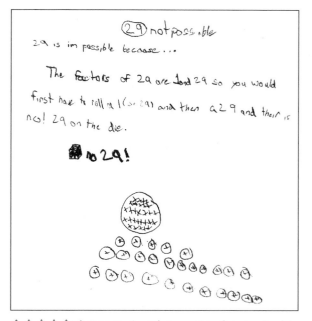

▲▲▲▲▲▲Figure 2–4   *Lisa wrote about why it's impossible to get a score of 29 on a round of* **Circles and Stars.**

EXTENSIONS

For a homework assignment after introducing the game, ask the children to teach someone at home how to play *Circles and Stars* and to play at least one game of seven rounds. If the children don't have paper at home, have them take some from class or prepare two booklets in advance.

Some students may not have dice at home; show them how to cut slips of paper, number them from 1 to 6, put them in a bag, and draw one out to get a number. Remind them to replace the slip of paper each time before drawing out another number. Children may want to draw dots on the slips of paper to make them look more like dice. After children have played the game at home, have them report about their experiences, telling with whom they played and the responses they got.

If you think it would be useful, send home a short letter to parents informing them about the purpose of this assignment. For example:

Dear Parent,

Circles and Stars introduces multiplication as a way of adding the same number over and over. Drawing stars in circles gives children a visual model for the idea of multiplication as repeated addition. Please play at least one game with your child. Later in this unit, we will investigate the scores for a round and find which scores are more likely to come up than others, which will introduce your child to ideas about probability.

For another version of the game, have students use spinners with the numbers 0 to 9 on them. This increases the range of scores possible in a round and gives children experience with multiples of zero, seven, eight, and nine.

Questions and Discussion

▲▲

▲ *What if children get tired of playing the game for so many days?*

My experience has been that children don't tire of the game in a few days, and many stay interested for much longer. While this game is a game of luck only, children seem to enjoy predicting what they'll need to win. Also, they seem to find it satisfying to write multiplication equations to describe what occurred. However, if you find your students' enthusiasm for the game waning, then after the first two days, wait a few days or a week and engage the class in another multiplication activity before discussing the class chart of *Circles and Stars* data.

▲ *When Josh stated that it's not possible to get seven stars, it wasn't obvious to all of the other students why this was so. Why didn't you discuss this further with the class?*

There has always been a range of mathematical interests and abilities in the classes I've taught. My goal is to provide learning opportunities that are accessible to all students while also challenging those who might be ready for more. When I raised the question to the class about ways to draw seven stars, I predicted that some children would be satisfied merely to notice that a score of 7 never came up while others would be interested in thinking about why this was so. I didn't feel the need to resolve the issue for all of the students at that time.

CHAPTER THREE
AMANDA BEAN'S AMAZING DREAM

Overview

The story *Amanda Bean's Amazing Dream,* by Cindy Neushwander, presents children with an engaging and persuasive argument for why they should learn about multiplication. The illustrations are an extra bonus, providing a rich collection of contexts for solving multiplication problems. The series of experiences in this chapter draw from the book and involve children in representing situations with multiplication equations and calculating answers to multiplication problems in several ways.

Materials

▲ *Amanda Bean's Amazing Dream,* by Cindy Neushwander
(New York: Scholastic, 1998)

Time

▲ at least five days, spread over several weeks

Teaching Directions

1. Read *Amanda Bean's Amazing Dream* aloud and discuss the story with the class.

2. Show the children the first spread in the book and draw their attention to the pink building on the left side. Draw one of the windows on the chalkboard and point out to the children that there are three panes across and six panes down. Ask two questions: "How many panes are in the window altogether? What multiplication equation can you write?" Have several children explain their reasoning for figuring out the answer. Record their explanations on the board along with the appropriate multiplication equations. Point out that it's possible to look at the problem as six rows with three panes in each, which is six threes or 6×3, or three rows with six in each, which is three sixes or 3×6.

3. Again, show the children the same spread from the book, this time drawing their attention to the orange building on the right side with windows that have two panes across and three panes down. Draw one of the windows on the chalkboard and ask the same two questions: "How many panes are in the window altogether? What multiplication equation can you write?" Again, record students' responses.

4. Show the children the next spread in the book, which shows Amanda in a bakery. Draw the children's attention to the top tier on the baker's cart, which has a tray of two rows of brownies with seven in each row. As for the two previous problems, ask two questions: "How many brownies are on the tray all together? What multiplication equation can you write?" Again, record their responses.

5. Continue on subsequent days with other problems from the book. You can do two or three problems a day and fit them in along with other instructional activities. Choose from the following ideas, presented in the order that they appear in the story. For each problem, remember to ask students to write the multiplication sentences that match the situation.

How many lollipops are there in all?

How many cakes are in the bakery cabinet?

How many flowers are on all of the cakes together?

How many cookies are on the second tier of the baker's cart?

How many cookies are on the next-to-bottom tier of the baker's cart?

How many plants are in the garden?

How many tiles are on the countertop?

How many pickles are there in the jars altogether? How many olives? Tea bags?

How many books are in the library shelf?

How many wheels do the sheep's bicycles have in all?

How many balls of yarn do the sheep have altogether?

How many knitting needles do the seven grandmas have?

6. From time to time, instead of using one of these problems for a whole-class discussion, ask children to solve a problem on their own.

Teaching Notes

In the story *Amanda Bean's Amazing Dream,* Amanda is a child who loves to count anything and everything. She counts panes in windows, books on library shelves, cookies on trays, tiles on a countertop, and much, much more. But sometimes Amanda just can't count fast enough. Her teacher tries to persuade her that multiplying might help, but Amanda isn't convinced—until she has an amazing dream about eight sheep on bicycles and seven speed-knitting grandmas. Only then does Amanda realize that multiplication can be valuable to learn. The situations in the story provide a variety of contexts that can help cement the idea for children that equal groups are essential to the idea of multiplication. Children also learn that representing situations may or may not call for a specific order of the factors.

For example, we can think of a window that has two panes across and three panes down either as two threes or three twos, and we can represent the problem as either 2 × 3 or 3 × 2. When representing the number of wheels on eight bicycles, however, we typically think of eight groups of two wheels, or eight twos, and the correct way to write this is 8 × 2. If, however, we thought of the wheels in two groups, the front wheels and the back wheels, then we would have two eights, which we would represent as 2 × 8. What's important is that children can represent a problem situation in the way they interpret it. Also, it's important for children to know that when figuring the answer to a problem such as 8 × 2, it's all right to add eight twos or two eights. Understanding the commutative property of multiplication helps develop children's flexibility when computing.

When I did this lesson with a third-grade class, I didn't introduce the experiences on consecutive days. Rather, I interspersed them with other instructional activities. Not only does this help maintain children's interest in using the book for multiplication problems, but it also helps children connect these experiences with *Circles and Stars, Patterns in Multiples,* and the other activities they are exploring.

The Lesson

▲▲

DAY 1

After reading the book aloud to the class, and before launching into a mathematical discussion, I talked with the children about the story. "What did you like about it?" I asked.

"I like the way the sheep said 'm-u-l-t-i-p-l-y,'" Aaron said, imitating the way I had bleated the word when I read it.

"I like the way Amanda said, 'I'm Amanda Bean and I count anything and everything,'" Ruthie said.

Jay said, "The book teaches you that you can't always count. When it's big, you have to multiply."

Peter said, "I like that she learned a lesson."

Bo said, "I like how she ended wanting to learn multiplication."

Jessica said, "I like the ending when she said, 'and I don't count sheep.' I thought that was funny."

I then opened the book to the first spread and pointed to the pink building on the left-hand side. "How many windows do you see on this building?" I asked.

"Six," Sally answered.

I said, "Let's look at the windowpanes in each window. There are three panes across and six panes going down." As I sketched one of the windows on the board, Ruthie said, "It's three horizontally and six vertically."

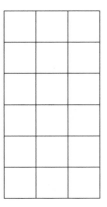

"How many panes does the window have altogether?" I asked. I waited until more than half the students had raised their hands and then called on Lydia.

"It's three times six and that's sixteen," she said. After noticing that several of her classmates quickly raised a hand to disagree, she added, "Oh, wait." I asked the others to put their hands down and give Lydia a chance to think. Lydia then said, "It's eighteen."

"Are you sure about that?" I asked. Lydia nodded yes. I wrote on the board:

$3 \times 6 = 18$

"Can you explain how you know that eighteen is correct?" I probed. Lydia was quiet for a moment and then she shrugged. She seemed to have lost her confidence.

"You're right that eighteen is correct," I said to confirm her answer. "But remember, it's important to be able to explain why an answer makes sense. Do you want to try or would you rather hear someone else's idea?"

"I want to hear someone else's idea," Lydia responded.

Amelia reported, "You can go six plus six and then add six more."

"How much is six plus six?" I asked.

"Twelve," Amelia answered.

"And six more?" I asked. Amelia used her fingers to count on from twelve to eighteen. I wrote on the board:

$6 + 6 = 12$

$12 + 6 = 18$

"You have three sixes, like in *Circles and Stars*," Alicia added.

"I know another way," Evan said. "You write six threes in a line going down and then add them." I wrote:

```
     3
     3
     3
     3
     3
   + 3
```

"Now what?" I asked. Eddie answered, "You count up the threes—three, six, nine, twelve, fourteen, no fifteen, . . . eighteen." I recorded the total:

```
     3
     3
     3
     3
     3
   + 3
    18
```

Jessica said, "You could write the sixes like that, too. You write three of them. It's eighteen." I wrote:

```
     6
     6
   + 6
    18
```

"All of these ways explain how to figure out the number of windowpanes," I said, bringing their attention back to the problem. "Lydia thought about the problem as 'three times six,' which means three groups of six, or three sixes." I pointed to the columns of panes on the window I had drawn on the board to show the three sixes and wrote on the board:

$3 \times 6 = 18$

I continued, "Evan's idea also works. He thought about the problem as six threes, and that makes sense if I count each row of panes, not the vertical columns." Again, I pointed to show what I was referring to and wrote on the board:

$6 \times 3 = 18$

"Solving the problem both ways is a good way to check that you figured right," I concluded.

"I can do it a different way," Tomas volunteered. "Can I come up and show?" I agreed. Tomas started at the top of the window and began by counting the panes in the two left columns. He said as he pointed, "Two, four, six, eight, ten, twelve, and then I add on six more to get eighteen."

"How many twos did you count first?" I asked. Tomas again counted the panes by twos and then said, "Six twos."

"And then what did you do?" I asked.

"Twelve and six more makes eighteen," he said. I added to what I had written:

2, 4, 6, 8, 10, 12

6 × 2 = 12

12 + 6 = 18

I then said, "I know another way to write a math sentence to show Tomas's idea." I wrote:

(6 × 2) + 6 = 18

I explained, "This tells me that first Tomas figured out six twos and then he added six more to get eighteen. Notice that the only part I could write as multiplication was when I had groups that were the same size, all twos. That's an important idea about multiplication—you have to have equal groups. When adding, you can use all different numbers, but when multiplying, you add the same number over and over."

The idea of equal groups is an important aspect of multiplication. I didn't expect that my explanation at this time would necessarily help or be sufficient for all children, but I knew that I would reinforce the idea whenever the opportunity became available, connecting it as often as possible to the children's thinking.

I opened the book and again showed the children the first spread of illustrations. I pointed to the orange building on the right-hand side and drew one of the windows on the board.

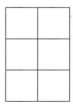

"I have two questions," I said. "How many panes are in the window altogether? How can I write a multiplication sentence to represent the problem?"

"I don't get it," Jessica said.

"Listen to someone else's idea and see if that helps," I said. I called on Alicia.

"There are six," Alicia said. "It's two times three." I wrote on the board:

2 × 3 = 6

"How did you figure?" I asked.

"I added three and three," she said, moving her finger up and down in the air to indicate that the threes represented the three panes in each of the two columns.

"What if I wrote this?" I said and wrote on the board:

3 × 2 = 6

"Then it's three twos," Jay said. "It's the same answer; you go two, four, six."

"Who can see how we could think of the windowpanes as three twos?" I asked.

"You go down from the top," Marea said, "two, four, six."

I looked over at Jessica. "I get it now," she said.

There are other problems we could have talked about on this spread, but I decided that moving to another page would help me to hold their interest. I'd return to this page on another day. The next spread in the book shows Amanda in a bakery. She is looking at the cakes in the cabinet while the baker is rolling in a five-tier tray of brownies, bread, and cookies.

"There are lots of possible multiplication problems we could think about from this page," I said to the class. I pointed to the first tier on the baker's cart. "Let's think about the brownies on this tray. There are two rows of brownies on the tray. Let's count and see how many brownies there are in each row." The children counted along with me to find that there were seven brownies in each row.

"I have two questions," I said as I did for the illustration of windowpanes. "How many brownies are on the tray altogether? What multiplication sentence can you write to represent the problem?"

A few children raised their hands immediately. To give more children a chance to think through the problem, I said to the class, "Talk to your neighbor about how many brownies are on the tray and what multiplication sentence you can write." The room got noisy as children shared ideas. After a few moments, I called them back to attention.

"Raise your hand if you think you know how many brownies are on the tray," I said. Now many more hands went up. I called on Sergio.

"Fourteen," he said. The others murmured their agreement.

"How did you figure that out?" I asked.

"We did seven plus seven," he said. I wrote on the board:

7 + 7 = 14

"Did anyone figure in a different way?" I asked.

Lydia said, "I counted by twos because there are two rows."

"Count out loud so we can all hear what you did," I said.

Lydia counted, "Two, four, six, eight, ten, twelve, fourteen." I wrote on the board:

2, 4, 6, 8, 10, 12, 14

"Now about my other question," I said. "What math equation can we write?"

Aaron said, "Two times seven."

"Does this equation match what Sergio did or what Lydia did?" I asked.

"It matches Sergio's," Aaron answered, "because it's two sevens."

"It could be seven times two," Alicia said. "Then you count by twos like Lydia did." I added to what I had written on the board to show which multiplication equation matched each way of figuring. I wrote:

7 + 7 = 14   *2 × 7 = 14*

2, 4, 6, 8, 10, 12, 14   *7 × 2 = 14*

"You can look at the brownies on the tray either way," I said, "but you should be sure that you know what you're describing when you write an equation."

I asked the same two questions about the cakes in the cabinet on the left side of the page. There were three shelves of cakes with three cakes on each shelf. The multiplication equation was easy to write since both factors were the same.

DAY 2

I continued presenting multiplication problems from illustrations in *Amanda Bean's Amazing Dream*. I began by showing the class the spread of Amanda and eight sheep bicycling. Some children giggled.

"Who remembers what was happening in this part of the story?" I asked. Hands shot up.

Amelia answered, "The sheep were bicycling by and Amanda was trying to count how many there were."

"That's not it," Aaron said. "She knew there were eight sheep and she wanted to know how many wheels there were on the bicycles."

"Oh yeah," Amelia said.

"Have you ever seen a sheep riding a bicycle?" I asked the class.

"It was just a dream!" Ruthie said.

"A really bad dream," Raul added.

"Writers can invent things with their own imaginations, so it's OK to have sheep riding bicycles," Jessica said.

"I didn't know it was a dream right away," Greta said.

"How did you find out that Amanda was dreaming?" I asked.

"At the end," Greta said. "Her mother woke her up and comforted her."

"I'm interested in the problem Amanda was thinking about: How many wheels are there on eight bicycles? I'm also interested in the multiplication equation that describes the problem. So my two questions are: How many wheels are there? What multiplication equation can we write? Talk to your neighbor about both of these questions."

After a few moments, I asked the children for their attention. "Who would like to answer?" I asked.

Bo said, "It's eight times two and it's sixteen." I wrote on the board:

8 × 2 = 16

"Tell us why the equation makes sense and how you figured the answer," I said.

"There are eight twos, so it's eight times two," Bo said. "And I know that's sixteen."

"How do you know it's sixteen?" I probed.

"Because eight and eight is sixteen," he answered. I find that it's common for children to switch the factors in a multiplication problem, as they often do with the addends for addition problems, to find the answer in the way that's easiest for them. Children seem intuitively to understand the commutative property of multiplication. I addressed what Bo had done.

"So you figured it this way?" I asked, writing on the board:

8 + 8 = 16

Bo nodded.

"We did it a different way," Amelia said. "We counted by twos."

"Did you get sixteen?" I asked.

Amelia nodded and counted by twos to sixteen. I recorded on the board:

2, 4, 6, 8, 10, 12, 14, 16

"So Bo added two eights, and Amelia counted eight twos," I said.

"I have another way," Lydia said. "Can I come up?" I agreed and Lydia came up and wrote:

2 + 2 + 2 + 2 + 2 + 2 + 2 + 2

She talked aloud as she explained how she combined pairs of twos to make four fours, then pairs of fours to make two eights, and then the two eights to get sixteen. She recorded as she explained:

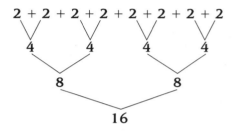

"These three ways convince me that the answer is sixteen," I said. "An important idea about multiplication is that you can switch the numbers around when you figure. This bicycle problem is about eight twos, because each bicycle has two wheels. That's why we write 'eight times two.' But you can find the answer either by figuring eight twos or two eights. You'll get the same answer both ways."

I turned back to the page about the bakery. "Let's do one more problem together," I said, "and then you can try one on your own." I directed the children's attention to the tray of cookies that had three rows with six cookies in each. After showing the class the illustration from the book, I drew a sketch of the tray on the board.

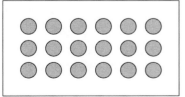

"Who knows the two questions I'm going to ask?" I said.

"How many cookies are there in all?" Greta said.

"And you want us to tell you the multiplication equation," Jay added.

"I know," Sally said, "it's six times three equals eighteen." I wrote on the board:

$6 \times 3 = 18$

I looked back at Sally for an explanation. "OK," she said, "see the three cookies in a row? Can I come up and show?" I agreed. Sally came up and pointed to the three cookies on the left side of the tray. "There's three and three and three," she said, pointing each time to the next three cookies and continuing for the entire tray. "So that's six of them, so you write six times three." Sally returned to her seat.

"And how did you get eighteen?" I asked.

"It's the same as the windowpanes," she said grinning.

"If I didn't remember that, how could I figure?" I asked.

"Count by threes," several children answered in unison. I had the class count with me as I recorded:

3, 6, 9, 12, 15, 18, 21, 24

I had kept writing because the children had continued to chant. But then Jay blurted out, "You went too far."

The room got quiet. He said, "You only need six of them. You should stop at eighteen." Jay came up and counted six of the numbers in the sequence to show where we should have stopped. I erased the two last numbers.

"You could do it the other way, too," Amelia said. "You could count the sixes. There are three of them."

"Tell us some more," I said.

Amelia added, "You go six, twelve, eighteen. You're just counting the cookies the other way." I wrote on the board:

6, 12, 18

"If you count three sixes, the equation should be the other way," I said.

"It should be three times six," Peter said. I wrote on the board:

$3 \times 6 = 18$

I then presented the children with a problem to solve. I chose to have them find the number of cookies on the remaining tray of cookies in the illustration.

"They're chocolate chip cookies," Chuck said.

"Those are my favorite," Raul added.

I had the children count with me to determine the number of cookies across and down the tray. "Let me draw a picture of this tray on the board so you can all see it," I said. I drew a 4-by-7 array on the board.

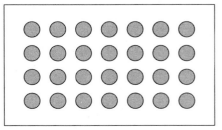

"Remember, you have to answer two questions," I said. I wrote on the board:

How many cookies are on the tray?

What multiplication equation can you write for the problem?

The problem was accessible for all the children and they worked well. Aaron wanted to draw the cookies and used centimeter squares to do so. "It's neater this way," he said. Others followed his suggestion, cutting out their arrays and pasting them on their papers. Most children figured out the problem by adding four sevens and then seven fours. Some also added fourteen twos. Figures 3–1 through 3–4 show how some students figured out this problem.

DAY 3

I took a break from the book for several days before using it again for a similar lesson. I wanted to persist with more experiences that would help the students link situations to multiplication equations and figure answers in several ways, but I didn't want them to tire of the book.

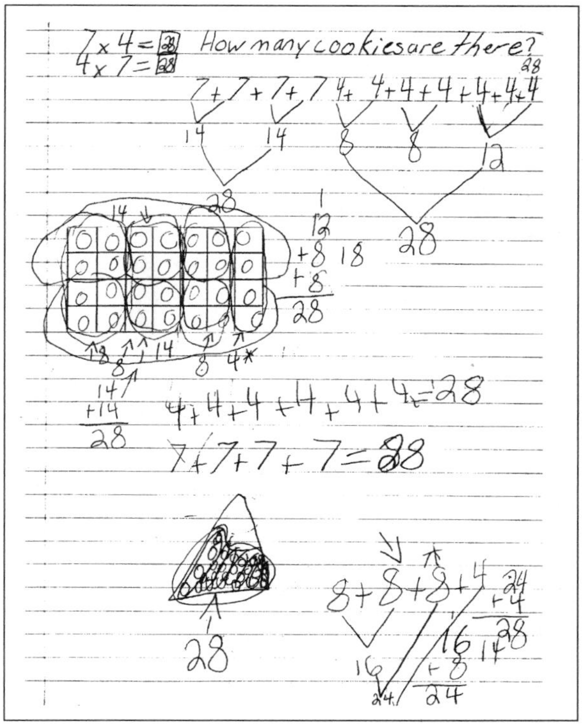

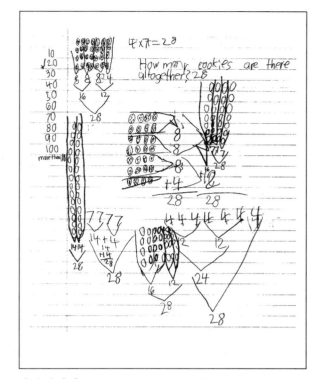

▲▲▲▲▲▲Figure 3–1 *After adding four 7s and seven 4s to figure the number of cookies, Marea also computed the problem as three 8s plus 4. Her illustration explains why this makes sense.*

▲▲▲▲▲▲Figure 3–3 *Bo made drawings to show the different ways he thought about the cookies on the tray.*

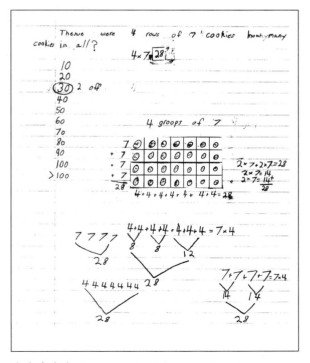

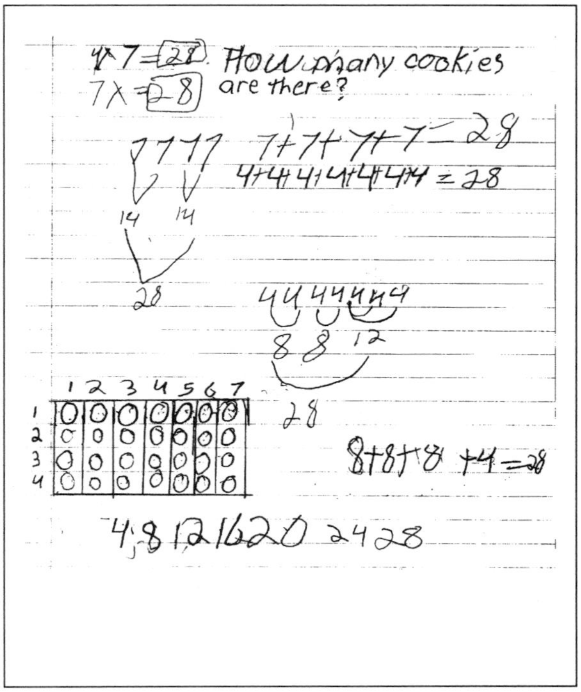

▲▲▲▲▲▲Figure 3–2 *Aaron made an estimate first before figuring how many cookies were on a tray with 4 rows and 7 cookies in each.*

▲▲▲▲▲▲Figure 3–4 *Raul figured the answer of 28 in five different ways.*

On the day I returned to the book, I opened it to the spread that shows Amanda in the library and pointed to the bookcase in the middle of the left-hand page. I reread the first paragraph of the text: "I walk to the library to check out a book. One bookcase has seven shelves and nine books on each shelf. I am Amanda Bean and I count anything and everything."

With the children, I counted the books on the top three shelves to verify that there were nine on each. I said, "Amanda would count all of the books, one by one. But since there are nine books on each shelf, I think this could be a multiplication problem. To figure out how many books there are in all, what multiplication equation could we write? And how could we figure out the total number of books?"

Aaron said, "You could write nine times nine." He immediately corrected himself. "No, that's not right, it should be nine times seven." I recorded Aaron's idea on the board:

9×7

When I turned around, several other children had raised their hands. Rather than ask Aaron to explain, I called on Lydia. "I agree," she said. "It's nine times seven."

Kelly had a different idea. "I think it should be seven times nine," she said. I wrote on the board:

7×9

"It can be both," Ruthie said. "When we do cookies or windows, you can do it both ways."

"I don't think so," Jay said. "I think it has to be seven times nine because you have seven nines, not the other way around."

"I agree with Jay," Jessica said. So did Marea, Tomas, and Sergio.

I said, "Remember, seven times nine means seven nines, and nine times seven means nine sevens. Another way to think about it is to read the times sign as 'groups of,' so we have seven groups of nine. Which fits the bookshelf?"

Aaron said, "I change my mind. The bookcase has nine books seven times. So that's seven nines. It has to be seven times nine."

I realized that some children were still confused, but I pressed on. "That's right. Each shelf holds a group of nine books, and there are seven shelves, so there are seven groups of nine and you write that as seven times nine. But you can figure out the answer either way, by thinking of seven nines or nine sevens. Who has an idea about how to find the answer?"

"It's sixty-three," Sergio answered. "My mother taught me a trick. You go seven minus one is six and then six plus three is nine, so the answer is sixty-three." A few of the other children also had learned this trick. Alicia showed it by using her fingers.

"How else can we figure the answer?" I asked.

Ruthie came to the board, wrote seven 9s, did some adding, and then was stuck:

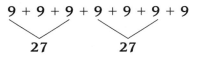

Lydia came up to help. She began as Ruthie did but added pairs of nines, then added three eighteens, and finally added nine more to get sixty-three.

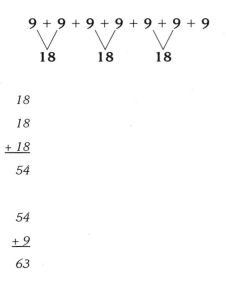

Amelia then came up and finished what Ruthie had started, adding twenty-seven and twenty-seven to get fifty-four and then adding nine more as Lydia had done.

Kelly solved the problem by adding nine sevens. She added groups of three sevens to get three twenty-ones and then added twenty-one three times to get sixty-three.

Sergio had another idea. He said, "You add twenty and twenty and twenty and get sixty, and then three more makes sixty-three." When I asked him where the twenties came from, he looked confused.

I said, "The problem is about seven shelves with nine books on each shelf. I agree that your arithmetic is right, but I don't see how it connects to this particular problem."

Jay had a way to bail out Sergio. "Nine and nine is eighteen, right?" he asked me. I nodded and he continued. "So you take two from the bottom shelf to make twenty. Then the next two shelves are the same—nine and nine and two from the bottom. And you do the next two shelves the same. Then you have three books left on the bottom shelf." I looked at Sergio.

"I don't get that at all," he said.

I said, "Keep in mind, Sergio, that when you multiply, you have to make equal groups, and you should be able to tell us where in the problem those equal groups are. Jay was trying to make groups of twenty books."

I then shifted the discussion. "Let's look at the sheep again," I said. I opened the book to the spread with the eight sheep in the barn, each holding five balls of yarn. I read what Amanda said: "'Oh, no!' I cry out. 'Now I must count the yarn, too! I am Amanda Bean and I count anything and everything. First it was wheels. Then it was legs. Now it's balls of yarn!'"

I asked the same two questions: "What multiplication equation can we write? And how many balls of yarn are there altogether?"

"That's an easy one," Marea said. "You just have to count by fives eight times." As Marea counted, I recorded on the board:

5, 10, 15, 20, 25, 30, 35, 40.

"Why is it so easy to count by fives?" I asked.

"They all end in five or zero," Raul answered.

"You could add up all the fives," Lydia said.

"How many fives?" I asked.

"Eight of them," Lydia answered. I wrote:

$5 + 5 + 5 + 5 + 5 + 5 + 5 + 5$

"How would you add them?" I asked.

"Two fives are ten, so you have ten plus ten plus ten plus ten, and that's forty," she said.

"What about the multiplication equation?" I asked. "How can I write that we have eight fives and that makes forty altogether?"

Bo said, "It's eight times five." As I wrote that on the board, he added, "It's equal to forty."

$8 \times 5 = 40$

No one mentioned adding five eights and I didn't suggest it.

THE NEXT FEW WEEKS

From time to time during the next few weeks, I'd take part of a math class and engage the students again in a problem from *Amanda Bean's Amazing Dream.* Sometimes I led a class discussion about a problem; other times I asked the children to work individually to solve one. With time and practice, the children all made progress.

Questions and Discussion

▲▲▲

▲ *Sometimes you have children come to the board to record and explain their thinking, and sometimes the children just explain and you do the recording. How do you decide which is better?*

The more recording that children actually do, the better. I try to do enough recording on the board to model for children how they might record to keep track of their own thinking. Then as often as possible, I give children opportunities to record during lessons. When children write on the board, they get valuable practice and also provide another model for their classmates.

▲ *Why do you insist on the correct order of the factors if it doesn't matter for finding the products?*

It's important for the children to understand the meaning of the mathematical representation for multiplication, that 6 × 4, for example, means six groups of four, or six fours. It's also important for children to connect correct mathematical representations to problem situations. Finally, we want children to understand that the commutative property of multiplication results in the same answer no matter the order of the factors. The activities in this lesson aim at developing understanding of all of these concepts.

A caution: Be sure to listen to children's explanations before you pass judgment on a multiplication sentence. A colleague told me that her class was discussing how many wheels there were on seven tricycles. Most children thought that the appropriate sentence was 7 × 3, to show seven groups of three. One girl, however, thought that 3 × 7 could make sense if you thought of the front wheels together as a group of seven, the left rear wheels as another group of seven, and the right rear wheels as a third group of seven.

CHAPTER FOUR
MULTIPLICATION STORIES

Overview

This lesson gives children experience connecting real-world situations to multiplication equations. It also gives children experience estimating answers to multiplication problems and calculating accurate answers in several different ways. The lesson helps develop children's understanding of multiplication, their number sense, and their ability to compute accurately.

Materials

▲ *Multiplication Stories* worksheet (see Blackline Masters)

Time

▲ two class periods; can be repeated

Teaching Directions

1. Begin listing on the board the multiples of ten. Ask the children to say the numbers along with you as you write them. Tell the children that you're going to write a problem and they are to think about which of the numbers on the list would be a good estimate for the answer.

2. Write the problem on the board: *There are 7 tricycles. How many wheels are there altogether?* Talk with children about the usefulness of making estimates as a way to begin thinking about the solution to a problem. Ask children to choose an estimate from the list. Put a check mark next to each of the choices they make.

3. Next ask the children how you might write the problem with a math equation that uses multiplication. If the children don't know what to do, this is a good time to connect the problem to the appropriate representation and explain that 7×3 means seven groups of three or seven threes.

4. Ask for volunteers to figure out the answer and explain their reasoning. Have the children record on the board or ask them to explain and you can record their thinking on the board. Talk about how their answers relate to the estimates they made.

5. Explain the individual assignment. For the multiplication equation $8 \times 4 = \square$, they are to make an estimate, write a problem that fits the equation, and figure the answer. Draw a sample worksheet on the board or an overhead transparency or distribute a copy to each student. Also, if you have taught the *Things That Come in Groups* lesson (see Chapter 1), suggest to the children that they can look over the class lists for ideas.

Multiplication Stories

Estimate   Equation   _____
10
20
30   Problem   _____
40   _____
50   _____
60   _____
70   _____
80   _____
90   _____
100   _____
>100

Figuring

6. The next day, have students share the different problems they wrote for the equation, their solutions, and their methods for figuring. Point out that many different situations can be represented by the same multiplication equation, but they all have to do with equal groups.

7. If you think it's necessary, do another problem with the class to be sure that the children understand what they are to do. Then have them work individually, choosing their own equations and writing their own problems.

Teaching Notes

The lesson begins with the teacher presenting the class with a problem situation: *There are 7 tricycles. How many wheels are there altogether?* The children are asked to represent the problem with a multiplication equation: $7 \times 3 = \square$. After choosing an estimate for the answer from a list of multiples of ten, children present their strategies for calculating the exact answer.

Children often are discouraged when their estimates don't match the accurate solution. Asking children to choose an estimate from the multiples of ten is useful for helping children realize that estimates don't have to be exact and generally aren't. Also, children who might already know the exact answer to a problem still have to think about which multiple of ten is closest, which both draws on their number sense and gives them experience that will be useful later when they learn about rounding numbers. After children arrive at an answer, discuss the estimates they made—how close they were to the solution, what they learned from solving the problem, and what ideas they have for making reasonable estimates in the future.

After investigating the tricycle problem, children think of other problems that also can be represented by $7 \times 3 = \square$. Children then work individually to write a problem for $8 \times 4 = \square$, make an estimate, and then use several different methods to calculate the answer. Children repeat the assignment for other multiplication equations.

The lesson presents the opportunity to talk with children about the power of mathematical representation. Having children think of problem situations other than tricycles for $7 \times 3 = \square$, and later share their different problem situations for $8 \times 4 = \square$ and other equations, helps them realize that the same equation is effective for interpreting a wide variety of situations.

It's important to emphasize that the common characteristic of all problem situations that relate to multiplication is that they involve equal groups. Children typically solve multiplication problems by adding, but these problems differ from other addition problems in that the same addend is repeated a certain number of times.

The Lesson

▲▲▲

DAY 1

I began the lesson by listing a few of the multiples of ten on the board, saying them as I wrote them, "Ten, twenty, thirty." I stopped, asked the class to say the pattern along with me, continued until one hundred, and then wrote *more than 100* at the end of the list:

10

20

30

40

50

60

70

80

90

100

more than 100

"Who knows what an estimate is?" I asked.

"It's a guess," Alicia answered.

"It's something you think but it might not be for sure," Jay added.

No one had another idea to contribute, so I said, "I'm going to write a problem on the board. I'd like you to think about which of the numbers I listed would be a good estimate for the answer." I then wrote on the board:

There are 7 tricycles. How many wheels are there altogether?

"Which number on the board do you think is closest?" I asked.

"Twenty," Sergio said. I put a check mark next to 20 on the list.

"I think forty," Peter said. I put a check mark next to 40 as well.

Alicia said, "Thirty."

Lydia said, "Ten." I put check marks next to each of those numbers.

"We'll see which of these estimates is closest to the answer when we figure it out," I said. "But before we talk about how to figure, I'm interested in writing the problem with a math equation that uses multiplication. Who has an idea about how to do this?"

"You can write seven times two," Jessica said. I wrote on the board:

$7 \times 2 = \square$

Even though Jessica's suggestion wasn't correct, I wrote it on the board to give Jessica a chance to reconsider and to see how others might react. No one raised a hand to offer a comment and Jessica seemed satisfied.

"Why did you put the seven in your equation?" I asked Jessica.

"There are seven tricycles," Jessica responded.

"And what about the two?" I asked.

"Because a tricycle has two wheels," she said.

"No, it doesn't," Aaron blurted out.

"Oh yeah, oh yeah," Jessica said. "The two isn't right."

"What shall I write instead of the two?" I asked.

"Change it to a four," she said.

"That's not right," Amelia said. "A tricycle has three wheels, Jessica."

"It has one front wheel and two back wheels," Kelly added.

Jessica was now flustered. I waited a moment to give her time to think. Finally, Jessica hit her head with the palm of her hand and said, "I get it. It should be a three." I revised what I had written on the board:

$7 \times 3 = \square$

"So tell us again what the seven stands for?" I asked.

"There are seven tricycles and each tricycle has three wheels, so it's seven times three," Jessica answered.

"That's right," I confirmed. "I can also read the equation as 'seven groups of three' or 'seven threes,' which makes sense

because we're thinking about seven tricycles with three wheels each."

"I know a way to get the answer," Amelia said.

"That's just what we're going to do next," I said. "We have a problem, an estimate, and an equation. Now we have to figure out the answer. What's your idea, Amelia?"

"You draw three circles to be the wheels, and you draw that seven times," Amelia explained.

"Like this?" I asked, after drawing seven groups of three circles on the board:

OOO OOO OOO OOO
OOO OOO OOO

"Yes, but you can put a circle around each of the threes to show it better," Amelia said. I revised my drawing by circling each group of three circles. Amelia nodded to confirm that I had done what she was thinking.

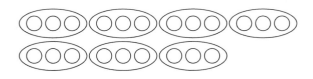

"So how many wheels are there?" I asked.

Amelia continued, "I'll count by threes—three, six, nine, twelve, fifteen, eighteen, twenty-one." She used her fingers to help with the last two numbers. I recorded on the board:

3, 6, 9, 12, 15, 18, 21

"Making a picture is often a useful help for figuring," I said. "Who has another idea about how to figure out the answer?"

I called on Alicia. "Can I come to the board?" she asked. I nodded yes.

Alicia came up and said, "Seven and seven is fourteen, and I know that fourteen and six makes twenty." She wrote on the board:

7 + 7 = 14

14 + 6 = 20

Alicia was then stuck. By focusing on writing on the board, it seemed that she had lost the idea she had had. She started to erase what she had written, but I stopped her and suggested that she see if someone in the class had an idea that could help. Alicia turned to the class. Aaron raised a hand.

"It has to be twenty-one," Aaron said, "because seven is one more than six, so seven plus seven plus seven is twenty-one."

"I don't get it," Alicia said.

I added to what Alicia had written to represent Aaron's idea:

7 + 7 = 14

14 + 6 = 20

14 + 7 = 21

7 + 7 + 7 = 21

Alicia still wasn't sure. "Let's hear other ideas," I said, "and that might help." Alicia nodded and returned to her seat.

Ruthie had a different approach. "I know three times three is nine," she said, "and that's three tricycles. You do it again for three more tricycles, and you have eighteen, and then you add on three more wheels for the last tricycle."

"Let me see if I can record your idea on the board," I said. I wrote:

3 × 3 = 9

3 × 3 = 9

9 + 9 = 18

18 + 3 = 21

Ruthie nodded. To show the class another way to represent Ruthie's idea, I said, "I can write this a shorter way." I wrote:

(3 × 3) + (3 × 3) = 18

18 + 3 = 21

Lydia had another idea. "You can add three seven times," she said. She came to the board and wrote:

3 + 3 + 3 + 3 + 3 + 3 + 3

Then she proceeded to combine the numbers:

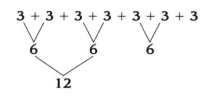

"I know that three and six is nine, so I have to add twelve and nine," Lydia said. "That's hard."

Can you add twelve and ten?" I asked.

"It's twenty-two," Lydia answered quickly, then she added "Oh yeah, that helps." She wrote on the board:

3 + 6 = 9

12 + 10 = 22

12 + 9 = 21

"So Sally, Alicia and Aaron, Ruthie, and Lydia all got the same answer of twenty-one," I said.

"I know another way," Alicia said. I was interested to hear how Alicia was now thinking. She came to the board and wrote with confidence, explaining as she did so:

7 + 7 = 14

15 + 5 = 20

14 + 6 = 20

20 + 1 = 21

"That's good!" Jay said.

"What made you write 'fifteen plus five equals twenty'?" I asked Alicia, interested in finding out why she was so confident now.

"It's an easy one," Alicia said, "and I could change it."

"Ah, so you used something you already knew," I commented. Alicia nodded.

"Starting with something you know is a very useful strategy when you have to figure out an answer," I said, "as long as what you know connects to the problem you're trying to solve." I still wasn't sure what had caused Alicia's new confidence, but I didn't pursue her thinking any more. Marea had her hand raised.

"I have a way that's like Lydia's, but I figured differently," she said.

"Did you get the same answer?" I asked.

"Yes," Marea said. She came to the board and wrote:

3 + 3 + 3 + 3 = 12

12 + 3 + 3 + 3 = 21

She then explained, "I knew that four threes make twelve, so then I had to add on three more."

"How did you know that you had to add on three more threes?" I asked.

"Because there are seven tricycles, and I only used up four of them. There were three more," Marea answered. She returned to her seat.

"I know another way to show your idea, Marea," I said. "First you figured four threes and then you added on three more threes. See if this makes sense to you." I wrote on the board:

$(4 \times 3) + (3 \times 3) = 21$

"That's OK," Marea responded.

I then pointed to the multiples of ten I had listed. "So which estimate is closest?" I asked.

"Twenty," Tomas said. "It's only one away."

I then said, "Suppose I hadn't started with the tricycle problem but instead started by writing 'seven times three equals blank' on the board. What other problems could I have written?"

Peter said, "There were seven tennis ball cans. How many balls were there?" I wrote this on the board.

Aaron said, "There are seven poison oak plants. How many leaves are there?" I wrote this on the board.

Greta said, "There were seven lily pads and there were three frogs on each of them." I wrote this on the board and then said to Greta, "What question are you asking?"

"How many frogs are there?" she answered. I added this to complete her problem and reminded the children, "A problem needs to end in a question so we know what we're trying to figure out."

I summarized what we had done. "There are four parts to what we just did. There's a problem." I pointed to the problem I had written about the seven tricycles. "There's an equation," I continued, pointing to the equation. "We made an estimate and you figured the answer in several different ways." I pointed to the estimates and the students' calculations.

I then explained to the children what they were to do individually. "Now you'll do a paper like this on your own on which you'll show an equation, a problem, an estimate, and how you figured the answer." I drew a sample on the board to show them how to organize their papers.

"Do we write the numbers like that?" Tomas wanted to know, referring to the list of the multiples of ten.

"Yes," I said, "and you'll also write this equation." I added $8 \times 4 = \square$ to the sample paper I had drawn.

"For your work, I chose an equation, and your first job is to write a problem that matches it. If you'd like, check for ideas on the lists we made for *Things That Come in Groups*. Make an estimate by checking which multiple of ten you think is closest to the answer, and then figure out the answer in several different ways. Remember, figuring different ways gives you a check and is a good way to be sure that your answer is right."

A few children had questions. "What do we put for a title?" Jessica asked.

I thought for a moment. "Let's call this paper 'Multiplication,'" I said.

"Can we write any problem we want?" Eddie asked.

"As long as it's a situation about eight groups of four," I said.

Observing the Children

There was the typical confusion that exists when children begin a new assignment. As I began circulating around the room, Greta called me over and whispered, "Can I do lily pads and frogs?"

"Do you think they work?" I asked her.

"They work for anything," she told me.

The class had previously experienced the *Things That Come in Groups* lesson, so it wasn't hard for them to think of situations for groups of four. Pets were a common theme. Alicia wrote: *There were 8 kittens and each kitten had 4 legs. How many kitten legs in all?* Jessica also used kittens' legs (see Figure 4–1). Marea wrote: *There was 8 dogs and they all had 4 legs. How many legs all together?* Carlos wrote: *There was 8 people thay all have four pets. How many pets wher all togther.*

Cars and trucks were another theme among the boys. Sergio wrote: *There wer 8 cars. How many weels* (see Figure 4–2). Tomas and Aaron used the same situation. Bo wrote: *There were eight trucks with four wheels each. How many wheels are there all there together?* Bo drew the trucks and carefully labeled them—Safeway, Big 4 Rents, Web Van, and so on (see Figure 4–3).

Other problems varied. Sally wrote: *There were 4 bees on 8 flowers. How many bees all together?* (see Figure 4–4). Jay referred to kikuzaras, the four-pointed origami stars he had learned to make: *There are 8 kikuzaras and each kikuzara has 4 points how many kikuzara points in all?* Peter wrote: *There were eight baseball dimonds. 4 bases on each dimond. How many bases in all?*

Several children wrote about frogs and lily pads. Evan's problem indicated his lack of understanding about multiplication. He wrote: *There were 8 frogs on lieypads and 4 on land how many frogs in all.* Although Evan's calculations were correct, his paper showed how a child can be able to compute correctly but not yet have developed adequate understanding of the concept. Evan's paper indicated to me that I needed to talk with him individually.

Most children calculated by adding eight fours and four eights. Some also showed how they counted by fours to get thirty-two. Some drew a picture and then counted by fours or twos.

For two of his six methods for figuring the points on the eight kikuzaras, Jay had unique ideas. He wrote: *5 + 5 + 5 + 5 + 5 + 5 + 5 + 5 = 40 five is one more then 4 so take away one from five eights take away 8 from 40 and get 32.* For his next method, he wrote: *3 + 3 + 3 + 3 + 3 + 3 + 3 + 3 = 24. 3 is one less then 4 so add 8 ones to 24 and get 32.*

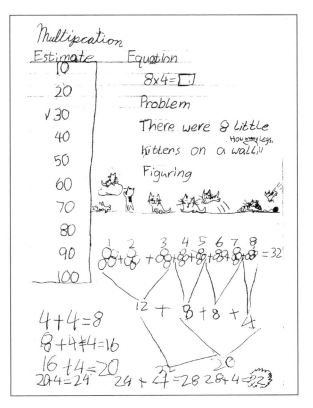

▲▲▲▲▲▲**Figure 4–1** *Jessica's paper showed several different ways to figure the number of legs on 8 kittens.*

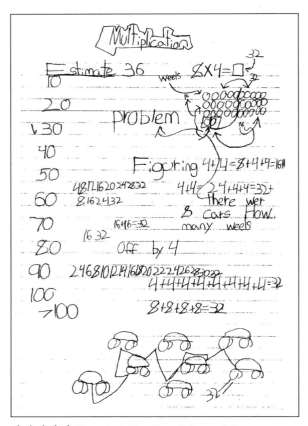

▲▲▲▲▲▲Figure 4–2 Sergio's problem was similar to Bo's problem, but his methods for finding the answer differed.

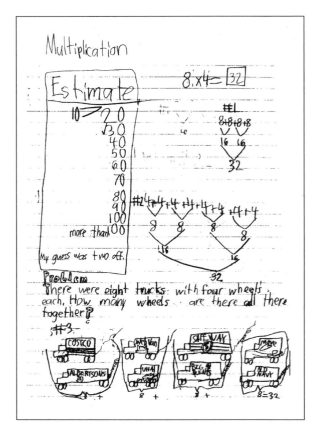

▲▲▲▲▲▲Figure 4–3 Bo solved his problem by adding four 8s, then eight 4s, and then making a drawing to count the wheels on the trucks.

Lydia was interested in explaining how she made her estimate of thirty. "I knew the answer was thirty-two," she told me. She showed me that she had written *7 × 3 = 21* and then, underneath, *8 × 3 = 24.* "I started with what I knew from the other problem," she explained. She also wrote: *7 is one less than 8 and 3 is one less than 4.* Then she reasoned that to find the right answer, all she had to do was increase each digit in twenty-one, making it thirty-two! While her reasoning had no mathematical grounding, it worked in this particular instance (see Figure 4–5).

I thought about how to respond to Lydia. First of all, I wanted her to know that I was pleased to see that she was trying out the strategy of starting with what you know. But I also wanted her to see the flaw

in her idea in this particular case, so I gave her an example that would present a contradiction.

"I see that you know how much seven times three is," I commented.

"It's twenty-one," Lydia said.

"Do you know how much six times two is?" I asked.

Lydia thought for just a moment and then said, "It's twelve."

I wrote on her paper:

6 × 2 = 12

7 × 3 = 21

"OK?" I asked her. She nodded.

"But if I used your idea for figuring out the answer to seven times three from six times two, I'd say that since seven is one more than six and three is one more than

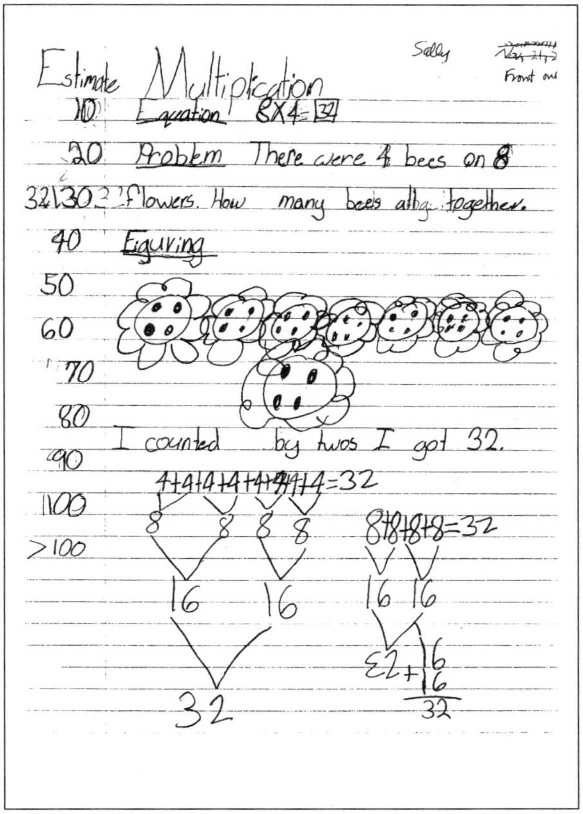

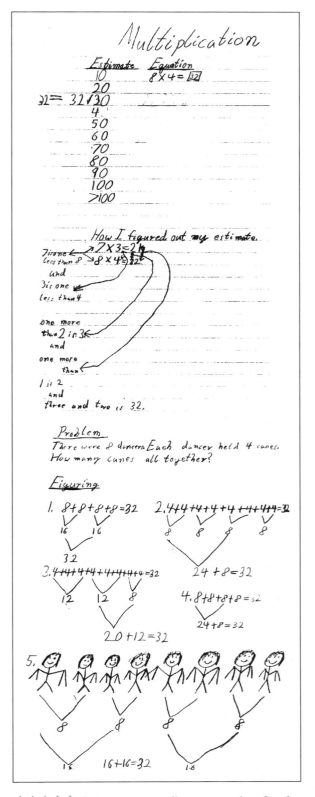

Figure 4–4 *Sally figured how many bees there were altogether if there were 4 bees on each of 8 flowers.*

two, the numbers in the answer should each be one more, and that would give me twenty-three, not twenty-one."

"Hey," Lydia said. "It wouldn't work. I don't get it. It worked over here." She pointed to the example she had done.

"Yes, you got lucky there," I said. "But a strategy has to work for everything in order for it to be a method you can count on."

"I guess so," Lydia said. She wasn't too concerned, and because the rest of her work was fine, I wasn't concerned either. But the encounter reminded me of several things. One is the importance of reading children's work carefully. Another is the importance of thinking about the mathematics sufficiently to be prepared to present a counterexample, as I did with Lydia.

Figure 4–5 *Lydia's reasoning for deciding on an estimate worked in this problem, but it wasn't a correct approach!*

DAY 2

My plan for this day's class was to discuss another problem with the students so that I would have the chance to review several ideas. One idea was that the order of the numbers in a multiplication sentence usually matters when describing a situation, but the order doesn't matter when you think about how to calculate the answer. Another idea was that it's possible to break a problem into smaller pieces to figure an answer, a strategy that uses the distributive property. I wasn't concerned about teaching the property as much as offering children another alternative for computing.

On the board, I set up a sample paper as I had had them do the day before on their papers and wrote a problem in the appropriate place: *There are 5 spiders. How many legs do they have altogether?*

"What multiplication equation can I write to represent this problem?" I asked. I called on Aaron.

"It's forty," he said. Aaron didn't answer what I had asked, but I decided to continue with his line of thinking.

"Is that an estimate or a definite answer?" I asked.

"An estimate," Aaron answered. I checked 40 on the list and repeated the question I had asked first, "What multiplication equation can I write to represent this problem?"

"It's five times eight," Jay offered. I wrote on the board:

$5 \times 8 = \square$

"Can you explain your idea?" I asked.

"A spider has eight legs and there are five of them, so you go five times eight," Jay said.

"It's five eights," Kelly added.

I drew on the board five spiders, each with eight legs, and explained, "Five times eight means five groups of eight, or five eights."

"If you drew eight of them and they each had five legs, it would be eight times five," Lydia said.

"They wouldn't be spiders," Tomas said.

"They could be amoebas," Amelia suggested.

"Or spiders with some legs cut off," Jessica said giggling.

Before the conversation spun more off the track, I brought the children's attention back to the problem I had presented. I said, "How can we figure out the answer?"

Bo said, "For two spiders, you go eight plus eight and that's sixteen legs. Two more spiders have sixteen legs and sixteen plus sixteen makes thirty-two. Then I have to add on eight more legs." Bo paused while I recorded what he had suggested so far. I wrote:

2 spiders	$8 + 8 = 16$
2 spiders	$8 + 8 = 16$
4 spiders	$16 + 16 = 32$

Bo continued, "Take two off the thirty-two and put it on the eight to make ten. Then you add thirty and ten and you get forty." I didn't follow Bo's reasoning and asked him to repeat it. He did and I recorded what he said. I wrote:

$32 - 2 = 30$

$2 + 8 = 10$

$30 + 10 = 40$

5 spiders have 40 legs

Lydia went next. "You add five eights," she said. I wrote on the board:

$8 + 8 + 8 + 8 + 8$

Lydia then explained, "Two eights make sixteen and these two eights make sixteen. Then sixteen and sixteen makes thirty-two. And then you have to add thirty-two and the last eight to get forty."

Marea said, "You can count by fives. It's easier that way." As Marea counted, I recorded on the board:

5, 10, 15, 20, 25, 30, 35, 40

I then said to the class, "Five times eight is the correct equation for the spider problem, because we're talking about five groups of eight. But when you figure it out, it's OK to switch the order of the numbers so you have eight fives. This doesn't match the problem, but you'll get the same answer."

"It's like when you add," Alicia said.

"Yes," I confirmed, "you can switch the order of the numbers when you add and when you multiply. That's because addition and multiplication are what we call 'commutative.'" I wrote *commutative* on the board and asked the children to say it aloud. I find that if I introduce vocabulary in the context of their experience, it helps children learn it.

"I have another way," Jay volunteered.

"Do you want to come up and write or explain and I'll write?" I asked.

"You can write," Jay said. "You go five plus five plus five," he said, continuing until I had recorded eight fives:

$$5 + 5 + 5 + 5 + 5 + 5 + 5 + 5$$

Jay continued, "I know that five times four is twenty, and another five times four is twenty, so you have forty altogether." I wrote:

$$5 \times 4 = 20$$
$$5 \times 4 = 20$$
$$20 + 20 = 40$$

Ruthie raised a hand. "My way is like Jay's but a little different," she said. "I did five plus five is ten, five plus five is ten, five plus five is ten, and five plus five is ten. Then you go ten plus ten is twenty and you have two twenties and that makes forty."

Kelly had a different approach. "I used the eights," she began. "Ten times eight is eighty, and half of eighty is forty, so five times eight has to be forty." Most of the others had difficulty following Kelly's reasoning. I didn't discuss it further but acknowledged that it was a correct way to arrive at the answer.

I then showed the children the worksheet I had prepared. Although most of the children had done fine doing their own recording, I felt the worksheet would help those who labored with organizing their papers. Also, having the worksheet provided a way to structure the activity as a choice for when children had time available and needed a purposeful activity to do.

I gave the class directions. "On this paper, you can choose your own problems to work on. You can start either with a multiplication equation or by writing a problem. When you figure the answer, be sure to do so in more than one way so that you'll have a check."

Most children chose single-digit problems. Kelly, for example, wrote: *There were 9 dogs and each dog had 7 puppys. How many puppys in all?* Marea wrote: *There were 9 bumble bees. How many legs do they have all together?* Chuck was less confident in his numerical ability. He wrote: *Their were 5 people. they each had 2 snow skis, how many snow skis in all* (see Figure 4–6). Some children wanted more challenge. Tomas was interested in solving 50×3 and wrote: *There wer 50 non nativ black bares* [nonnative blackberries] *how meny leaves wer there all together.* Bo used the context of money and wrote: *There was sixty half dollars. How many dollars is there all together?*

This activity became one of the choice items, available for children when they had extra time. As a choice, they were again free to pick their own equations as well as write their own problems. See Figures 4–7 through 4–9 for more examples of students' work with this activity.

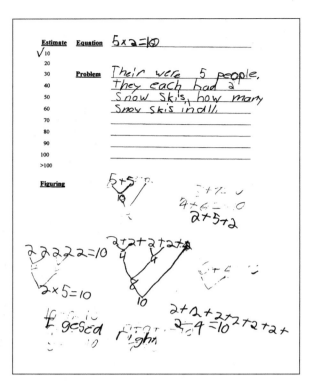

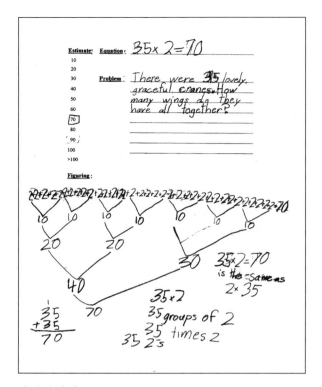

▲▲▲▲▲▲Figure 4–6   *Chuck struggled with learning and his paper showed his partial understanding and confusion.*

▲▲▲▲▲▲Figure 4–8   *Ruthie's paper showed that she understood the meaning of multiplication and the commutative property.*

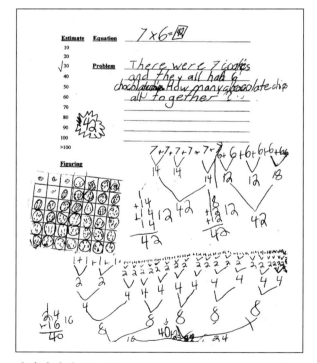

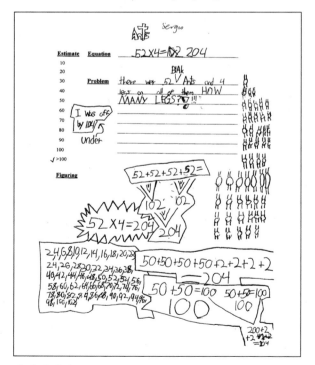

▲▲▲▲▲▲Figure 4–7   *Marea used squared paper to represent her problem about chocolate chips on cookies and then solved it in several ways.*

▲▲▲▲▲▲Figure 4–9   *Sergio was interested in challenging himself with larger numbers.*

Questions and Discussion

▲▲

▲ *When Jessica answered incorrectly and offered 7 × 2 to represent the problem with the tricycles, weren't you worried about her being humiliated or discouraged by calling attention to her error?*

There's no right way to handle a situation when a child answers incorrectly. However, I try to establish a culture in the classroom in which errors are viewed as opportunities for learning. We all make errors, I tell the children, and what's important is that we learn from them. Giving students a chance to rethink their ideas is important, as long as it's done in a supportive way.

▲ *Why do you have children make up their own problems?*

As with all topics, children learn about multiplication at their own rates. Class instruction needs to structure experiences that are accessible to all children, that provide opportunities for all students to learn, and that also can challenge those children who learn more quickly. This lesson addresses that need by allowing children to choose the numbers for the multiplication problems they tackle. My experience is that children choose numbers that are within their reach and of interest to them. Therefore, their work is not only useful for assessing their skills but also for getting a sense of their numerical comfort.

▲ *Wouldn't class discussions be easier if all the students worked on the same examples?*

I agree that class discussions about the same problem are extremely useful. To provide this experience, from time to time, I use one of the children's problems for a class discussion. Doing so acknowledges the child who created it while involving the entire class in thinking about another problem. I've found that often the child who chose the problem no longer remembers the answer and thus has the chance to participate fully in the discussion along with the others!

CHAPTER FIVE
WHICH HAS MORE?

Overview

This activity provides children experience comparing the results from two multiplication problems, both presented in contexts. The lesson gives children experience both representing problem situations that involve multiplication and computing accurate answers. Asking children to compare products helps build their number sense as children make estimates to predict which answer will be larger. Also, after the activity is introduced, children have opportunities to choose numbers for subsequent problems.

Materials

▲ *Which Has More Cookies?* worksheet (see Blackline Masters)

▲ *Which Has More Windowpanes?* worksheet (see Blackline Masters)

▲ *Which Has More Wheels?* worksheet (see Blackline Masters)

▲ optional: *Amanda Bean's Amazing Dream,* by Cindy Neushwander (New York: Scholastic, 1998)

Time

▲ one period to introduce, then several more to repeat

Teaching Directions

1. Draw on the board two windows, one with five rows of panes and four panes in each row, and the other with three rows of panes and six panes in each row.

2. With the children, count to determine the number of rows in each window and the number of panes in each row. Write on the board:

a window with 5 rows of panes with 4 panes in each row

a window with 3 rows of panes with 6 panes in each row

3. Ask: "Which window do you think has more panes?" Discuss the problem with the class, recording on the board to model representing methods of calculating.

4. Give the children directions about what they are to do individually: "Now you'll each solve two *Which Has More?* problems on your own. One is about cookies on trays, and the other is about wheels on bicycles and tricycles." Write on the board:

Which has more?

a tray with 3 rows and 8 cookies in each row or a tray with 4 rows and 6 cookies in each

the number of wheels on 5 bicycles or 7 tricycles

Remind the children to write the multiplication problems and to figure in more than one way to check their answers.

5. To follow up the lesson, have children make up their own *Which Has More?* problems using the worksheets to organize their work. If you wish, use the activity as a choice over the next several weeks.

6. As an extension to help children think about how multiplication and addition differ, present Tomas's idea. Tell the class: "Tomas decided to figure out which tray had more cookies—a tray with eight rows of cookies and four cookies in each row, or a tray with seven rows of cookies and five in each. He knew that in order to figure out which tray had more cookies, he had to compare the answers to two multiplication problems." Write on the board:

8×4

7×5

Then continue: "Tomas thought that the answers would be the same. He reasoned that since seven is one less than eight, and five is one more than four, the products should be the same. What do you think about Tomas's idea?" Discuss with the class.

Teaching Notes

Before teaching this lesson, make sure children have had experience with writing multiplication equations to represent situations and with computing answers. Introducing the activity to the whole class helps establish the procedure and prepares children to work independently. I presented this lesson using three contexts from *Amanda Bean's Amazing Dream.* Asking children to compare the number of windowpanes in two different-size windows or the numbers of cookies on two cookie trays gave them experience thinking about multiplication as arrays. Asking children to compare the number of wheels on different numbers of bicycles and tricycles gave them experience thinking about multiplication as repeated addition. It isn't necessary, however, to rely on the story of Amanda Bean. Using the context of different-size candy boxes, such as those the children explore in the *Candy Boxes* lesson (see Chapter 7), provides the same opportunity. You can also ask the children to compare scores for individual rounds of *Circles and Stars.* Or you can use any other context with which the children are familiar.

The extension to the lesson presents a way to stretch the children's thinking about how multiplication and addition differ. The situation suggested actually arose in one class I taught and was based on what one student, Tomas, had predicted. If no one in your class suggests this idea, you can offer your students the same experience by presenting Tomas's idea and asking them to consider it.

The Lesson

▲▲▲

To begin the lesson, I drew on the board two windows, each with a different number of windowpanes:

The children and I counted the number of rows in each window and the number of panes in each row. I recorded the counts on the board:

a window with 5 rows of panes with 4 panes in each row

a window with 3 rows of panes with 6 panes in each row

"Which window do you think has more panes?" I asked the class.

Amelia answered, "I think that the one with five rows has more because five rows is two more than three, and four is two less than . . . oops, now I think they are the same . . . no, no . . . oh, I'm confused."

I waited for a moment to see if Amelia wanted to continue. She seemed on the verge of offering another idea but then said, "Oh, let someone else go."

"Raise your hand when you have another idea and we'll listen," I told her. I called on Bo.

"It's equal," he said, "because five plus four is nine and three plus six is nine." I recorded on the board:

$5 + 4 = 9$

$3 + 6 = 9$

"Hmmm," I said, "I agree that five plus four is nine and three plus six is nine, but I'm not sure how that helps us figure the number of panes in the windows. I need to think some more about that."

Kelly had a more direct response. "That's not right, Bo," she said. "You have to multiply, not add. Five times four is twenty."

"Oh yeah," Bo said.

"What does the twenty tell you?" I asked Kelly.

"How many panes there are on that window," Kelly answered. "See, you go five, ten, fifteen, twenty." I wrote on the board:

$5 \times 4 = 20$

5, 10, 15, 20

"Let's check that answer by figuring the other way, adding up five fours," I said. I wrote on the board:

$4 + 4 + 4 + 4 + 4$

I asked the class to add along with me, "Four and four is eight, and four more is twelve, and four more is sixteen, and four more is twenty."

"Can I do the other one?" Alicia asked.

"What is your idea?" I asked her.

"Three times six is eighteen," Alicia said. "You go six plus six, and that's twelve, and then six more makes eighteen." I wrote on the board:

3 × 6 = 18

6 + 6 = 12

12 + 6 = 18

"So you added three sixes," I said, pointing out the three 6s I had used as addends. "Can anyone figure it another way?"

Sergio said, "Add six threes." I wrote:

3 + 3 + 3 + 3 + 3 + 3

"How will you do that?" I asked.

"Three and three is six," Sergio began, "then the next three and three is six, and then three and three is six." I recorded:

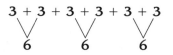

Sergio took a breath and said, "Six and six makes twelve." Then he counted on his fingers to find out that twelve and six more made eighteen. It was interesting to me that Sergio didn't make use of the information from when Alicia added three sixes, preferring to do it in his own way instead.

I said, "So you got the same answer adding three sixes as Alicia did by adding six threes. That's a good check." I pointed to the three 6s I had added previously. Sergio nodded.

"I can do it another way," Lydia said. "I know that three plus three plus three is nine. You do that two times and then nine plus nine is eighteen." I recorded:

3 + 3 + 3 = 9

3 + 3 + 3 = 9

9 + 9 = 18

"Solving problems in several ways is good for checking that our answers are right," I reminded the children.

"I have another way for the other one," Aaron said.

"For figuring five times four?" I asked.

"Yes," Aaron said. "You can add ten plus ten, and that's twenty." I wrote on the board:

10 + 10 = 20

"Can you help me understand how that relates to the windowpanes?" I asked.

"I split it in half down the middle," Aaron explained. "There's ten on the left and ten on the right." I drew a line to show Aaron's idea:

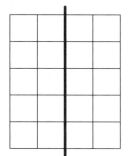

Aaron continued, "It's two tens. So five times four is the same as ten times two."

"Ten times two means ten twos," I said. "Aren't you thinking about two tens?" I probed. I wouldn't necessarily push every child this way, but Aaron was a keen thinker capable of this sort of precision.

"Oh yeah," he said, "it's two times ten." I recorded:

5 × 4 = 2 × 10

"Saying 'ten times two' would work also," I said, "if you were counting the panes by twos." I demonstrated how to do this.

"I have another way," Ruthie said. "It's sort of the same as the five fours, but different."

"What's your idea?" I asked.

"I added four and four and got eight, then four and four and got eight again. I know that eight and eight is sixteen, so four more makes twenty." I wrote on the board:

4 + 4 = 8

4 + 4 = 8

8 + 8 = 16

16 + 4 = 20

"Can I come up and write it a different way?" Ruthie asked.

"The same way of figuring?" I asked.

"Yes," she said.

"Let's see," I said. Ruthie came up to the board and wrote:

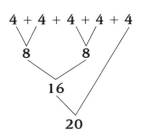

$$4 + 4 + 4 + 4 + 4$$

8   8

16

20

I brought the conversation back to the original problem and said, "So which window has more panes?"

"The first one," several children answered.

I then explained to the children what they were to do. "Now you'll each solve two *Which Has More?* problems on your own. One is about cookies on trays, and the other is about wheels on bicycles and tricycles. Watch as I write on the board." I wrote:

Which has more?

a tray with 3 rows and 8 cookies in each row or a tray with 4 rows and 6 cookies in each

the number of wheels on 5 bicycles or 7 tricycles

I told the children, "For each, be sure to write the multiplication problems. Also, do your figuring in more than one way so that you have a check on your answers."

"Is it OK to draw pictures?" Jessica wanted to know.

"That's fine, if it will help you solve the problem," I answered.

"What paper do we use?" Peter asked.

"I'll distribute lined paper," I said.

"Which do we do first?" Amelia asked.

"Start with the cookies," I suggested.

The children got to work. I realized after a moment that it might have been better if I had reversed the number of bicycles and tricycles. It seemed obvious to me that with more tricycles there would be more wheels. But only a few children saw the problem as obvious. Peter, for example, wrote: *I could tell*

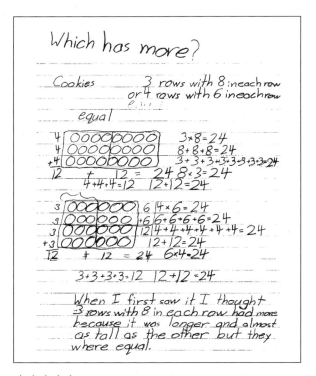

▲▲▲▲▲▲Figure 5–1 *Kelly's paper showed her clear understanding of how multiplication relates to the problem and her ability to compute. She was surprised to find that both trays held the same number of cookies.*

▲▲▲▲▲▲Figure 5–2 *Lydia's paper illustrated how she used the commutative property to figure the number of cookies on each tray in two ways.*

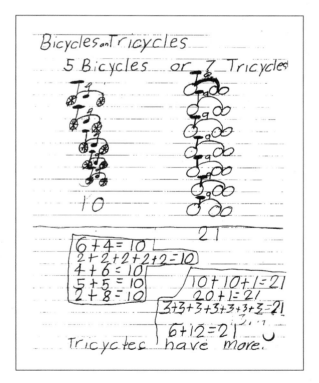

Figure 5-3 (Aaron's work):

Which Has More?
5 bicycles with 10 wheels
or 7 tricycles with 21 wheels

5 bicycles x 2 wheels=10 wheels!
5 +5 /10 or 5x2=10
5+5=10 or 5x2=10
2+2+2+2+2=10 or 2x5=10

7 tricycles x 3 wheels=21
3 +3 +3 +3 /9
3+ 3+ 3+ 3 /12
9 or 12
9+12=21

▲▲▲▲▲Figure 5–3 *Aaron showed that 7 tricycles have more wheels than 5 bicycles.*

Figure 5-4 (Amelia's work):

Bicycles and Tricycles
5 Bicycles or 7 Tricycles
10   21
6+4=10
2+2+2+2+2=10
4+6=10
5+5=10
2+8=10
10+10+1=21
20+1=21
3+3+3+3+3+3+3=21
6+12=21
Tricycles have more.

▲▲▲▲▲Figure 5–4 *Amelia answered the question correctly by counting the wheels she drew. She didn't use multiplication to represent the problem, but she wrote several addition sentences for each. This work is typical of children just learning about multiplication.*

Figure 5-5 (Ruthie's work):

Which has more
5 bicycles or 7 tricycles

5x2=10 is the same as 2x5=10 but we want the first question.

2+2+2+2+2=10 but if you were doing it the other way it would be......5+5=10. + A stick with the first problem

7x3=21 is the same as 3x7=21 but, we want the first question.

3+3+3+3+3+3+3=21 but if you were doing it the other way it would be..7+7+7=21. I'll stick with the first problem. tricycles had more

▲▲▲▲▲▲Figure 5–5 *Ruthie showed that she understood which is the correct way to use multiplication to represent the number of wheels on bicycles and tricycles.*

that when I first saw the question. I knew that the 7 tricycles had more wheels than the 5 bicycles because tricycles have more wheels than bikes and because there are more tricycles than bicycles. (See Figures 5–1 through 5–5 for other students' responses to these problems.)

After working on the cookie problem, Jay sidled up to me and said, "I think you made a mistake. They both have the same number of cookies."

"That's a good discovery," I said. "I chose those numbers purposely so you could see that different multiplication problems can produce the same answer."

"I won't tell," he whispered to me in a conspiratorial tone.

To follow up the lesson, I had children solve other *Which Has More?* problems, choosing the numbers they'd like to explore. I duplicated worksheets on which they could organize their problems. I then used this activity as a choice item for children to do when they had extra time (see Figures 5–6 through 5–10).

Which Has More?   53

Figure 5–6 (top left)

Which has More?
7 row with 6 cookies in each row
or 5 rows with 9 in each row

9   9   Less cookies
29   21+21=42
9   42
+12
42   This is an odd number
        6 X 7=42 acros
        7X6=42 is not the same
        number acros.

7+7+7+7+7+7=42
6+6+6+6+6+6=42

more cookies
8   10
           45   This an odd number
                so it is not divided
                into the same number
                5X9=45 on each side.
           12   9X5=45
5+5+5+5+5+5+5+5=45
9+9+9+9=45

              12
              15
              10
            +08
              45

▲▲▲▲▲▲**Figure 5–6** *For her own problem, Alicia compared 7 x 6 and 5 x 9. She tried, unsuccessfully, to split the cookies into four equal groups, but she was able to solve the problem correctly.*

Figure 5–7 (bottom left)

Which has more?
8 rows with 6 cookies in each row

6+6+6+6=24+
6+6+6+6=48

8x6 = 48

8+8+8+8+8+8=48

4 rows with 9 cookies in each row
4+4+4+4=16+4+
4+4+4+4=36
9+9+9+9=36

I thought that 9 x 4=36
and I was right
8 x 6
cookies would be higher
and I like doing *problem
that why make cookies because I love
doing cookies I love cookies and I love eating cookies

▲▲▲▲▲▲**Figure 5–7** *Marea compared a cookie tray with 8 rows and 6 cookies in each and a tray with 4 rows with 9 cookies in each.*

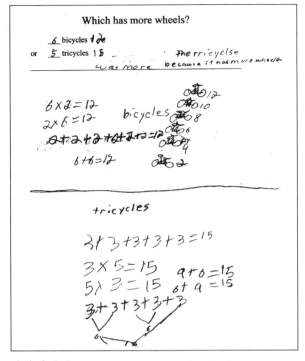

Which has more wheels?
6 bicycles 1 de
or 5 tricycles 1 δ   The tricycles
                was more because it had more wheels

6 X 2 = 12
2 X 6 = 12   bicycles
2+2+2+2+2+2=12
      6+6=12

tricycles
3+3+3+3+3=15
3 X 5 = 15   9+6=15
5 X 3 = 15   6+9=15
3+3+3+3+3

▲▲▲▲▲▲**Figure 5–8** *Raul decided to compare the number of wheels on 6 bicycles and 5 tricycles. He found out that the tricycles had more wheels.*

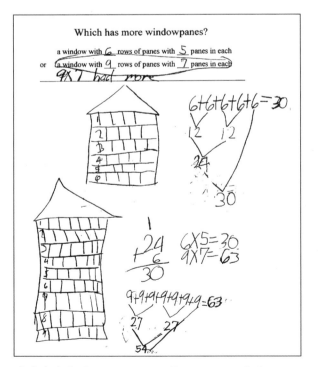

Which has more windowpanes?
a window with 6 rows of panes with 5 panes in each
or a window with 9 rows of panes with 7 panes in each
9X7 had more

6+6+6+6+6=30
      12
      24
      30

      24
    + 6
      30   6X5=30
                9X7=63

9+9+9+9+9+9+9=63
      27   27
         54

▲▲▲▲▲▲**Figure 5–9** *Sally compared the number of windowpanes in two windows, one with 6 rows and 5 panes in each, and the other with 9 rows and 7 panes in each.*

54   Lessons for Introducing Multiplication

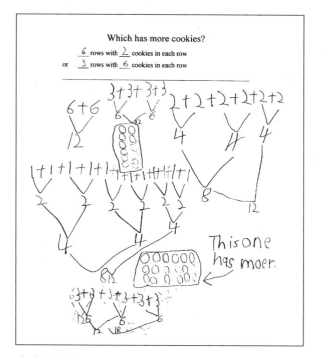

Which has more cookies?

_6_ rows with _2_ cookies in each row

or _3_ rows with _6_ cookies in each row

▲▲▲▲▲▲**Figure 5–10** _For his problem, Evan compared two cookie trays. While he drew the trays and solved the answers correctly, he didn't write multiplication problems to describe them._

EXTENSION

This extension is based on an experience that Tomas had when working on a _Which Has More?_ problem involving cookies on trays. I began the discussion by writing on the board:

$15 + 5 = 20$

$14 + 6 = 20$

I said to the class, "A student once told me that adding fourteen and six was hard, so she changed the problem to fifteen plus five because it was easier. Since she knew that fifteen plus five was twenty, she also knew that fourteen plus six was twenty. What do you think about her idea?" I gave the children a few moments to think about this and then called on Amelia.

"Six is one more than five, and fourteen is one less than fifteen, so it's right," Amelia said.

"You take one from the six and add it on the four in fourteen and it's fifteen, so they're the same," Bo said.

"I agree with her idea," Aaron said. "You're just moving stuff around."

There seemed to be general consensus that the idea was a good one. I then presented Tomas's experience. (I had talked with Tomas previously and he had agreed to my doing so. To use Tomas's idea in your class, you can present it as I did for the previous child's idea.) I said to the class, "Tomas decided to figure out which tray had more cookies—eight rows of cookies with four cookies in each row, or seven rows of cookies with five in each." I wrote on the board:

8 rows with 4 in each

7 rows with 5 in each

I continued, "Tomas knew in order to figure out which tray had more cookies, he had to compare the answers to two multiplication problems." I wrote on the board:

_8 × 4_

_7 × 5_

"Tomas thought that the answers would be the same," I said. "He reasoned that since seven is one less than eight, and five is one more than four, the products should be the same. I want to hear what you think about Tomas's idea. Then, in a bit, Tomas will tell you what he discovered." (See Figure 5–11 for Tomas's work on this problem.)

I called on Kelly first. "I agree with Tomas," she said. "They both are the same. It's like the adding problem."

Peter agreed and offered his reasoning. "If you add two even numbers, the answer is even," he began. (A week or so ago, we had been discussing what happens when you add even and odd numbers.) "And if you add two odd numbers, you still get an even number. You get twelve both times." Peter then stopped for a moment. "Uh oh," he said, "I just realized that we're timesing,

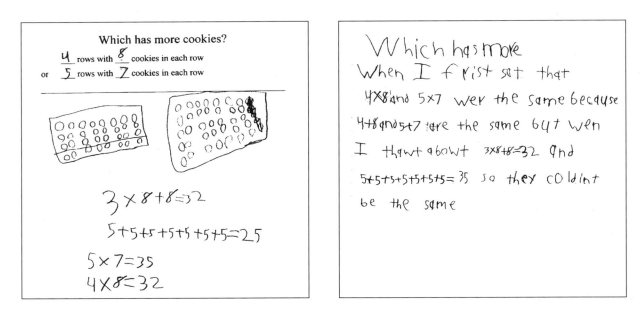

Which has more cookies?

__4__ rows with __8__ cookies in each row

or __5__ rows with __7__ cookies in each row

$3 \times 8 + 8 = 32$

$5+5+5+5+5+5+5=25$

$5 \times 7 = 35$

$4 \times 8 = 32$

Which has more

When I frist set that 4X8 and 5X7 wer the same because 4+8 and 5+7 are the same but wen I thawt abowt 3X8+8=32 and 5+5+5+5+5+5+5=35 so they coldint be the same

▲▲▲▲▲▲**Figure 5–11** *At first, Tomas thought that the two trays would hold the same number of cookies. His calculations proved him wrong.*

not adding. I think they are going to be thesame answers but bigger numbers."

Aaron had a different idea. "I disagree with Tomas's idea," he said. "I think that if you multiply even numbers you get an even answer and if you multiply odd numbers you get an odd answer. So they have to be different." I wrote on the board:

Odd + Odd = Even

Even + Even = Even

Odd × Odd = Odd

Even × Even = Even

"I don't think we've proved that multiplying two odd numbers produces an odd answer, but it's an interesting idea," I said.

Sergio then said, "I agree with Peter, it's just like adding but the answers get bigger."

Raul said, "I think it's the same because the top is more and the bottom is less in the first number and then the other way around." Raul's language was imprecise, but we all seemed to understand how he was reasoning.

Jay said, "I mainly agree with Aaron. Multiplication is like repeated adding. If you add seven plus seven, you get an even

answer, and that's two sevens. Wait, I'm mixed up."

Lydia said, "I can't decide yet. We aren't sure yet about odd times odd."

Ruthie said, "I think they are different but very, very close."

"Why do you think that?" I asked her.

"I'm not sure," Ruthie said.

"How close do you think the answers will be?" I asked.

"Maybe one or two, or maybe three," she replied.

Kelly said, "I'm changing my mind. I'm not sure now. I got plus and times mixed up. If it was plus, it would work."

Amelia said, "I know the answers, I think. I think they're one away, so they have to be different."

Peter said, "I still agree with Tomas and Sergio that they're the same. The eight is one more than seven and the four is one less than five."

Aaron said, "They're different. I'm sure of it. I figured them out."

Kelly added, "Me, too. They're three away."

The conversation was a lively one, but I interrupted it and said, "I have an idea to share. Whenever I have a problem to solve that I'm not sure about, I try to make a smaller problem just like it to help me think." I reminded the class that when we had talked about figuring out the tiles on a 12-by-12 countertop, we had had a long discussion about whether or not to count the corner tile twice when figuring out the number of tiles across and down. (See the *Tiles on the Countertop* activity in the Additional Activities section.) To help the children think about this problem, I wrote on the board:

4×1

3×2

"How much is four times one?" I asked the class. They chorused the answer. "And three times two?" I continued. They answered again. I wrote on the board:

$4 \times 1 = 4$ $1 + 1 + 1 + 1 = 4$

$3 \times 2 = 6$ $2 + 2 + 2 = 6$

"Who has an idea about why this problem with small numbers can help us think about Tomas's problem?" I asked.

Lydia answered, "They're not the same, but you did the same thing. Three is one less than four and two is one more than one."

"The answers are different," Sergio said.

"They're two away," Amelia said.

"When I try these easier problems and see that the answers are different, then I'm not sure that the answers to the other problems should be the same just because I made one factor larger and the other smaller. I'm mathematically suspicious," I said.

"Can I tell what I discovered?" Tomas asked. I agreed.

Tomas referred to his paper. He said, "I drew the cookie trays and then figured out the answers. Seven times five was easy because I counted by fives. I got thirty-five. Eight times four was harder, so I did three eights first and got twenty-four and then I added one more eight on to get thirty-two.

So I discovered that they were different." I wrote on the board:

$7 \times 5 = 35$

$8 \times 4 = 32$

"It was very interesting," Tomas added.

"But it still seems that they should be the same," Sergio said.

"That's what I think," Raul added.

"Now I see that they're three away, not one," Amelia said.

I attempted to give an explanation. "Multiplication and addition are related to each other, but they're also different, and it's sometimes tricky to think about them together." I wrote the two multiplication problems on the board as addition problems:

$7 \times 5 = 35$ $5 + 5 + 5 + 5 + 5 + 5 + 5 = 35$

$8 \times 4 = 32$ $4 + 4 + 4 + 4 + 4 + 4 + 4 + 4 = 32$

"Look," Alicia said, excitedly. "You can see that the top is more. If you take off one four so they both have seven, then the fives have to be more because they're bigger. And the extra four isn't enough to put one more on each of the fives."

I ended the discussion with one final comment. "One way that multiplication and addition are different is that when you add, you combine the two numbers. With seven and five, for example, you can count up seven and then add on five more. But you don't combine the two factors in multiplication problems. The first number tells you how many times to add the second number. In this problem, the seven tells us how many fives to add. So we use the numbers in different ways when we add and when we multiply."

I then structured the rest of the math period by offering the children choices. "You can try another *Which Has More?* problem as Tomas did, or you can write your ideas about whether or not multiplying two odds gives an odd, or you can play *Circles and Stars* with a partner." This array of choices was sufficient to meet all of the children's needs.

Questions and Discussion

▲▲▲

▲ *When Bo suggested the wrong idea, that you add the number of panes instead of multiplying, why did you record his idea on the board? Won't that confuse some of the children?*

I'm careful to write all children's ideas on the board and not to censor, just as I'm careful to question children when they are right as well as when they are wrong. Both actions contribute to building children's intellectual autonomy and encourage them to think critically about their ideas as well as the ideas of their classmates. Bo's arithmetic figuring was correct, but I didn't see how his idea related to the problem. (Nor did Bo.) Putting it on the board, however, honored his contribution and gave the entire class the chance to contemplate his reasoning. Also, sometimes a child does have a correct notion that I don't understand. For example, I didn't understand why Aaron thought that $10 + 10$ was a good way to figure the number of panes in the 5-by-4 window. If I had rejected his answer, I would have missed understanding his correct thinking.

▲ *What about the children who didn't participate in the discussion about 7×5 and 8×4? Was this time useful for them?*

It's always a judgment call about how long to let a discussion go when some children aren't engaged. But if the mathematics is important and at least half the class is actively participating, I tend to pursue a discussion. Even when children aren't sharing ideas, they still may be paying attention and learning. Hearing from their classmates is very important, I think. Also, I find that more and more children engage as they learn that having discussions like this is part of the culture of how we learn math and as they develop confidence in their own ideas.

CHAPTER SIX
BILLY WINS A SHOPPING SPREE

Overview

In this lesson, the children are introduced to Billy, a boy who won a twenty-five-dollar gift certificate to spend at the Science Museum Store. Billy must choose from a list of items that cost three dollars, four dollars, and five dollars. The children's task is to find different ways Billy can spend his money, write receipts showing the amount Billy spends in each price category, and figure out how much money, if any, is left over.

Materials

▲ Science Museum Store price list, 1 per student (see Blackline Masters)

Time

▲ two class periods

Teaching Directions

1. Tell the class that Billy is a fortunate boy who won a twenty-five-dollar shopping spree at the Science Museum Store. Post the price list of items he can buy or distribute a copy to each student. **Note:** I chose the particular items listed because they fit in the price range of three to five dollars, are familiar to children, and would probably be of interest to them. If you want to select different items, use a price list with at least three choices in each price category.

2. Explain to the class: "Billy can spend up to twenty-five dollars on any selection of the listed items. If he doesn't spend the entire amount, he can't keep the change."

3. Tell the children that they will work in pairs to find at least two different ways Billy might spend the money. For each, they should write about the choices they made and then prepare a receipt to show how much Billy spent and how much money, if any, is left over.

Science Museum Store
Price List

$3.00	$4.00	$5.00
1. Origami paper	1. Kaleidoscope	1. Koosh ball
2. Crystal and gem magnets	2. Large magnifying bug box	2. Glow-in-the-dark solar system stickers
3. Furry stuffed seal pups	3. Sunprint kit	3. Inflatable world globe
4. Prism	4. Inflatable shark	4. Wooden dinosaur model kit

4. Draw on the board a model of the receipt. Explain the "at" sign and show the class how to make it. Children enjoy learning new symbols such as this one. Rather than duplicating blank receipts for the students to fill in, having them prepare their own helps them learn how to organize their work on paper.

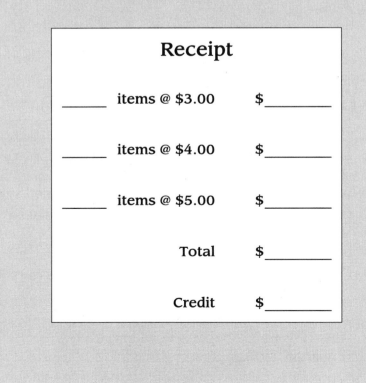

Receipt

_____ items @ $3.00 $_____

_____ items @ $4.00 $_____

_____ items @ $5.00 $_____

Total $_____

Credit $_____

5. Children may raise the question of sales tax. If so, respond by telling them that they can decide for themselves whether they want to account for tax in their figuring. Everyone need not deal with this in the same way.

6. In a class discussion, ask children to present how they decided Billy could spend the money. As they report, record their receipts on the board. Each time, ask the others to check that the mathematics on the receipt is correct.

Teaching Notes

The real-world aspect of this lesson serves to engage children's interest while giving them a context to apply multiplication. Having the children write receipts gives them an organized way to represent their choices numerically. Also, writing receipts provides a way to introduce the @ symbol, another way to bring real-world learning into a math lesson.

The extension suggested for an in-class or homework assignment asks students to find all the possible ways for Billy to spend exactly twenty-five dollars. Students typically search for solutions to this problem by trial and error, which gives them a good deal of practice with reasoning numerically. However, knowing if or when they've found all the possible solutions to this problem is generally beyond the ability of third graders. Still, it's beneficial for children to consider this question, as it introduces the ideas that problems can have more than one solution and that knowing when you have all the possible answers is part of thinking mathematically.

The Lesson

▲▲

DAY 1

When I introduced the activity, the children were interested in Billy and the options he had for his shopping spree. There was an outburst of chatter when I posted the price list.

"I love Koosh balls. They're so fun."

"I got a blow-up globe for my birthday."

"What's a sunprint kit?"

"I know. You make pictures in the sun."

"What kind of kaleidoscope is it?"

"I'd get the dinosaur kit."

After giving students a chance to express their ideas, I called them back to attention. I explained, "Your task with your partner is to decide how Billy might spend his money."

Alex raised his hand. "Could he buy different things?" he asked.

"Yes," I answered. "Billy can buy all different things or several of one thing. He can mix and match any way he likes, as long as he doesn't spend more than twenty-five dollars."

"Can he use some of his own money?" Lindsay asked.

I responded, "No, he can only spend up to twenty-five dollars."

The children again began talking with one another about the things Billy could buy. I asked for their attention.

"I have a few more directions to give you before you start to make your decisions," I said. I waited for them to listen.

"You must record in two different ways," I continued. "First, write about the items Billy will buy. Then make a receipt showing how much he spent and how much money, if any, is left over. Does anyone know what a receipt is?"

A few children raised their hands. I called on Josh. "It's what you get when you buy something so if you need to return it you can show you bought it," he said.

That's right," I said. "A receipt is a record of your transaction." I drew on the board a sample receipt form and explained how to use it to describe Billy's purchases.

"Could Billy just take the money?" Brandon asked.

I answered, "No, it's only store credit. Also, if he doesn't spend the entire twenty-five dollars, he doesn't get change; it remains as store credit."

Angie raised the issue of sales tax. She was a mature and precise child, and her question didn't surprise me. I told her she could decide to include tax or not, that it was up to her and Jennifer, her partner.

There were no more questions and the children got to work. The activity interested all of the children. Most took the decision about which items Billy might buy quite seriously. Some wrote in detail about what Billy bought.

Libby and Kristina, for example, wrote: *With the $25.00 Billy won, he can buy crystal and gem magnets, a furry stuffed seal pup, an inflatable shark, a large magnifying bug box, glow-in-the-dark solar system stickers, and a wooden dinosaur model kit. Billy wraped some of the wonderful toys he bought. He gave some of his friends a toy. His friends loved the presents he gave them. Billy was happy he gave his friends those toys.* Their receipt indicated he had bought two items at three dollars, two items at four dollars, and two items at five dollars for a total of twenty-four dollars.

Emily and Jenny reported a way for Billy to spend the entire amount. In their descrip-

tion, they chose more sophisticated words than they could spell. They wrote: *With the $25 Billy won, he can buy the following: 2 packs of Origami paper, a prism, a kaleidoscope, a sunprint kit, and a Koosh ball. We hope that Billy will have bundles of fun with these wonderful gifts. We know we would, and Billy was very fourtionate to recive these fabulise things that he would normally have to pay oodles of money to get. These wonderful things will surly bring him lots of joy and happiness.*

Koji and Sam kept a running total of the money Billy had available. They wrote: *Billy bought Orrigami paper. It costed him $3.00. He had $22.00 left. Then Billy bot a inflateble shark. It costed him $4.00 he had $18.00 left. Then Billy bought a Koosh ball. It costed him $5.00. He had $13.00 left. Then he bought another pack of origami paper. It costed him $3.00. He had $10.00 left. Then he boght a sunprint kit and it costed him $4.00. He had $6.00 left. Then he bought a prism. It costed him $3.00. He had $3.00 so he bought a Prism again.* Their receipt showed that he had no money left.

Figure 6–1 shows how Lisa and Kim itemized Billy's shopping list.

DAY 2

I initiated a class discussion for children to report what they had done. To help them prepare for the discussion, I asked partners to read aloud to each other what they had written. Then I gathered them to report.

As pairs reported, I recorded their receipts on the board. After recording each receipt, I turned to the class and asked, "Do you agree with the financial transaction on the receipt?" This encouraged children to think about the calculations, thus giving them practice with computing mentally.

After Libby and Kristina and Angie and Jennifer reported, Josh noticed that they both had purchased two five-dollar items. He commented, "Look, it's the same on

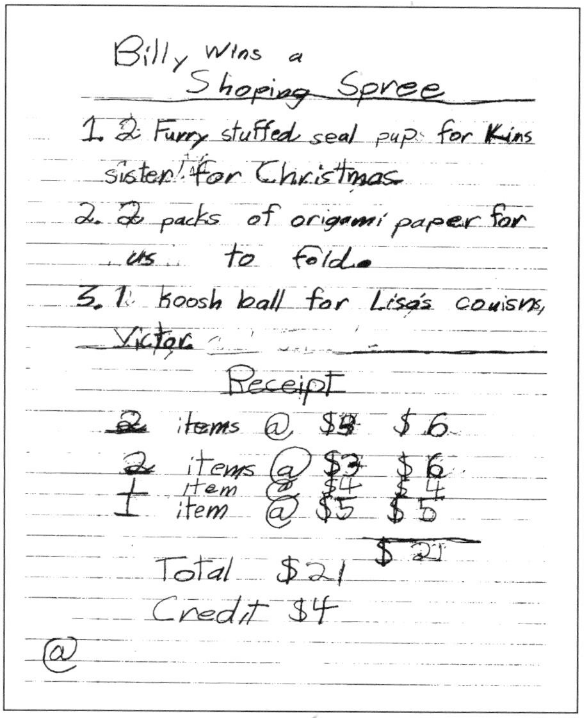

Billy Wins a Shoping Spree

1. 2 Furry stuffed seal pup for Kins sister for Christmas
2. 2 packs of origami paper for us to fold.
3. 1 Koosh ball for Lisa's cousins, Victor

Receipt

2 items @ $3 $6
2 items @ $3 $6
1 item @ $4 $4
1 item @ $5 $5
$21

Total $21
Credit $4
@

Figure 6–1 ***Lisa and Kim's description indicated that they forgot to purchase an item for $4, but then they squeezed one in on their receipt.***

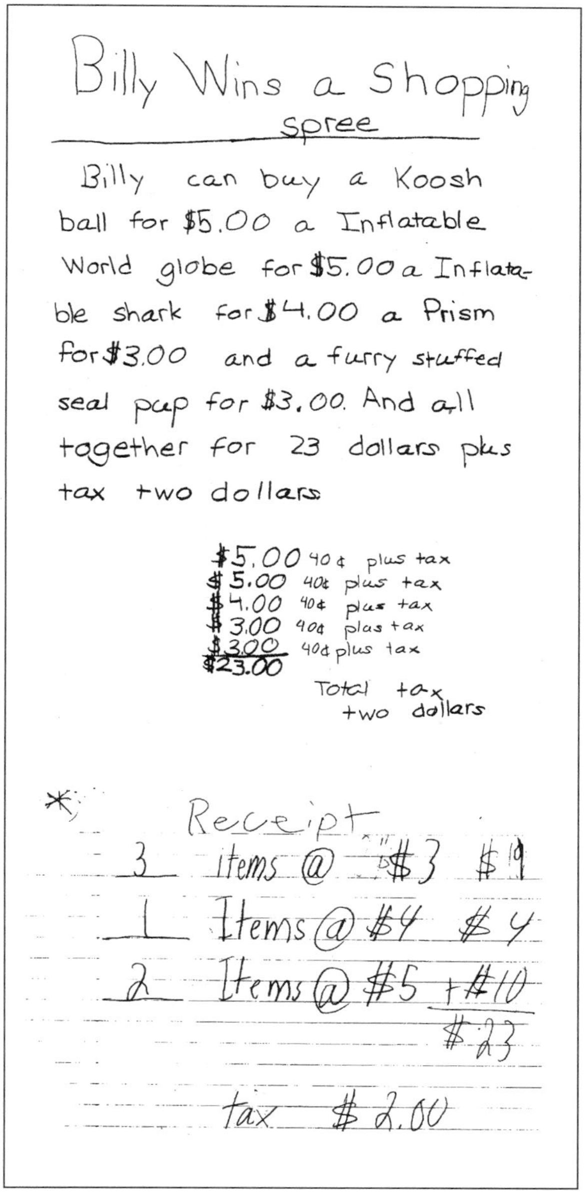

Billy Wins a Shopping spree

Billy can buy a Koosh ball for $5.00 a Inflatable World globe for $5.00 a Inflatable shark for $4.00 a Prism for $3.00 and a furry stuffed seal pup for $3.00. And all together for 23 dollars plus tax two dollars

$5.00 40¢ plus tax
$5.00 40¢ plus tax
$4.00 40¢ plus tax
$3.00 40¢ plus tax
$3.00 40¢ plus tax
$23.00
Total tax two dollars

Receipt

3 items @ $3 $9
1 Items @ $4 $4
2 Items @ $5 +$10
$23

tax $2.00

Figure 6–2 ***Angie and Jennifer were the only children in the class to use the remaining money for tax. Their work showed they didn't yet understand the proportional nature of sales tax.***

their receipts, but they bought different things." Angie and Jennifer had bought a Koosh ball and an inflatable world globe (see Figure 6–2), while Libby and Kristina had bought a Koosh ball and glow-in-the-dark solar system stickers.

Josh's comment sparked a search for other instances where receipts indicated the same thing but the actual purchases differed. I told the children, "The receipt gives you information about the money transaction, and your description tells what you actually bought."

Emily said, "The supermarket receipt tells you what you bought, too." A few of the other children were also familiar with these itemized receipts.

Tony then said, "The Koosh ball is the best thing to get." Several others agreed. I didn't want the discussion to center on favorite items, so I refocused the students on reporting their purchases and I returned to recording as they did so.

After all pairs had reported, I pointed to the receipt I had recorded on the board for the purchases Alex and Brandon had chosen—three five-dollar items, one four-dollar item, and two three-dollar items. "They found

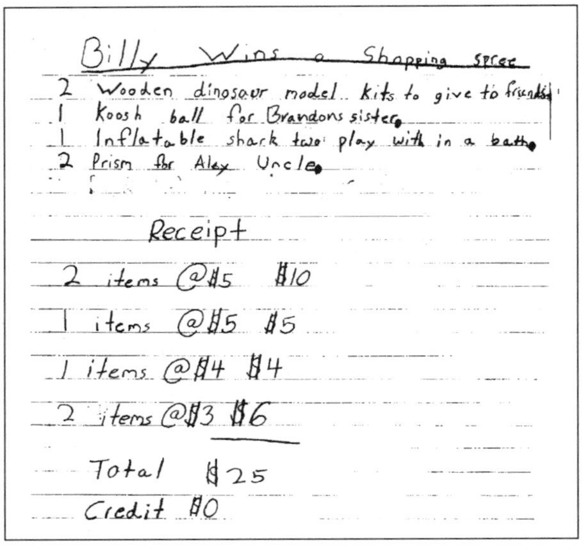

Billy Wins a Shopping spree
2 Wooden dinosaur model kits to give to friends
1 Koosh ball for Brandons sister
1 Inflatable shark two play with in a bath
2 Prism for Alex Uncle

Receipt
2 items @ $5 $10
1 items @ $5 $5
1 items @ $4 $4
2 items @ $3 $6
          Total $25
          Credit $0

▲▲▲▲▲▲**Figure 6–3** *Alex and Brandon found a way to spend exactly $25.*

a way for Billy to spend exactly twenty-five dollars," I said. (See Figure 6–3.)

"Let's see if you found other ways for Billy to spend exactly twenty-five dollars and have no money left over," I said.

As the children scanned the receipts I had written on the board, Angie said, "We did it with tax."

"Yes, you did," I commented. "Let's see if anyone spent exactly twenty-five dollars on the items, without extra for tax."

"Oh, Tanya and Rebecca did," Brian noticed. "They bought four items for three dollars, two for four dollars, and one for five dollars."

"We did, too," Michael said. "We did it like Alex and Brandon."

"We bought three Koosh balls," Tony added, grinning. "I told you the Koosh ball was best."

"You could have bought five Koosh balls, if you like them so much," Josh said.

"He wanted to, but I wouldn't let him," Michael said.

No other receipts indicated an exact total of twenty-five dollars.

EXTENSION

Ask children to find all of the different combinations of three-, four-, and five-dollar items that equal exactly twenty-five dollars. For this problem, ask children to focus on the number of items at a particular price, not the selection of particular items. For example, buying five Koosh balls is the same solution as buying three Koosh balls, an inflatable world globe, and a dinosaur model kit. In each case, Billy spends twenty-five dollars by buying five items for five dollars each.

This extension is also suitable for a homework assignment. If you assign it for homework, make sure each child has a price list to take home. You might also want to send home a note to explain the assignment to parents:

Dear Parent,

The children have been introduced to Billy, a fortunate (and fictitious) boy who won a $25 shopping spree at the local Science Museum Store. Using a price list that explained the possible purchases, the children decided how Billy might spend the money. They prepared receipts to record his purchases and indicate how much money was left. For homework, your child is to find ways for Billy to spend exactly $25. This assignment gives experience using multiplication in a problem-solving situation. Please offer your assistance if needed. (Note that your child should focus on the number of items at each particular price, not on the selection of particular items.)

Questions and Discussion

▲▲

▲ *Wouldn't it be easier to give the children duplicated forms for the receipt?*

It certainly would be easy to draw receipt forms, four to a page, and duplicate them for the children. However, I prefer to give children as many opportunities as I can to do their own recording. This form is fairly simple, and writing it themselves helps children learn to plan ahead and organize their papers. Also, writing their own receipts gives them the chance to practice writing the @ sign. Some of the children were familiar with the sign from e-mail addresses but hadn't had experience writing it. Also, this lesson provides another use for the symbol.

▲ *What do you do if children present a solution that has an error in it?*

I record just what is reported. Then I turn to the class and ask, "Do you agree with the financial transaction on the receipt?" This encourages children to check the calculation. If they notice a mistake, I make sure that the children who made it now understand the correct answer. Also, I'm sure to point out that making mistakes is part of learning math, and I emphasize the benefit of checking calculations.

▲ *Is it important to have the children work in pairs? This seems like a good individual assignment.*

The decision of whether children will work with partners or individually should depend on your goals. Working together gives children the chance to talk about what they're doing to solve the problem, and this interaction supports students' learning to reason and record. When children work individually, however, you have a way to assess each student's numerical reasoning and recording. The choice is yours. You might ask children to work together on one solution for how Billy might spend the money and then work on individual solutions. This way you offer them initial learning support and also an individual challenge.

CHAPTER SEVEN
CANDY BOXES

Overview

This activity introduces children to a geometric model for multiplication. Students investigate rectangular arrays as they research how to package candies. The "candies" are 1-inch square tiles that are packed one layer deep in rectangular boxes. Children use the tiles to identify the various dimensions of boxes that are possible for different numbers of candies. While helping students learn about multiplication from a geometric perspective, the activity also provides them experience with the concept of measuring area.

Materials

- ▲ color tiles (1-inch square tiles), at least 12 per student
- ▲ one-half-inch squares (see Blackline Masters)
- ▲ scissors, 1 pair per pair of students
- ▲ tape or glue
- ▲ optional: *Candy Box Research* directions, 1 per pair of students (see Blackline Masters)
- ▲ Optional: *More Candy Box Research* directions, 1 per pair of students (Blackline Masters)
- ▲ sheet of 18-by-72-inch chart paper, or several smaller sheets taped together, ruled into 2-inch columns numbered from 1 to 36

Time

- ▲ three class periods

Teaching Directions

1. Distribute tiles so that each pair of children has twenty-four. Explain to the class that the tiles are pretend candies that are packaged in one layer in rectangular boxes. Point out that candy boxes can also be square because squares are rectangles with the special quality that each of their sides is the same length.

2. Tell the class that a sampler box holds four candies. Ask each child to take four tiles and arrange them to fit into a box. Remind them that candies are packaged in only one layer.

3. Ask children to describe their arrangements. Draw them on the chalkboard. Typically, students produce the two possible options. If children find only one arrangement, however, show the other and have them build it with the tiles. If students suggest an L-shaped arrangement, remind them that the boxes must be rectangular or square.

4. Show the class how to label the sampler boxes you drew by writing 2 × 2 and 1 × 4 inside them. Read aloud what you wrote as "two by two" and "one by four," and explain to the class that the numbers refer to the number of units on adjacent sides. Then, using one-half-inch squares, cut out the two different arrays and label them as you showed.

5. Pose the *Candy Box Research* problem: *Each pair of students is the design research team of the candy company. The president of the company has asked for a report about the different boxes possible for six, twelve, and twenty-four candies.* You may wish to write the directions on the board or an overhead transparency or distribute a copy to each pair of students.

Candy Box Research

You need: color tiles
one-half-inch squares
scissors
tape

1. Use color tiles to build all the rectangular boxes possible for 6, 12, and 24 candies.

2. Cut out each box from one-half-inch squares and label its dimensions.

3. Write a memo to the president explaining what you've learned about possible boxes and what shape box you recommend. Include your cutout boxes with your memo.

6. The next day, have children report their findings and recommendations in a class discussion. To prepare for the discussion, have them first read aloud their memos to their partners.

7. Introduce the *More Candy Box Research* problem: *The president of the company wants customers to be able to buy any number of candies they like. The design research department now has to recommend boxes for all quantities of candies from 1 to 36.*

8. Post the chart paper ruled into columns numbered from 1 to 36. To demonstrate what children will do, post cutout rectangles for the numbers the class has already investigated: four, six, twelve, and twenty-four. Make sure that the rectangles you posted are correctly labeled.

9. Show the children the small bag you've prepared with slips of paper numbered from 1 to 36, except for 4, 6, 12, and 24. Tell them that they'll work in pairs, choose a number from the bag, and investigate the possible boxes for that many candies. You may wish to write the directions on the board or an overhead transparency or distribute a copy to each pair of students.

More Candy Box Research

You need: color tiles
             one-half-inch squares
             scissors
             tape
             bag with numbers

1. Pick a number from the bag.

2. Use the tiles to find all possible rectangles for that number.

3. Cut each rectangle you build out of one-half-inch squares and label.

4. Tape the rectangles on the class chart.

5. Repeat for another number from the bag.

---

10. When the chart is complete, lead a class discussion. Ask the following questions and list the numbers that answer each:

Which numbers have rectangles with a side that is two squares long?

Which numbers have rectangles with a side that is three squares long?

Four squares?

Five squares?

Which numbers have rectangles that are also squares?

Which numbers have only one possible rectangle?

If we continued the chart, would we ever find a number that had no rectangles? Why or why not?

Teaching Notes

It's important for children to have as many opportunities as possible to see how different mathematical topics relate to one another. This lesson helps build a connection between the numerical concept of multiplication and the geometric concept of area. Using the tiles gives children concrete assistance for developing understanding of this connection, and using the context of packaging candies links the activity to a real-world application.

To help children think about the number of candies in a rectangular box, relate the dimensions of the box to counting a number of equal groups. For example, the number of candies in a 3-by-5 box can be figured by thinking of three rows with five candies in each, or three fives. It can also be thought of as five rows with three in each, or five threes. Both ways produce the same answer of fifteen candies.

The Lesson

▲▲▲

DAY 1

I began the lesson by telling the class that we were going to pretend that the color tiles were candies made by a particular candy company. "The company always packs the candies in boxes one layer deep, and the boxes are always rectangular," I said.

I began distributing zip-top baggies with about fifty tiles in each to each group of four children. As I did so, I reminded the class about something we had discussed previously. "Candy boxes can also be square. Remember that a square is a special kind of rectangle. It's special because each of its sides is the same length."

When all of the tables had tiles, I continued. "The smallest candy box that the company makes is a sampler that holds four candies. Take four tiles and see how you might arrange the candies in one layer to fit into a sampler box."

The children had used the tiles for other activities before this lesson. Because of their prior experience, they were comfortable with the tiles, didn't need time to explore them, and quickly went to work on the task. In a few moments, almost all had their tiles arranged. As I looked around the room, I saw both 2-by-2 and 1-by-4 arrays as well as a few L-shaped arrangements.

I called on Angie, who was sitting near the back of the room. I said, "Angie, describe your arrangement of tiles so I can draw it on the board."

Angie said, "Well, I put two in a row and then underneath two more in a row." I drew a 2-by-2 array of squares on the board and looked at Angie. She nodded.

"Who arranged the tiles the same way Angie did?" I asked. More than half the students raised their hands.

I then showed the children how to record the dimensions. "Because there are two tiles on each edge, each side is two units long," I said. "I can write that this is two by two." Inside the square I wrote: 2×2. Also, I cut a 2-by-2 square from one-half-inch grid paper and labeled it.

"Can someone who arranged the tiles differently describe what you did so I can draw it on the board?" I asked.

I called on Koji. He said, "Mine goes in a straight line. There's four in a row." I drew a 1-by-4 rectangle.

"That's what I did," Brandon blurted out.

"Who else made this same arrangement?" I asked. About a dozen children raised their hands.

"I'll record this by writing 'one by four' inside," I said and wrote: 1 × 4. "Who can explain why "one by four" describes this rectangle?"

I called on Tanya. "Because it's just one row of four," she said. Using the same sheet of squared paper, I cut out and labeled a 1-by-4 rectangle.

"I know another way," Tony said. He had arranged his tiles into an L.

"That won't work for the candies," I said. "Candy boxes are always rectangular. They can be long rectangles, like Koji's, or a square, like Angie's. But they don't come in L shapes."

A few children were still rearranging tiles to see if they could find another shape, but most were satisfied that the two on the board were the only possibilities for four tiles.

I then told the children what they were to do. "You and your partner are a research team for a candy company. The president gave you a job to work on together. 'In our candy company,' the president said, 'we sell candy boxes in half-dozen, dozen, and two-dozen sizes.'" I stopped to be sure the children knew how many candies were in each box. All of them knew there were twelve in a dozen. They quickly figured out how many were in half a dozen and two dozen. I recorded the numbers of candies on the board: six, twelve, twenty-four.

I continued, "Just as with the sampler box, there are different rectangular shapes that would work for each of these numbers. The president wants you to investigate the different box shapes possible for each number. Use the tiles to experiment and then, with the same size squared paper that I used, cut out and label all the rectangles you find."

A few of the children began to talk and experiment with the tiles, but I asked them to stop and listen to my directions. "The president also wants you to write a memo that explains what you learned and what you recommend. Include your cutout rectangles to illustrate your recommendations." I distributed a copy of the directions to each pair of students and reviewed them with the class.

Observing the Children

The children went to work with enthusiasm. Rebecca and Karin decided to glue their cutout rectangles onto a 9-by-12-inch piece of construction paper. Others noticed and did the same. I often find that when ideas originate with the children, they spread through the class quickly and effortlessly, more so than they would have if I had suggested them. Also, most of the class wrote a separate memo for each number of candies. Again, I hadn't suggested this, but it seemed to make sense to the children.

As I circulated, I reminded some pupils to label their rectangles. I found that several still weren't sure how to do so, and I showed them how.

Josh and Tony's work was typical of many. They cut out, labeled, and glued their rectangles onto construction paper and wrote a separate memo for each number. For six candies, they wrote: *We did: We made all the possible boxes that were rectangle. We learned: that there are only 2 possible boxes for 6. We recomend: that you yuse the 1 × 6 becuse it just makes it seem bigger.* They reported similarly for the other two sizes.

Rebecca and Karin also displayed all their rectangles on construction paper and wrote separate memos for the three numbers. They wrote the following on their memo for six candies: *We did 6 × 1 and 2 × 3. We put six across and two rows of three across. We learned that you could only do two sides. We recommend 2 × 3 because it's the shortest one and it will fit in a mailbox.*

Lisa and Angie brought their work to me when they were finished. They had glued the rectangles on construction paper and prepared a one-page memo for all three numbers. They wrote: *We did 2 ways for 6 candies, 3 ways for 12 candies and 4 ways for 24 candies. We learned 9 diffrent ways to make rectangle boxes. We recomend the 4 × 6 for 24 candies, the 4 × 3 for twelve candies and the 2 × 3 for six candies.*

"I agree with what you learned," I said. "You found all the possible rectangles and showed them clearly. But your memo doesn't tell why you made the recommendations you did."

"What do you mean?" Lisa asked.

"Well," I said, "I'm interested in why you think the four-by-six is best for twenty-four candies and the four-by-three is best for twelve candies and the two-by-three for six candies. Why do you recommend those particular sizes?"

"I don't get it," Lisa said, reluctant to rethink her work. She had written the memo while Angie had cut and glued the rectangles.

"I know," Angie said, and the girls returned to their seats. In a while, they returned with a second sheet attached to their memo. This time, Angie had done the writing: *We recomend the 4 × 6 for 24 candies because it is rectangle and easy to carry. We recomend the 4 × 3 for 12 candies because it is easy to handel, unlike the longer boxes. We recomend the 2 × 3 for six candies because it can fit in small places and a little goes a long way.*

When Libby and Brian cut out the rectangles they found and labeled the dimensions, they also colored the individual squares on each rectangle to represent dif-ferent flavors. They labeled some of the rectangles *regular* and others *kid pack.* They wrote: *We made four differant flavors: cherry, bluebarry, mint, and banana. We made "kid packs" and regular packs. The differance between the two is regular packs have banana in them, and "kid packs" don't. We recomend what any other kid would recomend, "Kid Packs." We recomand "Kid Packs" because we think that bannana does not taste very good. Although blueberry and cheery taste devine. The size of "Kid Packs" that we recomend is the "24 × 1." We like that size because there is lots of blueberry and also lot's of cherry.*

I've learned not to be surprised by children's interpretations of situations. I never would have thought about flavors as descriptors, but then again, I had no firm idea about which shapes they should recommend, either. The important thing was their ability to find the rectangles and label them correctly. (Figure 7–1 shows how another pair of students got creative with this project.)

DAY 2

The next day, the children were eager to present their work. To help them prepare, I had partners read aloud to each other what they had written.

I began the discussion with an observation. "I noticed that everyone was working well together on this project. I'd like some general comments first. Did you like it or not? Why? Was it easy or hard? What were your reactions?"

I called on Sam first. "It was fun except for the writing part," he said. Sam is a reluctant writer but loves all spatial activities.

"It was kind of easy but kind of hard," Tanya said.

"What made it easy and what made it hard?" I asked. Tanya shrugged, but Emily had an idea.

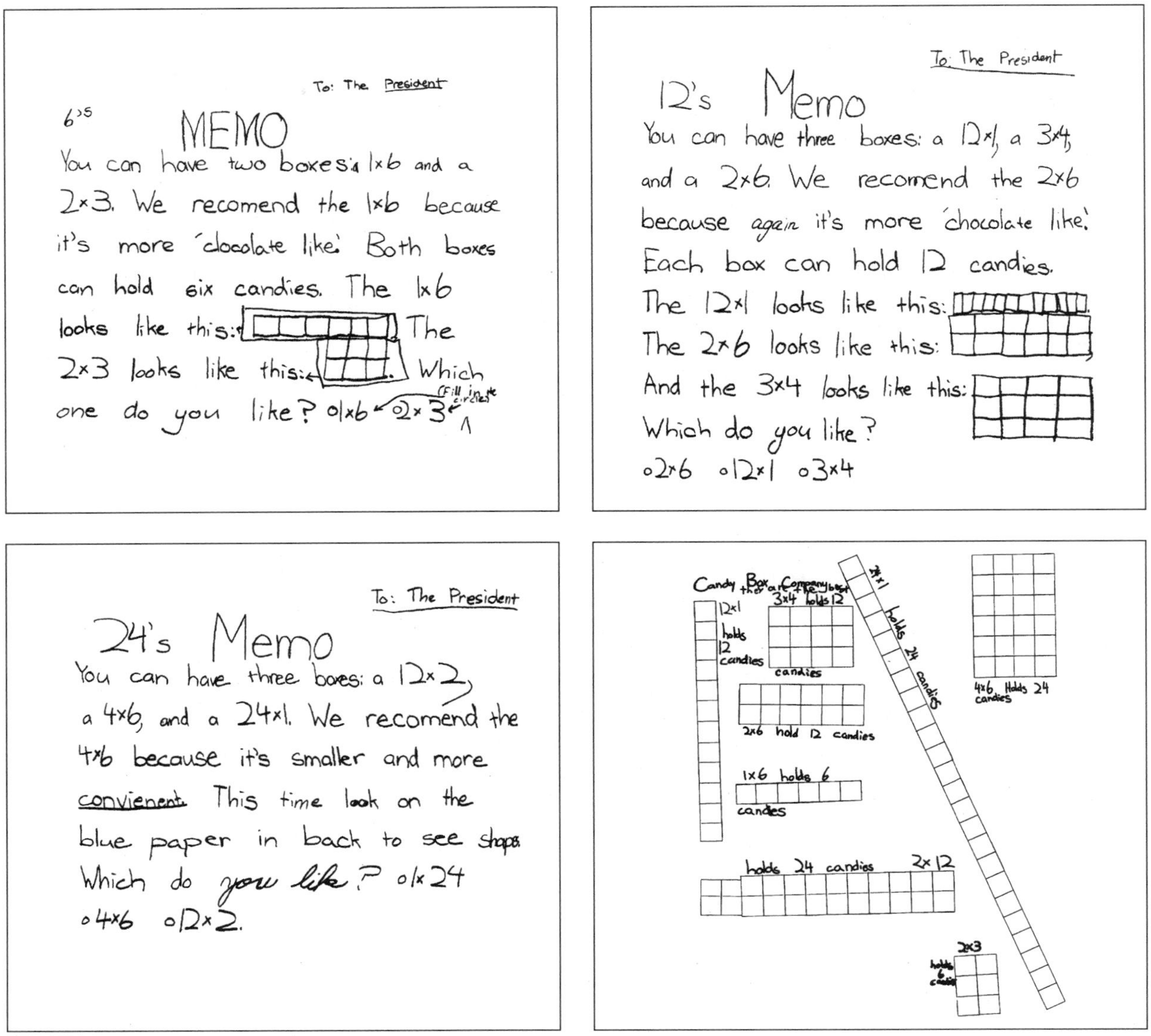

▲▲▲▲▲▲**Figure 7–1** *On their memos, Tanya and Jason asked for feedback from the president. To illustrate their memos, Tanya and Jason displayed their cutout rectangles.*

"It was easy to cut out the rectangles, but I wasn't sure if we had them all," she said. Emily was usually tentative and uncertain in math and came to me regularly for reassurance. Her ability surpassed her confidence, however, and I tried to help her see how capable she was.

"What did you do to be sure?" I asked.

"I checked with Libby," she said.

"Are you sure now you have them all?" I asked.

"Well, sort of," she replied.

"Any other reactions?" I asked.

I called on Jennifer. "The long one for twenty-four was hard," she said.

"How come?" I asked.

"The paper wasn't long enough," she said. "But then we figured out to cut another strip and glue them. It was messy."

"Anything else?" I asked.

"I liked it," Libby said. "Me and Brian did flavors. We had cherry, blueberry, mint, and banana."

"Yuck, banana!" Tony said.

Libby continued, "Well, those were only in the regular packs, not the kid packs."

The children started to talk among themselves about flavors. I called them back to attention and began to discuss the possible rectangles.

"Lisa and Angie reported that they found nine rectangles altogether for the three numbers," I said to the class. "Look at your work and see if you agree." That changed the children's focus from flavors back to the rectangles they had found. After they had a few moments to check, I heard murmurs of agreement.

"I'm interested in the shape you recommended for the largest box, the one with two dozen candies," I said. The children looked at their papers and a smattering of hands went up.

"You can read what you wrote or just explain," I added and called on Edna.

She read, "We recommend the six-by-four box that is most squarish, because it is easy to carry instead of a big long box."

Rebecca reported next. "We think so, too, because it isn't too long or too short," she said.

Josh then said, "We liked the one-by-twenty-four because it looks more interesting."

Sara reported for herself and Brandon. She read, "We think that the six-by-four is best because it is easier to handle unlike the other long boxes and because it can fit in many small rectangle spaces like if you wanted to give a present for someone special."

More Candy Box Research

After the children reported their recommendations for the other two box sizes, about half the math period remained. I introduced the next activity. The children watched as I taped up a 6-foot length of chart paper I had cut from a roll. I had ruled it into columns each about 2 inches wide and had numbered the columns from 1 to 36.

I said to the class, "The president of the company wants customers to be able to buy any number of candies they like. So the design research department now has to recommend boxes for all quantities of candies from one to thirty-six." To show the class how we would collect the information on the chart, I posted in the correct columns cutout rectangles for the numbers the class had already investigated—four, six, twelve, and twenty-four.

I then showed the class the paper bag I had prepared. I explained, "In this bag are slips of paper numbered from 1 to 36. But there are no slips for the numbers 4, 6, 12, and 24. Who thinks you know why I didn't make slips for those numbers?"

Several hands shot up and, after a moment, almost everyone had raised a hand. I asked Edna to explain. "We did those numbers already," she said.

"That's right," I said and then gave directions for what they were to do. "You and your partner will pick a number from the bag and investigate the possible boxes for that many candies. As you did with the others, you'll cut the boxes from one-half-inch grid paper and label them. Then you'll post your rectangles on the chart in the correct column." I stopped talking to distribute a copy of the directions to each pair of students.

I explained the last direction. "If you have time, and there are numbers still in the bag, pick another slip and investigate the boxes for that number."

The children didn't have any questions about the directions. Because of their previous experience making rectangles for four, six, twelve, and twenty-four candies, the children were familiar with the procedure for this activity. Everyone understood what to do, and I didn't have to address the kinds of procedural concerns that typically come up when I introduce a new task.

As I watched the class work, I noticed that students used different methods for finding rectangles. Many used trial and error. Libby and Kristina, for example, picked the number sixteen. They each counted out sixteen tiles and worked in a seemingly random manner to arrange them into a rectangle. Libby found a solution first; she built a 4-by-4 array. She showed it to Kristina, who then built the same array, as if to verify that it would work with her tiles as well. Then Kristina began to rearrange the tiles in search of another shape. Libby cut the 4-by-4 square out of the squared paper and went back to working with tiles. Eventually, they found the three rectangles for sixteen.

In contrast, Michael and Brian worked together in a very methodical way. They had picked the number twenty-eight. After making and cutting out a 1-by-28 rectangle, they arranged the tiles in two rows to get the 2-by-14 array. Then they tried an arrangement in three rows, which didn't work because one tile was left over at the end. They continued with four rows, and so on.

Josh made use of his keen number sense. He and Tony picked the number fifteen. Tony began to arrange his tiles into two rows. "It's not even, so two rows won't work," Josh told Tony. Tony continued anyway, putting the tiles in two rows until he proved to himself it couldn't be done. Josh, meanwhile, went on independently and found the 3-by-5 rectangle.

None of the children knew for sure when they had found all the possible rectangles. I noticed that some rectangles were missing for some of the numbers on the chart. I decided to deal with this in a class discussion.

The period ended before the children finished the investigation. "You'll get back to work on it tomorrow when we start math class," I told them.

DAY 3

The children got to work and completed their investigations in the first part of the period. Then I gathered them for a class discussion, making sure that everyone could see the chart. I asked, "Which numbers have rectangles with a side that's two squares long?"

As the children looked, they suggested numbers in random order—6, 10, 4, 20, and so on. I said, "I'd like to list the rectangles, but in order, starting with the smallest number that has a rectangle with two squares on a side." That refocused the children. I listed as they reported—2, 4, 6, 8, 10, 12, up to 36.

"They're all even!" Tony said, surprised. Several others expressed their surprise at this.

"They're all two-times numbers," Josh said.

"I don't get that," Angie said.

Josh explained, "Two times three is six, two times four is eight, like that."

"Oh yeah," several others said. These responses revealed to me that many of them didn't see a relationship between multiples and rectangles. While the children were able to chant "two, four, six, eight, ten" and so on, they seemed to know the sequence as a familiar chant, not as a mathematical pattern. An activity such as this can help them understand that sequence more mathematically.

I continued asking other questions, creating a list of numbers for each and talking about the patterns in the sequences: "Which numbers have rectangles with a side that's three squares long?" "Which have sides with four squares?" "Five squares?" "Which numbers have rectangles that are also squares?" "Which numbers have only one rectangle?"

For the list of numbers with square rect-angles—1, 4, 9, 16, 25, and 36—the children had difficulty finding a pattern. They looked for a while, and finally Angie raised her hand. "I don't think there's any pattern," she said. Several others nodded their agreement.

"I don't either," Alex added. "They don't skip evenly."

"Sometimes you can see a pattern more easily if you look at it geometrically instead of numerically," I said. "Watch as I demonstrate a pattern with the tiles." I put out one blue tile to represent the first square number. I then added red tiles across the top and one side to make a 2-by-2 square.

"How many red tiles did I add to build the next larger square?" I asked.

The children answered, "Three."

I then added yellow tiles across the top and side to make a 3-by-3 square. "How many yellow tiles did I add?" I asked.

The children answered, "Five."

I continued in this way, adding different-colored tiles to change each square into the next larger square and asking the children each time how many tiles I had added. Some of them caught on to the pattern, that I added the next larger odd number each time, and were fascinated by it. Others didn't react.

Then I brought the children's attention to the numbers that had only one rectangle. "Except for the number one, these are called 'prime numbers,'" I said. The children liked learning the name for this set of numbers.

I asked the children about thirty-seven, the next number after those on the chart. "Do you think thirty-seven is prime?"

The children discussed this among themselves. Alex raised his hand and asked, "Well, is it one of those prime numbers?"

I didn't give Alex the answer he wanted. "I'm not going to tell you," I said. "But, if you come up with an answer and explain your reasoning to me, I'll give you honest feed-back. I don't want just to tell you the answer; I want you to try and make sense of the situation for yourself. Talk about it with others who are interested."

At this time, none of the children had a strong enough number sense or understanding of multiplication to answer the question. But I left it as a challenge to see what would happen. This was a judgment call on my part. I decided that the information was not of value to them without the understanding, and I knew they would encounter prime numbers again in the next several grades. It wasn't necessary to resolve this now.

EXTENSIONS

Interested students can investigate the candy boxes for other numbers as well. For students ready for a further challenge, pose the following problem: *A woman came to the store requesting a box of candies that could be shared equally among all the people coming to visit. She wasn't sure whether there would be three, four, five, or six people sharing the box. What size box should she buy that would work for any of these numbers?*

Questions and Discussion

▲▲

▲ *If my class hasn't had much previous experience with the tiles, what should I do before initiating this lesson?*

In my experience, if children haven't had time to explore a material, it's difficult for them to focus on a specific task. I've learned to provide time for them to become familiar with a material and satisfy their curiosity before using it for an investigation. I've found with tiles that some children gravitate toward standing them on end and arranging them in lines to try to topple them like dominoes; others try making their initials or other shapes. Sometimes I tell the children that I know the material is new for them and I'm going to give them five minutes to explore it before we get to work. Then I set a kitchen timer. "When it rings," I tell the class, "I'll ask you to end your own exploration and listen to the problem I'd like you to solve."

▲ *Why did you have the children read their papers aloud to each other before the class discussion?*

I find it a good idea in general for students to read their work aloud to their partners before a class discussion. Reading their work aloud helps children revisit their thinking and, sometimes, reconsider their ideas. Also, it helps them edit their work, as they often find that there are missing or incorrect words in their writing.

CHAPTER EIGHT
HOW LONG? HOW MANY?

Overview

This lesson provides children experience with multiplication in a geometric context. After rolling a die to determine the dimensions, children build rectangles using Cuisenaire rods and then trace them on a 10-by-10-centimeter grid until no more space is available. The activity encourages students to think strategically as they consider where to place their rectangles so that they can cover as much as possible of the grid. A follow-up problem-solving activity provides additional multiplication practice and helps build children's number sense.

Materials

▲ Cuisenaire rods
▲ dice, 1 per pair of students
▲ *How Long? How Many?* record sheet, several per student (see Blackline Masters)
▲ optional: directions for activity, 1 per pair of students (see Blackline Masters)
▲ for extension: centimeter squares, at least 1 sheet per pair of children (see Blackline Masters)

Time

▲ three class periods; additional time for repeated play

Teaching Directions

1. Introduce the activity to the class. Tell them that they will build and then trace rectangles on a 10-by-10-centimeter grid, trying to cover as much of the grid as possible.

2. Either write the directions on the board or an overhead transparency or distribute a copy to each pair of students. Explain and model what to do by rolling a die twice, building the rectangle, and drawing and labeling it on the top grid of a record sheet.

How Long? How Many?

You need:　　Cuisenaire rods
　　　　　　　a die
　　　　　　　How Long? How Many? record sheet
　　　　　　　a partner

1. Each partner uses a different record sheet.

2. On your turn, roll the die twice. The first roll tells how long a Cuisenaire rod to use. The second roll tells how many rods to take.

3. Arrange the rods into a rectangle. Trace it on your grid. Write the multiplication equation inside.

4. When one person is blocked and can't place a rectangle because there's no room on the grid, you both stop.

5. Figure out how many squares on your grid are covered and how many are uncovered. Check each other's answers.

---

3. Point out that the name of the activity, *How Long? How Many?*, is helpful for remembering that the first roll of the die tells *how long* a rod to use, and the second tells *how many* rods to take. Also, explain to the children that they will work with partners, but that they should each draw on their own record sheet, using the top grid for the first round and the bottom grid for a second round. Instruct the children to play at least two rounds.

4. After the children have done the activity several times, initiate a class discussion, drawing from the questions that follow. For each question, give all who want to answer a chance to respond.

What's the greatest number of squares you covered on a grid?

What's the greatest number anyone in the class covered?

For each round, how did you figure out the number of covered and uncovered squares?

What's the greatest number of turns you had on any one round? The least number?

What do you think are the greatest and least number of turns possible? Explain your idea.

What strategies did you figure out for covering as many squares as possible?

What did you like about the activity?

What does this activity have to do with multiplication?

5. Introduce a follow-up problem-solving activity. Choose one of the students' papers and tell the class the number of squares that were covered on one round, or use the number sixty-seven from Rebecca's paper as I do in the vignette. Discuss with the class what the student might have rolled. Model for students how to draw and label the rectangles on a 10-by-10-centimeter grid, record the corresponding multiplication sentences, and check their solutions by adding. Do this for at least two different solutions. See Figures 8–1 and 8–2 for samples of completed papers.

Teaching Notes

This lesson provides experience that is similar to what *Candy Boxes* provides—a geometric interpretation of multiplication. However, the activities differ in that the explorations with candy boxes focus children on arranging individual square tiles, each with the value of one square unit, into rectangular arrays. When they record the multiplication equations for candy boxes, the children typically count the number of tiles in each direction to determine the factors. In *How Long? How Many?*, children don't construct rectangles from squares; the rolls of the die determine the dimensions of the rectangles. In addition to giving children experience thinking about the relationship between multiplication and the area of rectangles, the lesson also provides them problem-solving experience. Thinking about how to place rectangles on a grid to cover the maximum number of squares possible involves children's spatial reasoning ability. Also, thinking about the rectangles to use to cover a specific number of squares on a 10-by-10 grid engages students with a problem that has more than one solution.

After introducing the activity to the class, repeated experiences are appropriate and valuable. The activity is suitable for choice time.

The Lesson

▲▲

DAY 1

I began by telling the class that I was going to introduce a new multiplication activity. "It's called *How Long? How Many?* and you work with a partner," I said.

I showed the children a sample of the record sheet they would use to play and explained, "For this activity, you draw rectangles on these grids. You roll a die and use Cuisenaire rods to determine their size and shape. You and your partner take turns, each building on your own sheet."

I then modeled for the children what to do. "On your turn, you roll the die twice. The first roll tells *how long* a Cuisenaire rod

you'll use for this round. The second roll tells *how many* of that length rod to take."

I rolled the die and a 3 came up. "This means that I'll use the rod that's three centimeters long, the light-green rod." I held up one of the light-green rods and then rolled the die again. This time, a 4 came up.

I said, "The second roll tells me how many to use, so I take four light green rods." I fished out the rods I needed.

"Now I have to arrange the rods into a rectangle," I continued. I arranged the rods into a rectangle, matching their long sides. I held it up for the class to see.

"Who can tell me the dimensions of this rectangle?" I asked. I called on Edna.

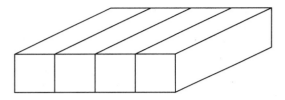

"It's four on one side and three on the short side," she said.

"Yes, it's four centimeters by three centimeters," I said, confirming what Edna had said but including the units as well.

"Or it's three by four," Tony added.

"Yes, you could say either," I responded and then asked, "If I place this rectangle on one of the grids on the recording sheet, how many squares will it cover? Think about that for a moment and then raise your hand when you're ready to answer and explain how you figured."

After more than half the students had raised hands, I called on Lisa. She said, "It would cover twelve squares because you have four of them and they are three each and three plus three plus three plus three makes twelve."

"Or you could just do four times three," Josh said.

"Or three times four equals twelve," Maria said.

"What I do next is to trace this rectangle somewhere on the first grid. Then, inside the rectangle, I write the multiplication sentence." I did this and then showed my paper to the class.

I said, "While you're tracing and writing on your paper, it's important that your partner watches and agrees that what you're drawing and labeling is correct. Then you watch as your partner takes a turn. Your partner rolls the die twice to find out how long a rod to use and how many to take, then traces and labels it on his or her paper. Then, when it's your turn, do the same thing again."

"When you go again do you use the bottom part?" Sam asked.

"Not yet," I answered. "You draw on the same grid until you're blocked. At some

4 × 3 = 12

point, one of you will roll the die twice and the rectangle you build won't fit on the grid. There won't be enough room. Then you're both finished for that round. Well, you're both finished rolling and drawing, but you each have to figure out how many squares you covered and how many are still uncovered. You write those numbers on the recording sheet in these spaces." I pointed to where they should record these numbers.

I then said, "Try to cover as many squares as you can before someone is blocked, and then you figure out how many squares are covered and uncovered."

There were no other questions and the children began. As with all new activities, some children were confused at first. But they soon caught on and took to the activity. They enjoyed making the rectangles and deciding where to trace them. As I circulated, I reminded children about recording the multiplication sentences in the rectangles they drew.

As the students worked, they became more aware of how to place the rectangles effectively. For example, Koji and Sam had the shortest round in the class; they each had one turn before Koji was blocked. On his turn, he had first rolled a 6 and then a 1. He had placed one dark-green rod vertically near the middle of the grid. On his next turn, he rolled two 6s, and there was no room for a 6-by-6 rectangle.

[grid with a tall shaded rectangle labeled 1 × 6 = 6]

"Bad luck," Koji commented.

Sam rolled his eyes and pointed to the place Koji had drawn his rectangle. "That wasn't bad luck!" he said. Koji's strategy improved after that.

When students completed a round, I checked to see if they correctly figured the number of covered and uncovered squares. I could easily see if their numbers were correct by checking that the sum of covered and uncovered squares was one hundred. This method wasn't obvious to the children, however. When I revealed to Kristina how I knew her figuring was incorrect, she was so excited that she went around the room, checking to see if others' scores added to one hundred. Soon, more of the children became interested and began to check. This provided unexpected but valuable practice adding to one hundred. This kind of incidental learning is always a welcome treat.

At the end of the class, I interrupted the students and told them that they would continue with the activity the next day.

DAY 2

The next day, the children eagerly returned to *How Long? How Many?* I let them play for

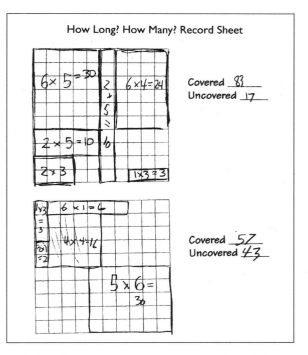

▲▲▲▲▲**Figure 8–1** *In two rounds, Michael covered 56 and 73 squares. In his first round, he arranged two yellow rods end to end to make a 1–by–10 rectangle instead of a 2–by–5 rectangle.*

about half of the period, leaving half an hour for a class discussion. Before beginning the discussion, I had children change partners and compare papers. I instructed them, "Look to see how many squares you each covered and left uncovered. Also, compare the rectangles you drew and compare their sizes and shapes."

After a few moments, I initiated a discussion by asking who had the most turns before being blocked. We learned that Emily and Jenny did; they each drew nine rectangles before Emily was blocked. Emily had covered eighty-one squares and Jenny had covered forty-four.

Sara and Tony covered the greatest number of squares in one round, eighty-eight of the one hundred squares. They were surprised to learn that they had done so with different assortments of rectangles. Lisa and Maria made the same discovery with the different ways they each covered sixty-six squares. No one had covered all one hundred squares.

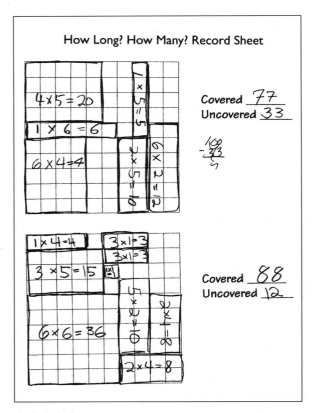

How Long? How Many? Record Sheet

$4 \times 5 = 20$
$1 \times 6 = 6$
$6 \times 4 = 4$

Covered 77
Uncovered 33

100
-77 (written over)
3

$1 \times 4 = 4$ $3 \times 1 = 3$
$3 \times 5 = 15$ $3 \times 1 = 3$
$6 \times 6 = 36$
$2 \times 4 = 8$

Covered 88
Uncovered 12

▲▲▲▲▲▲**Figure 8–2** *On her second round, Sara covered 88 squares, the highest number of squares covered in the class.*

"Is it possible to cover all one hundred squares?" I asked. Josh said, "If you kept rolling fives."

"Tell more about your idea," I probed.

"Five times five is twenty-five, and four twenty-fives make a hundred," Josh elaborated.

"You'd never roll all those fives in a row," Brian said.

"I know," Josh said, grinning.

"It's unlikely," I agreed.

Kristina raised a hand and reported what she had been delighted to discover. "The covered ones and uncovered ones have to add up to one hundred," she said.

"Can you explain why?" I asked.

"Because there are a hundred squares altogether," she said.

I then said, "Here's a problem for you to think about. If someone covered fifty-eight squares on his or her grid, how many squares would be left uncovered?" I think

it's important to continue to reinforce children's addition and subtraction skills, even while they're studying multiplication. I gave the class a few moments to think quietly and then called on several children to respond. I recorded their ideas on the board.

Tony went first. He said, "I added two to fifty-eight and got sixty. Then sixty plus forty is one hundred, so forty plus two is the answer. It's forty-two." I wrote on the board:

$58 + 2 = 60$

$60 + 40 = 100$

$40 + 2 = 42$

Emily used a different approach. She reported, "Five and five makes ten, so I know that fifty plus fifty equals one hundred. Then I did fifty minus eight and I got forty-two." I recorded on the board:

$5 + 5 = 10$

$50 + 50 = 100$

$50 - 8 = 42$

Even though Emily's answer was correct, I wasn't clear about how she had reasoned. I asked her to explain it again to help me understand.

"Fifty-eight is eight too big to add to fifty to get one hundred, so I had to take off eight," she explained.

Tanya then said, "I know that eight plus two is ten, so fifty-eight plus two is sixty. One hundred minus sixty is forty, and forty plus two is forty-two." I recorded:

$8 + 2 = 10$

$58 + 2 = 60$

$100 - 60 = 40$

$40 + 2 = 42$

Before I ended class, I explained the directions for a second version of the activity (see Extension on page 86). This new version became an option for children during choice time.

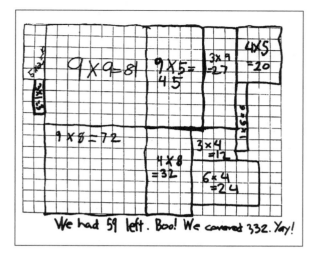

The grid contains handwritten notation including:
$9 \times 9 = 81$, $9 \times 5 = 45$, $3 \times 9 = 27$, $4 \times 5 = 20$, $9 \times 8 = 72$, $3 \times 4 = 12$, $4 \times 8 = 32$, $6 \times 4 = 24$

We had 59 left. Boo! We covered 332. Yay!

▲▲▲▲▲▲Figure 8–3 *When Emily and Jenny tried the new version of the activity, using a full sheet of centimeter-squared paper and a 1–10 die, they took eleven turns before being blocked.*

DAY 3

I waited a week or so to give the children time to play both versions of the activity on their own. Then I introduced a problem for them to solve. I began by reviewing one of the directions. "Who can explain how you know when a round is over?" I asked.

Lisa answered, "You can't do anything after you roll."

"There's no room," Edna said.

"It won't fit," Sam said.

Josh added, "I always thought that two sixes were good luck, but it isn't always."

I posted a blank recording sheet for the first version of the activity and wrote *67* in the space for the number of squares covered for the first grid. I said, "I noticed that on one of her rounds, Rebecca covered sixty-seven squares before she rolled numbers that were too big and she was blocked from fitting in the rectangle. What do you think Rebecca could have rolled in order to cover sixty-seven squares before she was blocked? Think for a moment, and then raise your hand if you have an idea about how to solve this problem."

I waited a few moments and then called on Maria. "If you split sixty in half, you get

thirty. So I think her first two rolls could be six and five, so you make a six-by-five rectangle."

"Where on the grid would you draw it?" I asked.

"In the corner on the left at the top," she answered. I drew and labeled the rectangle.

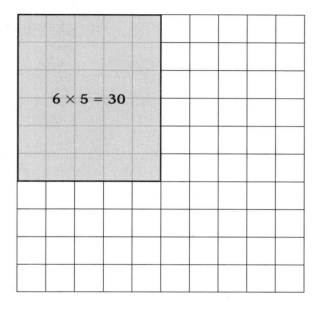

$6 \times 5 = 30$

I turned back to Maria. She said, "We need thirty-seven more, but you can't split seven in half." She paused and then continued, "Oh, I know, you can do another six-by-five right next to what you did. That gives us sixty." I drew and labeled another rectangle as Maria had suggested.

"Uh oh, we need seven more, and there's no seven on the dice," Maria said. "I know, do a two-by-two."

"Where?" I asked.

"In the bottom corner on the left," Maria answered. I did as she instructed.

Maria finished, "Now we have sixty-four and we need three more. Do a one-by-three, and draw it just above the square at the bottom." I did this and also wrote a multiplication equation for each rectangle, and then added the numbers for each rectangle to check that we had covered sixty-seven squares.

"I know another way we could do seven," Alex offered. "You could roll a five and a one, and then a two and a one."

6 × 5 = 30   6 × 5 = 30

6 × 5 = 30   6 × 5 = 30

1 × 3 = 3

2 + 2 = 4

"Or you could do one times three and one times four," Edna said.

"Or one times six and one times one," Angie added.

James raised a hand with a big grin. "You could do one times one, and one times one, and one times one, and one times one, until you get to seven."

I recorded their suggestions to model for them how to represent their ideas mathematically. I recorded Maria's idea first and then the others.

$(2 \times 2) + (3 \times 1) = 7$

$(5 \times 1) + (2 \times 1) = 7$

$(1 \times 3) + (1 \times 4) = 7$

$(1 \times 6) + (1 \times 1) = 7$

$(1 \times 1) + (1 \times 1) + (1 \times 1) + (1 \times 1) + (1 \times 1) + (1 \times 1) + (1 \times 1) = 7$

"Can anyone think of a different way to cover sixty-seven squares?" I asked. I called on Kim. As she described possible rolls, I again recorded on the board, using the grid on the bottom half of the recording sheet I had posted.

5 × 5 = 25   5 × 5 = 25

1 × 2 = 2

1 × 5 = 5

2 × 5 = 10

I then said, "Maria covered sixty-seven squares in four rolls and Kim did it in five rolls. What do you think would be the greatest number of rolls you'd need to cover sixty-seven squares?"

James's hand shot up, and then others did also. I called on Brian. "You'd roll only ones, over and over," he said.

"That would do it," Edna answered.

"That would be really hard to do," Josh said. "You can't roll all of those ones."

"I agree that it's very unlikely," I said.

"How many rolls did Rebecca use?" Elena wanted to know.

Rebecca went to her folder and got out the paper she had done. "I drew six rectangles," she reported. (See Figure 8–4.)

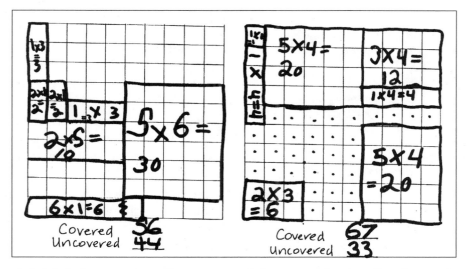

▲▲▲▲▲▲**Figure 8–4** *Rebecca covered 67 squares in six rolls. She used dots to keep track as she counted the uncovered squares.*

I then explained to the children what they were to do individually. "On a *How Long? How Many?* record sheet, figure out two different ways to cover exactly seventy-eight squares before you roll two sixes and are blocked," I said. I posted a blank record sheet and wrote *78* in the two spaces for covered squares.

I then pointed to the record sheet I had used for Maria's and Kim's solutions and reviewed what they were to do. "You'll draw and label the rectangles, record the sentences, add to check that you've covered the right number, and then figure out how many squares are uncovered."

The children were interested in the problem. As I circulated, I checked their calculations. The children's typical strategy was to start with larger rectangles and keep figuring how much more they needed to reach seventy-eight. Most did it with four, five, or six rectangles. I had to remind a few children that six was the largest number on the die and, therefore, they couldn't use 7-by-5 or 8-by-1 rectangles. Figures 8–5 through 8–7 show how some students handled this problem.

Over the next few weeks, I occasionally gave children other numbers to tackle. The more problems like this that they did, the more adept they became at predicting what rectangles they could use.

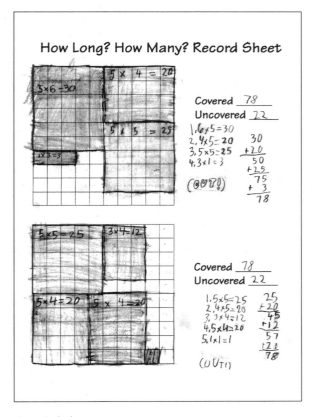

▲▲▲▲▲▲**Figure 8–5** *Alex covered 78 squares first with four rectangles and then with five.*

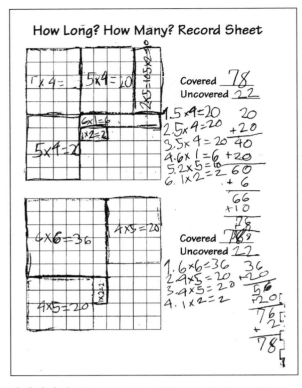

How Long? How Many? Record Sheet

Covered _78_
Uncovered _22_

1. 5×4=20   20
2. 5×4=20   +20
3. 5×4=20   40
4. 6×1=6   +20
5. 2×5=10   60
6. 1×2=2   + 6
                66
               +10
                78

Covered _78_
Uncovered _22_

1. 6×6=36   36
2. 4×5=20   +20
3. 4×5=20   56
4. 1×2=2   +20
                76
                +2
                78

▲▲▲▲▲▲**Figure 8–6** *Libby used six and four rectangles to cover 78 squares.*

My Stragety to get 78 in three steps

First I tried the highest number I could (36.) I put it in the left hand corner. Next I tried the next highest number I could and that was 24. Now I had 60. I needed 18 to get to 78. I thought what 18 devided into 2 was and that was 9. I couldent have nine because the die only goes to 6. Then I thought what else could equal nine. I came up with six, So next I wrote 3×6 on the paper and I colored it in.

▲▲▲▲▲▲**Figure 8–7** *Brian wrote about his strategy for covering 78 squares with only three rectangles.*

EXTENSION

For another version of *How Long? How Many?*, children use a spinner or a die with numbers from 1 to 10. This generates more sizes of rectangles than a standard die. Also, partners trace their rectangles on the same $8\frac{1}{2}$-by-11-inch sheet of centimeter squares. Explain that they take turns spinning the spinner or rolling the die twice, first to determine *how long* a rod to use and second to determine *how many* rods to take. Then, together, they decide where to place the rectangle. The goal is to work together to cover as much of the paper as possible. When they're blocked, they record the number of covered and uncovered squares.

Give the children additional problem-solving challenges related to the activity, such as the examples that follow. For each, ask the students to show their solutions on a 10-by-10 grid.

How could you cover all 100 squares in six turns? Is there more than one way to do this?

What's the least number of turns you need to cover 66 squares?

How could you cover 72 squares in eight turns? Is there more than one way to do this?

After five turns, a student had 58 squares uncovered. What might the student's grid look like?

Questions and Discussion

▲▲

▲ *In my class, a student rolled a 5 and then a 4. I had expected her to build a 5-by-4 rectangle, but instead she built and placed a 2-by-10 rectangle. How should I handle this?*

I think that the student's decision is mathematically legitimate since she made a rectangle using the four rods. Should this occur, I'd take the opportunity to discuss it. I'd point out that different-shape rectangles can cover the same number of squares and, therefore, have the same area. The criterion for this activity is that the rectangle has to fit on the 10-by-10 grid.

▲ *How do you handle careless errors, where students draw wrong rectangles or incorrectly calculate the number of uncovered squares?*

If I notice errors when I'm circulating, I point them out and ask children to make corrections. I know that it's difficult to spot all of these situations during class. I find errors when I review their papers later, and then I talk with the children. Also, I often have children look at one another's papers to see if the work makes sense; in this way, children participate in monitoring each other while they get the advantage of seeing how others handle an assignment.

▲ *I find that some children, when they draw a rectangle, continue to count squares one by one to find out how many they covered. How can I encourage them to learn the facts?*

The benefit of having the squares to count is that children have a way to verify the number of squares in a rectangle, which is a useful check for children as they are learning multiplication. It may help, however, to encourage children to make predictions about the number of squares in a rectangle before counting. Also, encourage children to count in more than one way—by twos, threes, fives, or whatever makes sense for a given rectangle. Finally, from time to time, put a rectangular array on the board and ask the students to share their strategies for finding the number of squares. Be sure to emphasize the way to record the number of squares for a rectangle. For example, if a rectangle is 5 by 7, it can be recorded as $5 \times 7 = 35$ or $7 \times 5 = 35$. And remember that children learn on their own schedules. Putting together all the different ways to think about multiplication is complex, and children do so at their own pace.

CHAPTER NINE
ONE HUNDRED HUNGRY ANTS

Overview

The children's book *One Hundred Hungry Ants,* by Elinor J. Pinczes, provides an engaging context for helping children relate multiplication to rectangular arrays and think about the factors of one hundred. The book is also an effective springboard for involving children in thinking about the factors of numbers other than one hundred. As an extension, the lively marching verses can inspire children to write their own versions of the story, using animals and numbers of their own choosing. (**Note:** A lesson based on this book is also included in *Teaching Arithmetic: Extending Multiplication, Grades 4–5* and offers older students a chance to investigate the commutative property of multiplication; prime, composite, and square numbers; and products for different combinations of odd and even factors.)

Materials

▲ *One Hundred Hungry Ants,* by Elinor J. Pinczes (New York: Houghton Mifflin, 1993)

Time

▲ two class periods

Teaching Directions

1. Read *One Hundred Hungry Ants* aloud to the class and invite children's reactions to the story.

2. Begin a class discussion by asking the children how the ants first reorganized. Draw on the chalkboard a row of one hundred dots to represent how the ants began marching, then draw two rows of fifty dots each to represent how they first reorganized. Record: $1 \times 100 = 100$ and $2 \times 50 = 100$. Ask: "Who can explain why these multiplication equations describe how the ants started marching and what happened when the ants reorganized?"

3. Ask the children how the ants reorganized next. Again, draw dots on the chalkboard to represent four rows with twenty-five in each. Ask for a volunteer to give the matching multiplication sentence: $4 \times 25 = 100$. Repeat for five and ten rows.

4. Next ask: "Why didn't the littlest ant suggest reorganizing the one hundred ants into three rows?" Give all children who are interested the opportunity to respond. Record to model how to represent their ideas mathematically. Emphasize that when the ants march, each row should have the same number of ants in it.

5. After the class resolves why it wasn't possible for the ants to get into three equal rows, continue discussing the story. Draw dots on the board and write the related multiplication equations to represent the ants in five and ten rows. Discuss with the class why it wasn't possible for the ants to be organized into six, seven, eight, or nine rows.

6. Pose the following problem: *If only 10 ants were marching to a picnic, could they reorganize into two rows and have an equal number of ants in each?* As you did before, record by drawing dots and writing the matching multiplication sentence. Continue investigating with the class to see if ten ants can be organized into three rows, four rows, five rows, and so on up to ten rows, drawing dots and writing the multiplication sentence for each number of rows. When a number isn't possible, model for the children writing *won't work* and a number sentence that explains why. For example, a possible equation to represent what happens when ten ants try to organize into three rows is: $(3 \times 3) + 1 = 10$.

7. Pose a similar problem for the children to solve independently: *Investigate what happens when 12 ants try to organize into two rows, three rows, four rows, and so on, up to 12 rows.* Direct children to draw the array and write the sentence for each number of rows.

8. As a follow-up activity, ask children to choose another number of ants to investigate in the same way, to see if they can organize into two rows, three rows, four rows, and so on.

9. For an extension, encourage children to write their own stories using the structure of *One Hundred Hungry Ants,* choosing their own animals, story lines, and numbers to investigate.

Teaching Notes

In *One Hundred Hungry Ants,* one hundred ants are hurrying single file in one long row to a picnic. Feeling hungry and worried that their progress is too slow, the littlest ant suggests that they reorganize themselves into two rows with fifty ants in each. The ants scurry into the new formation, but soon afterward the littlest ant stops them again, still worried that their progress is too slow and all of the food will be gone before they arrive. So the ants reorganize into four lines with twenty-five in each. Still unsatisfied, the littlest ant has them reorganize twice more, once into five rows with twenty ants in each, and finally into ten rows with ten ants in each. But all of this reorganizing is for naught—the ants arrive too late for any food at all!

After hearing the story, children can consider several questions: How come the littlest ant didn't suggest reorganizing the one hundred ants into three rows? What other numbers of rows would have worked so that the same number of ants would be in each? If there were twelve (or twenty-four, fifty, or any other number) of ants, how could they reorganize into equal rows? In considering questions like these, children think about factors and rectangular arrays.

The Lesson

▲▲▲

After I read *One Hundred Hungry Ants* aloud, several children offered comments. Tomas said, "The littlest ant didn't have such a good idea."

"He kept stopping them too much," Sergio added.

"I liked how they all chased him at the end," Jessica said.

"He should have just had them all run to the picnic," Evan said.

"I liked how they all said 'a hey and a hi dee ho,'" Greta said.

"They should have seen the other animals walking away with food," Alicia said, referring to the illustrations.

I then said, "Let's talk about how the ants reorganized. When the littlest ant interrupted them the first time, how many rows did they get into?"

Aaron answered, "Two rows and there were fifty ants in them."

I quickly drew dots on the board to represent what happened, first drawing one row of one hundred dots and then the two rows with fifty dots in each.

I wrote next to what I had drawn:

$1 \times 100 = 100$

$2 \times 50 = 100$

"Who can explain why my multiplication sentences describe how the ants started and what happened when they reorganized?" I asked.

Jay said, "When they started, all of the one hundred ants were in one row, so it's one times one hundred."

Alicia said, "Two times fifty means two lines of fifty, and that's what they did."

"It's two fifties," Ruthie added.

"It's fifty plus fifty," Amelia said.

"Then what happened in the story?" I asked.

"The littlest ant stopped them again and they got into four rows," Sally said.

"Raise your hand if you remember how many ants were in each row when there were four rows," I said. After more than half of the children had raised their hands, I said, "Let's say the answer quietly together."

"Twenty-five," they chorused. I drew dots to illustrate this configuration.

"What multiplication sentence can I write next to what I drew?" I asked.

Raul said, "You write 'four times twenty-five.'"

"Can you finish the sentence?" I asked him.

Raul nodded. "You write 'equals one hundred.'" I wrote on the board next to the four rows of dots:

$4 \times 25 = 100$

"Four times twenty-five means four twenty-fives," I said, "and that's how the ants lined up this time."

I pointed to the arrays of dots I had drawn on the board and said, "The littlest ant organized the one hundred ants first into two rows, and then into four rows. Why didn't he ask them to get into three rows?" I waited a few moments for the children to think and then called on Sally.

"Maybe he just skipped it so he could go faster," she said.

Marea had a different idea. "There would be an odd number if they lined up, so you wouldn't have equal groups."

"Is twenty-five even or odd?" I asked Marea.

"It's odd," she answered.

"When the ants were in four groups, there was an odd number in each group," I said.

"That was OK because they were equal," Marea clarified. "They wouldn't be equal with three lines." Marea was using "odd" to mean "not equal," a common usage of the word in the way that we use "even" to mean "the same."

Jay said, "Thirty-three times three is ninety-nine, so one ant would be left over. It wouldn't have a group so it doesn't work." I wrote on the board:

$33 \times 3 = 99$

$(33 \times 3) + 1 = 100$

Lydia said, "The extra ant could be the leader in the front."

Kelly said, "Or you could have a row of thirty-three, another row of thirty-three, and a row of thirty-four." I recorded:

$33 + 33 + 34 = 100$

Ruthie added, "That's two thirty-threes and a thirty-four." I wrote:

$(2 \times 33) + 34 = 100$

Bo said, "You could write 'two times thirty-three' and then 'one times thirty-four.'" I wrote:

$(2 \times 33) + (1 \times 34) = 100$

"What about if the littlest ant wanted each of the three rows to have the same number of ants in it?" I asked.

"It wouldn't work," Peter said.

"You can't do it," Greta added.

"So what happened in the story next?" I asked.

"He got them into five groups," Jessica said. Again, I drew an array of dots on the board and wrote the multiplication sentence.

"You have to write five times twenty equals one hundred," Kelly told me. I wrote on the board:

$5 \times 20 = 100$

"And then?" I asked.

"They got into ten groups of ten," Peter answered. "It's ten times ten." I drew the dots on the board and recorded the sentence.

"Why didn't the littlest ant suggest that they get in six groups?" I asked. "Or seven, eight, or nine groups?" A few children were clear that there wouldn't be equal groups, but others weren't sure. Some children lacked the number sense to know how to think about one hundred in groups of six, seven, eight, or nine. Also, it's difficult to visualize grouping one hundred. Rather than pursue this question in more depth, I switched to a smaller problem that I felt would be accessible to all of the children.

"Suppose only ten ants were marching to a picnic," I said. I stopped to draw a row of ten dots and record $1 \times 10 = 10$ next to it.

I then asked, "Could the ants reorganize into two rows and have an equal number of ants in each?"

"There would be five in each," Tomas said.

"That's two times five," Aaron said. I recorded on the board, modeling for two rows the way I would soon ask them to organize their papers for another problem.

Rows
1 ·········· $1 \times 10 = 10$
2 :::::: $2 \times 5 = 10$

"What about three rows?" I asked, adding a 3 to my list on the board. Most children knew that it wouldn't work, but fewer of them were able to offer a reason.

"Three and three and three makes nine," Lydia said, "and there's one extra that doesn't fit."

"Three times three equals nine," Ruthie said. "You need ten and you can't get it."

Jay said, "I know that one hundred can go into tens, like the ants did. But one hundred can't go into threes, so I don't think that ten will go into threes either." I crossed out the 3 and wrote *won't work* and the sentence *(3 × 3) + 1 = 10* next to it.

"So what do you think about four rows for ten ants?" I asked Jay.

"It works for one hundred," he said slowly, thinking. After a moment he added, "Nope, it won't work for ten. My idea doesn't work."

"It's useful at times to see the relationship between numbers, like one hundred and ten, but you have to be careful when you do this and check your ideas," I said.

I turned to the class and asked, "Do you agree with Jay that you can't organize ten ants into four equal rows?"

"Now there are two extras," Jessica said.

I drew two rows with four ants in each. "That takes care of eight ants," I said, "and there are two extras, as Jessica said." I drew the extra two dots and recorded:

(2 × 4) + 2 = 10

I continued talking with the children about organizing ants into five, six, seven, eight, nine, and ten rows. Each time, I drew an array of dots and recorded a sentence to describe what I had drawn.

AN INDIVIDUAL ASSIGNMENT

I then gave the children a problem to work on individually. I said, "Now you'll try a problem on your own, investigating how twelve ants might be reorganized into different numbers of rows, each with an equal num-

Rows

$$1 \times 10 = 10$$
$$2 \times 5 = 10$$
$$(3 \times 3) + 1 = 10$$
$$(4 \times 2) + 2 = 10$$
$$5 \times 2 = 10$$
$$(6 \times 1) + 4 = 10$$
$$(7 \times 1) + 3 = 10$$
$$(8 \times 1) + 2 = 10$$
$$(9 \times 1) + 1 = 10$$
$$10 \times 1 = 10$$

ber of ants." I told the children to organize their papers as I had shown on the board for ten ants. (See Figures 9–1 through 9–3.)

For most of the children, investigating ways to organize the twelve ants into one, two, three, four, five, and six rows was easy. I noticed that some had to struggle after that. Students were able to figure out that it wasn't possible to organize the ants into any number of groups larger than six except for twelve. They had different ideas about what to draw and how to explain why it wasn't possible.

For a follow-up experience, children chose their own numbers and repeated the activity. I suggested that they choose a number no larger than twenty-five, and their choices ranged from fourteen to twenty-four.

In a class discussion, Alicia was surprised to find out that while sixteen ants could reorganize in five different ways, twenty-two ants, which Peter and Lydia chose to investigate, could be organized in only four ways (see Figures 9–4 and 9–5). "I thought that bigger numbers would have more ways," she said.

12 Ants

Rows

1 . . . . 1 group of 12 1×12=12

2 ...... 6+6=12 2×6=12

3 .... 3×4=12

4 ... 4×3=12

5 5+5=10 and another 5 added to that would equal 15.

6 .... 6×2=12

7 Won't Work .... 2×7 is 14.

8 won't work .... 2×8 is 16.

9 won't work .... 2×9 is 18.

10 won't work .... 2×10 is 20.

11 won't work .... 2×11 is 22.

12 . . . . 1 group of 12

▲▲▲▲▲▲Figure 9–1 *Peter's paper showed that he recorded that 2 multiplied by all numbers from 7 to 11 would result in more than 12 ants.*

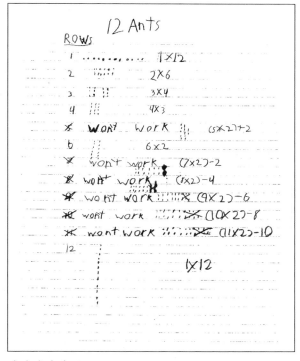

12 Ants

Rows

1 . . . . 1×12

2 ...... 2×6

3 .... 3×4

4 ... 4×3

5 Won't work (5×2)+2

6 6×2

7 won't work (7×2)−2

8 won't work (8×2)−4

9 won't work (9×2)−6

10 won't work (10×2)−8

11 won't work (11×2)−10

12 1×12

▲▲▲▲▲▲Figure 9–2 *Tomas drew arrays for the larger numbers, as Peter did, but he also used subtraction to show the number of extra ants there were in each.*

12 ants

1 . . . . 1×12=12

2 ...... 2×6=12

3 .... 3×4=12

4 ... 4×3=12

5 won't work (5×2)+2=12

6 6×2=12

7 won't work (7×1)+5=12

8 won't work (8×1)+4=12

9 won't work (9×1)+3=12

10 won't work (10×1)+2=12

11 won't work (11×1)+1=12

12 12×1=12

▲▲▲▲▲▲Figure 9–3 *Kelly's arrays and equations explained clearly what occurred for each number of rows.*

Amelia and Kelly reported that for twenty ants, the problem they worked on, they found six ways. Greta reported that she had found eight ways to organize twenty-four ants.

Then Bo said, "You should be glad you didn't pick seventeen. There were only two ways."

"What ways?" Jay asked.

"One long row of all of them, or a line of seventeen across," Bo answered. Several of the students were interested in looking at Bo's paper (see Figure 9–6).

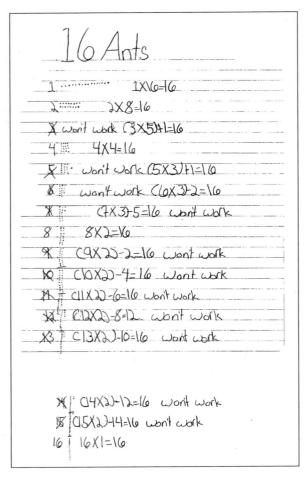

16 Ants

1 .... 1X16=16
2 .... 2X8=16
X̶ won't work (3X5)+1=16
4 ▦ 4X4=16
X̶ won't work (5X3)+1=16
6̶ won't work (6X3)-2=16
X̶ (7X3)-5=16 won't work
8 ▦ 8X2=16
X̶ (9X2)-2=16 won't work
1̶0̶ (10X2)-4=16 won't work
1̶1̶ (11X2)-6=16 won't work
1̶2̶ (12X2)-8=12 won't work
1̶3̶ (13X2)-10=16 won't work

X̶4̶ (14X2)-12=16 won't work
1̶5̶ (15X2)-14=16 won't work
16 16X1=16

▲▲▲▲▲▲**Figure 9–4** *Alicia learned that 16 ants could be organized in five different ways.*

22 Ants

1 .... 1X22
2 .... 2X11
X̶ won't work (3X7)+1
X̶4̶ won't work (4X5)+2
X̶5̶ won't work (5X4)+2
X̶6̶ won't work (6X3)+4
X̶7̶ won't work (7X3)+1
X̶8̶ won't work (8X2)+6
X̶9̶ won't work (9X2)+4
1̶0̶ won't work (10X2)+2
11 11X2
1̶2̶ won't work (12X1)+10
1̶3̶ won't work (13X1)+9

22 Ants

1̶4̶ won't work (14X1)+8
1̶5̶ won't work (15X1)+7
1̶6̶ won't work (16X1)+6
1̶7̶ won't work (17X1)+5
1̶8̶ won't work (18X1)+4
1̶9̶ won't work (19X1)+3
2̶0̶ won't work (20X1)+2
2̶1̶ won't work (21X1)+1
22 .... 22X1

▲▲▲▲▲▲**Figure 9–5** *Lydia found the four ways to organize 22 ants.*

17 Ants

#1. 1×17=17 OOOOOOOOOOOOOOOOO

#2. won't work (5×2)+7 OOOOOOOOO OOOOOOO It will not work because ten ants are in the top row and seven ants are in the bottom row.

#3. won't work (3×5)+2 OOOOO OOOOO OOO It will not work because there are three rows with five ant and one row with two ants.

#4. won't work (7×2)+3 OOOOOOO OOOOOOO OOO It will not work because fourteen ants are on the top row and three ants are on the bottom.

#5. won't work (5×3)+2 OO OOOOO OOOOO OOOOO It won't work because the top row has two ants and there are three rows with five.

#6. won't work (4×4)+1 OOOO OOOO OOOO OOOO O It will not work because there are four rows of ants with four ants in row.

#7. won't work (7+10) OOOOOOOOOO OOOOOOO It won't work because the top row has ten ants and the bottom row has seven ants.

#8. won't work (8×2)+1 OOOOOO OOOOOO OOOOO It will not work because there is two rows of six and one row of five.

#9. won't work (9+8) OOOOOOOOO OOOOOOOO It will not work because the top row has nine ants and the bottom row has eight ants.

#10. won't work (10+7) OOOOOOOOOO OOOOOOO It won't work because the top row has ten ants and the bottom row has seven ants.

#11. won't work (11+6) OOOO OOOO OOOO OOOO O because there are four rows of ants with four ants in each row and one row with one ant.

#12. won't work (12+5) OOOOOOOOOOOO OOOOO

#13. won't work (13+4) OOOO OOOOOOOOOOOOO

#14. won't work (14+3) OOO OOOOOOOOOOOOOO

#15. won't work (15+2) OO OOOOOOOOOOOOOOO

#16. won't work (16+1) O OOOOOOOOOOOOOOOO

#17. 17×1=17 O
O
O
O
O
O
O
O
O
O
O
O
O
O
O
O
O

▲▲▲▲▲▲**Figure 9–6** *Bo was surprised to find out that 17 ants could only line up in two ways—1 row of 17 ants or 17 rows with 1 ant in each.*

One Hundred Hungry Ants 95

EXTENSION

Encourage children to write their own stories similar to *One Hundred Hungry Ants*, choosing their own animals and numbers. Have children who are willing share their stories, reading them aloud for others to hear or exchanging them with partners. When children in my classes wrote stories, they usually chose larger numbers. (See Figures 9–7 through 9–9.)

18 Penguins

There are 18 penguins. All of the Penguins are going to a icekating party. The oldest penguin yelled 'No No No! We're going way to slow! So they scattered into two lines of 9. A few minutes later the oldest penguin yelled "No No No! We are going way to slow! So they scattered into three lines of six. Then they came to a slipecy muddy spot they were all falling down the oldest penguin said, "Lets try four groups" all the penguins tried but it did not work. All the penguins said we only have 10 minutes. Lets get in one line of 18. They scattered in one line. But when they got there all the people were leaving.

▲▲▲▲▲▲**Figure 9–7** *Greta found out that 18 penguins couldn't get into four equal groups.*

40 Pigs

There were 40 pigs and they all wanted to go to Angle island. They only have a little boat. "Who are we going to get there," said the litteist pig. "I have a idea we can get two boats and we can go in 20's. So 20 pigs got in one boat and the other pigs got in the other boat. "I'm squished," shrect the litteist pig. I have a idea," said the smartis pig. We can get 4 boats and go in 10's. That sounds like a grat idea," said the oldist pig. So they got 4 boat 10 pig got in one boat, the other pigs got in the other boat, and the other 10 pigs got in the other boat, and the last grop of 10 got in the last boat. "I'm squished," yelled the merist pig. I have a idea," said the smartist pig. We can get 8 boat and we can go in 5. So they got 8 boats and 5 pigs got in one boat and the other 5 got in the other boats and all of the pigs got in their boat. Was that feels good said the littleis pig. And they selled to Angle Islaend.

▲▲▲▲▲▲**Figure 9–8** *Sally wrote about 40 pigs organizing into 2, 4, and 8 boats to sail to Angel Island.*

80 Snakes

80 snakes slitherd along in a line to a party. All of a suden the smartist snake moaned "we are going to slow, if we get in two lines we will get there faster." So they had two groops of 40. "I'm bored" said the snake in the back of the line. "If we get in groops of 4 we will get there faster." So they went in 4 groops of 20. "The lines going to slow" said the dumist snake. "If we get in lines of 5 we will get there faster". said the dumist snake agean." So they went in 5 lines of 16. "I'm tierd" yaunded a snake. "If we go in groops of 8 we will get there faster." So they went in 8 rows of 10. "I'm stuck here" said a snake in the middle of the line. "If we get in groops of 10. we will get there faster." So they went in 10 groops of 8. "Its going to slow" said a snake. "If we go in groops of 16 we will get there faster." So there was 16 lines. with 5 snakes in them. "This is to slow" said a snake. "If we get in groops of 20." So there were 20 lines with 4 snakes in each. "Its to slow" said a snake. "If we go in lines of 40 we will get there faster." So they got in 40 lines. with 2 snakes in each line. STOP! said the slowist snake. "Its going to fast." "If we get in lines of 80 we will get there are own speed" so they got in 80 lines with one snake in each line. They finally got to the party. and every thing was gone. It was all gone, no snakes, no mouse tail spaggety, no nothing. So they walked home like turtles.

▲▲▲▲▲▲Figure 9–9 *Aaron's story about 80 snakes provided a complete analysis of the possibilities.*

Questions and Discussion

▲▲▲

▲ *Is it really necessary to draw all of those dots for one hundred ants? It seems cumbersome and I'm not sure of the advantage. Aren't the illustrations in the book sufficient?*

I felt that this visual representation would be useful, especially to the children who didn't see numerical relationships easily. Also, taking the time to draw the dots gives all children a way to think about the meaning of one hundred, a quantity that is large enough to be difficult to grasp.

▲ *When you asked the students how many ants there were in four, five, and ten rows, why did you have them say the answers together?*

When I ask a question that requires a simple answer that most of the children know, asking them to say the answer together gives more of them a chance to participate. Also, answering in a group is safer for some children than being put on the spot alone.

CHAPTER TEN
PATTERNS IN MULTIPLES

Overview

The charts from the whole-class lesson *Things That Come in Groups* are a rich resource for generating lists of multiples from real-world contexts. From these class charts, the children choose items that interest them, list at least twelve multiples, then color them on 0–99 charts. They write about the patterns they notice both in the list of multiples and in the visual display on the 0–99 charts.

Materials

▲ charts from the whole-class lesson *Things That Come in Groups*

▲ 0–99 charts, at least 2 per student (see Blackline Masters)

▲ optional: directions for activity, 1 per student (see Blackline Masters)

Time

▲ at least three class periods—one to introduce, additional time for repeat experiences, and one for a class discussion

Teaching Directions

1. Tell the students that they will use items from the *Things That Come in Groups* charts to investigate patterns in the multiples of different numbers.

2. Using eyes as an example, pose a problem: *How many eyes do six children have?* Ask six students to come to the front of the room and have the class count their eyes. Count by ones. Count by twos. Write the multiplication sentence on the board: $6 \times 2 = 12$. Explain how this equation relates to the problem: "Six times two means six children have two eyes each; six twos equal twelve eyes altogether."

3. Repeat the problem with eight children: How many eyes do eight children have? Have two additional students come to the front, then count again. Record

99

the multiplication sentence; $8 \times 2 = 16$. Again, explain how the sentence describes the situation. Have the children be seated.

4. Ask the class: "How many eyes do three children have?" If the first child you choose answers and explains correctly, ask if others thought about the problem in a different way and give them the opportunity to answer and explain. Ask all children who respond to explain the reasoning they used to get their answers. Then ask someone to give the multiplication sentence that matches the problem. Record it on the board: $3 \times 2 = 6$.

5. To model how they are to look for patterns in multiples, demonstrate for the children how to organize information about people and eyes. Draw on the chalkboard:

people	eyes

Ask the class how many eyes one person has. Record this information on the table, as well as the multiplication equation: $1 \times 2 = 2$. Explain that the expression $1 \times 2 = 2$ tells that one child with two eyes equals two eyes altogether.

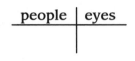

people	eyes
1	2

$1 \times 2 = 2$

Now ask: "How many eyes do two people have?" Record the information, write the multiplication equation, and have someone explain how the equation relates to the situation of two people having four eyes.

Continue until you've recorded information for twelve people. It's likely that the children will predict the numbers as you write them. Ask them to explain how they know what comes next. Encourage them to think about different ways to figure it out.

6. Introduce what happens when a number is multiplied by zero. Ask: "If there weren't any people in the room, how many eyes would there be?" Ask for a volunteer to tell the multiplication sentence you should write. Add this information to the top of the chart.

7. Point to the multiples 0, 2, 4, 6, 8, and so on and ask the class to read them aloud with you. Then ask the children what patterns they notice in the numbers. To prompt them, ask them to look first at the pattern of digits in the ones place of the multiples, and then the digits in the tens place. Ask them what other patterns they notice. As in other situations, accept all their ideas.

8. Show the class another way to look at the patterns. Post a 0–99 chart and color the multiples of two from 0 to 24. Have the children describe visual patterns they notice and then tell you the other numbers to color. This is an opportunity to talk

people	eyes	
0	0	$0 \times 2 = 0$
1	2	$1 \times 2 = 2$
2	4	$2 \times 2 = 4$
3	6	$3 \times 2 = 6$
4	8	$4 \times 2 = 8$
5	10	$5 \times 2 = 10$
6	12	$6 \times 2 = 12$
7	14	$7 \times 2 = 14$
8	16	$8 \times 2 = 16$
9	18	$9 \times 2 = 18$
10	20	$10 \times 2 = 20$
11	22	$11 \times 2 = 22$
12	24	$12 \times 2 = 24$

0–99 Chart

0	1	2	3	4	5	6	7	8	9
10	11	12	13	14	15	16	17	18	19
20	21	22	23	24	25	26	27	28	29
30	31	32	33	34	35	36	37	38	39
40	41	42	43	44	45	46	47	48	49
50	51	52	53	54	55	56	57	58	59
60	61	62	63	64	65	66	67	68	69
70	71	72	73	74	75	76	77	78	79
80	81	82	83	84	85	86	87	88	89
90	91	92	93	94	95	96	97	98	99

about even and odd numbers. Point out that all the multiples of two are even and that zero is also an even number.

9. Explain the assignment. You may want to write the directions on the board or an overhead transparency or distribute a copy to each child. Tell children they are to investigate at least two numbers. You may choose to have the children work individually, with partners, or first with partners and then on their own.

Note: If you decide that students need more preparation before investigating multiples independently, do a second investigation of multiples with them, perhaps on another day. Use a different number, selecting an item from another list.

10. After children have investigated as least two multiples, one with partners and one on their own, initiate a class discussion. Begin by posting a 0–99 chart for each of the numbers from two to twelve, with multiples colored. (See pages 103–104.)

Use the following discussion guidelines:

> Which numbers have all even multiples?
>
> Which numbers have all odd multiples?
>
> Which numbers have some even and some odd multiples?
>
> On which charts was the number zero colored? (This gives you the chance to reinforce that any number times zero is zero.)
>
> Are there any numbers that aren't colored on any of the charts?
>
> Some people say that the multiples of five are easy to remember. Why do you think they say that?
>
> Some people say that the tens are even easier. Why do they think that?
>
> Which other numbers have easy multiples?
>
> Which have hard multiples?
>
> On the chart with multiples of two, more numbers were colored in than on the chart with multiples of ten. Why is this so? What do you notice about how many numbers are colored in on other charts?

Be sensitive to the children's level of interest during a discussion. It's not necessary to discuss all the questions in one day. If the students' interest wanes, don't push, but return to the discussion on another day. Also, be sure to ask children what they may have noticed that you didn't ask about.

Grid 1 (top left):

0	1	2	3	4	5	6	7	8	9
10	11	12	13	14	15	16	17	18	19
20	21	22	23	24	25	26	27	28	29
30	31	32	33	34	35	36	37	38	39
40	41	42	43	44	45	46	47	48	49
50	51	52	53	54	55	56	57	58	59
60	61	62	63	64	65	66	67	68	69
70	71	72	73	74	75	76	77	78	79
80	81	82	83	84	85	86	87	88	89
90	91	92	93	94	95	96	97	98	99

Grid 2 (top right):

0	1	2	3	4	5	6	7	8	9
10	11	12	13	14	15	16	17	18	19
20	21	22	23	24	25	26	27	28	29
30	31	32	33	34	35	36	37	38	39
40	41	42	43	44	45	46	47	48	49
50	51	52	53	54	55	56	57	58	59
60	61	62	63	64	65	66	67	68	69
70	71	72	73	74	75	76	77	78	79
80	81	82	83	84	85	86	87	88	89
90	91	92	93	94	95	96	97	98	99

Grid 3 (middle left):

0	1	2	3	4	5	6	7	8	9
10	11	12	13	14	15	16	17	18	19
20	21	22	23	24	25	26	27	28	29
30	31	32	33	34	35	36	37	38	39
40	41	42	43	44	45	46	47	48	49
50	51	52	53	54	55	56	57	58	59
60	61	62	63	64	65	66	67	68	69
70	71	72	73	74	75	76	77	78	79
80	81	82	83	84	85	86	87	88	89
90	91	92	93	94	95	96	97	98	99

Grid 4 (middle right):

0	1	2	3	4	5	6	7	8	9
10	11	12	13	14	15	16	17	18	19
20	21	22	23	24	25	26	27	28	29
30	31	32	33	34	35	36	37	38	39
40	41	42	43	44	45	46	47	48	49
50	51	52	53	54	55	56	57	58	59
60	61	62	63	64	65	66	67	68	69
70	71	72	73	74	75	76	77	78	79
80	81	82	83	84	85	86	87	88	89
90	91	92	93	94	95	96	97	98	99

Grid 5 (bottom left):

0	1	2	3	4	5	6	7	8	9
10	11	12	13	14	15	16	17	18	19
20	21	22	23	24	25	26	27	28	29
30	31	32	33	34	35	36	37	38	39
40	41	42	43	44	45	46	47	48	49
50	51	52	53	54	55	56	57	58	59
60	61	62	63	64	65	66	67	68	69
70	71	72	73	74	75	76	77	78	79
80	81	82	83	84	85	86	87	88	89
90	91	92	93	94	95	96	97	98	99

Grid 6 (bottom right):

0	1	2	3	4	5	6	7	8	9
10	11	12	13	14	15	16	17	18	19
20	21	22	23	24	25	26	27	28	29
30	31	32	33	34	35	36	37	38	39
40	41	42	43	44	45	46	47	48	49
50	51	52	53	54	55	56	57	58	59
60	61	62	63	64	65	66	67	68	69
70	71	72	73	74	75	76	77	78	79
80	81	82	83	84	85	86	87	88	89
90	91	92	93	94	95	96	97	98	99

Grid 1 (top-left)

0	1	2	3	4	5	6	7	8	9
10	11	12	13	14	15	16	17	18	19
20	21	22	23	24	25	26	27	28	29
30	31	32	33	34	35	36	37	38	39
40	41	42	43	44	45	46	47	48	49
50	51	52	53	54	55	56	57	58	59
60	61	62	63	64	65	66	67	68	69
70	71	72	73	74	75	76	77	78	79
80	81	82	83	84	85	86	87	88	89
90	91	92	93	94	95	96	97	98	99

(Shaded: 0, 8, 16, 24, 32, 40, 48, 56, 64, 72, 80, 88, 96)

Grid 2 (top-right)

0	1	2	3	4	5	6	7	8	9
10	11	12	13	14	15	16	17	18	19
20	21	22	23	24	25	26	27	28	29
30	31	32	33	34	35	36	37	38	39
40	41	42	43	44	45	46	47	48	49
50	51	52	53	54	55	56	57	58	59
60	61	62	63	64	65	66	67	68	69
70	71	72	73	74	75	76	77	78	79
80	81	82	83	84	85	86	87	88	89
90	91	92	93	94	95	96	97	98	99

(Shaded: 0, 9, 18, 27, 36, 45, 54, 63, 72, 81, 90, 99)

Grid 3 (middle-left)

0	1	2	3	4	5	6	7	8	9
10	11	12	13	14	15	16	17	18	19
20	21	22	23	24	25	26	27	28	29
30	31	32	33	34	35	36	37	38	39
40	41	42	43	44	45	46	47	48	49
50	51	52	53	54	55	56	57	58	59
60	61	62	63	64	65	66	67	68	69
70	71	72	73	74	75	76	77	78	79
80	81	82	83	84	85	86	87	88	89
90	91	92	93	94	95	96	97	98	99

(Shaded: 0, 10, 20, 30, 40, 50, 60, 70, 80, 90)

Grid 4 (middle-right)

0	1	2	3	4	5	6	7	8	9
10	11	12	13	14	15	16	17	18	19
20	21	22	23	24	25	26	27	28	29
30	31	32	33	34	35	36	37	38	39
40	41	42	43	44	45	46	47	48	49
50	51	52	53	54	55	56	57	58	59
60	61	62	63	64	65	66	67	68	69
70	71	72	73	74	75	76	77	78	79
80	81	82	83	84	85	86	87	88	89
90	91	92	93	94	95	96	97	98	99

(Shaded: 0, 11, 22, 33, 44, 55, 66, 77, 88, 99)

Grid 5 (bottom-left)

0	1	2	3	4	5	6	7	8	9
10	11	12	13	14	15	16	17	18	19
20	21	22	23	24	25	26	27	28	29
30	31	32	33	34	35	36	37	38	39
40	41	42	43	44	45	46	47	48	49
50	51	52	53	54	55	56	57	58	59
60	61	62	63	64	65	66	67	68	69
70	71	72	73	74	75	76	77	78	79
80	81	82	83	84	85	86	87	88	89
90	91	92	93	94	95	96	97	98	99

(Shaded: 0, 12, 24, 36, 48, 60, 72, 84, 96)

Teaching Notes

This activity engages children in examining numerical patterns (from the lists they make), visual patterns (from the 0–99 charts), and verbal patterns (from the descriptions they give). It's typical for children to be confident using one or two of these approaches to describing patterns, but not all three. The activity is extremely useful for helping children build on their strengths and develop areas that are weaker.

When children are putting their ideas about patterns into words, encourage them to find their own ways to describe mathematical relationships and to listen to their classmates to get other perspectives. Expect their descriptions to be incomplete or imprecise. As often as possible, use new words in the context of activities to help children integrate new terminology into their vocabularies.

Aside from dealing with multiples of numbers, this activity also provides a way to talk about zero as a multiple of all numbers. Zero often gets shortchanged in math instruction, sometimes erroneously treated as a placeholder instead of a number. This may be because it's not a counting number and isn't used in general conversation as frequently as other numbers. Whenever you can, include zero in class discussions; children need to become familiar with its special properties. For additional ideas for dealing with zero, see "Multiplying by Zero" on page 126.

The idea of prime numbers can emerge from this activity. The numbers that aren't colored on any chart are prime numbers larger than 12. It's valuable to make connections among activities. The numbers in *Candy Box Research* with only one rectangle are also prime; these also include prime numbers less than 12—2, 3, 5, 7, and 11. Note that even though the number 1 has only one possible candy box, it's not considered to be prime because it has only one factor, not two as required for prime numbers. Although many of the children won't be interested in or able to understand this, it's worth mentioning for the one child whose mathematical imagination might be captured. This is the time when a light touch is important, so you don't want to make children feel they have to understand this.

After introducing the activity to the class, repeated experiences are appropriate and valuable. The activity is suitable for choice time.

The Lesson

▲▲▲

DAY 1

I began the lesson by telling the children that they would be using ideas from the *Things That Come in Groups* class charts for a new investigation. I said, "This new investigation is called *Patterns in Multiples.*" I wrote the name of the activity on the board.

I then posed a problem. I said, "One of the items we listed on our twos chart is 'eyes.' Let's find out how many eyes six children have." I asked six children seated near the front to come up and face the class. For some children, the answer was obvious, and some raised their hands immediately. But having the six children come up gave time for others to think, and I noticed a few children counting before raising their hands.

I asked again, "How many eyes do the six children have?" and then called on Michael.

"Twelve," he answered.

"Raise your hand if you agree," I said. Most of the children did so.

"How did you figure it out?" I asked Michael.

"It was easy. I just knew," he said.

"What did you know?" I probed.

Michael quickly counted by twos. "Two, four, six, eight, ten, twelve, like that," he said.

I responded, "Ah, so you counted by twos to find out that six twos are twelve. Did anyone figure it out another way?"

"I counted by ones," Rebecca said.

"Did you also get twelve?" I asked. She nodded.

"Any other way?" I asked. There were no responses. I wrote on the board:

$6 \times 2 = 12$

I said, "This multiplication sentence, 'six times two equals twelve,' is a mathematical way to write that six children with two eyes each have twelve eyes altogether. The equation states that six twos equals twelve."

I then asked Maria and Koji to join the children at the front of the room. I said, "Now there are eight children here. Let's count together quietly to see how many eyes they have altogether." As I pointed to each child, the students counted along with me. I then wrote on the board:

$8 \times 2 = 16$

"Who can read this mathematical sentence?" I asked.

Elena responded, "Eight times two is equal to sixteen."

"And that means that eight twos are sixteen," I added.

I asked the children up at the front to take their seats. When they were settled, I asked the class, "How many eyes do three children have? Raise your hand when you've figured out the answer to this question." I waited, and soon everyone but Brandon and Libby had raised a hand.

"Brandon, have you figured it out yet?" I asked.

"Oh yeah," he said and raised a hand.

"Libby?" I asked.

"I think I know but I'm not sure," she said.

"Let's say the answer together in a whisper voice," I said to the class. When they said, "Six," Libby grinned.

"I was right," she said.

"What multiplication sentence matches this problem?" I asked.

"Three times two equals six," Brian answered. I wrote on the board:

$3 \times 2 = 6$

I then drew a table on the board and labeled the left column people and the right column eyes. I wrote *1* in the people column and asked, "How many eyes does one person have?" I recorded, showing them how to write the answer and the multiplication sentence.

people	eyes	
1	2	$1 \times 2 = 2$

I then wrote *2* in the people column of the chart, the answer, and the corresponding multiplication sentence. I continued in this way down to twelve people. For three, six, and eight, we were able to use the information we already had figured out.

"They go up by twos," Alex said.

"And the people go up by ones," Lisa added.

I squeezed in the number zero above the one in the people column. The children giggled.

"That's easy," Josh said. "It's zero eyes."

"What's the multiplication sentence?" I asked.

Angie answered, "Zero times two equals zero." I recorded this to complete the chart.

"You noticed that the numbers in the eyes column go up by twos," I said. "Let's look just at the numbers in the ones place and see what pattern there is." I pointed to the numbers on the 0–24 people/eyes chart as the children read them aloud, "Zero, two, four, six, eight, zero, two, four, six, eight, zero, two, four." A few children continued counting even though we had reached the end of the column.

I stopped them. "You're right about how the pattern would continue," I said. "Let's look at the pattern in the numbers in the tens column." I began with ten and the children read the numbers, "One, one, one, one, one, two, two, two."

"There would be two again two more times, for twenty-six and twenty-eight," Josh said.

Tony added, excitedly, "Then it would go to three—three, three, three, three, three."

"How many threes?" I asked.

Several children counted on their fingers. Lisa answered, "There would be five of them—thirty-two, thirty-four, thirty-six, thirty-eight. Oops, that's only four."

I waited a moment while Lisa counted again, and I wrote the numbers on the board—*32, 34, 36, 38.*

"You forgot thirty," Rebecca said.

"Oh yeah," Lisa said. "I knew there were five."

"Let's look at the numbers again and see which are even and which are odd," I said. We looked and saw that they were all even.

I then posted a 0–99 chart on the board. "Another way to look for patterns is to color in the numbers from the eyes column. I'll color them as you read them." As I did so, several children made comments.

"They're stripes," Libby said.

"They go down straight," Kim said.

"What would the chart look like if we continued the pattern?" I asked. It was obvious to the children that the stripes would continue to the bottom of the chart. I completed coloring the chart.

"Who can describe the pattern if we go horizontally, across the rows?" I asked.

0	1	2	3	4	5	6	7	8	9
10	11	12	13	14	15	16	17	18	19
20	21	22	23	24	25	26	27	28	29
30	31	32	33	34	35	36	37	38	39
40	41	42	43	44	45	46	47	48	49
50	51	52	53	54	55	56	57	58	59
60	61	62	63	64	65	66	67	68	69
70	71	72	73	74	75	76	77	78	79
80	81	82	83	84	85	86	87	88	89
90	91	92	93	94	95	96	97	98	99

"They go color-skip-color-skip, like that," Maria said.

"And what pattern goes vertically, down the columns?" I asked.

Michael answered, "Stripe, no stripe, stripe, no stripe, stripe, no stripe."

"What about a pattern on the diagonal, going from zero at the top left down to ninety-nine at the bottom right?" I asked, pointing to illustrate what I meant by "on the diagonal." The children were interested in this pattern and fascinated to see that it alternated between being colored and not.

"Look!" Koji said. "They're doubles. Can I come up and show?" I agreed, and Koji pointed out that, except for zero, the numbers on the diagonal had both digits the same—eleven, twenty-two, thirty-three, and so on.

I then explained to the children what they were to do. I had duplicated the directions, and now I distributed one copy to each pair of children. I also distributed blank 0–99 charts. "You and your partner will first agree on an item from the *Things That Come in Groups* chart and do exactly what we did for the eyes. You'll make a table and list at least twelve multiples. Color them in on a zero through ninety-nine chart and then continue the pattern to the end of the chart. Finally, write about the patterns you see on your list and on the zero through ninety-nine chart. When you've done this together, then you'll work individually on another pattern. You'll each choose another item from the chart, for a different number, and investigate the patterns of the multiples."

I put the extra copies of the 0–99 chart in a visible location and the children got to work. I circulated, answering questions and helping as needed. The children worked for the remainder of the period.

DAY 2

Before class began, I chose a few completed papers to use as models of work that was done correctly and also to present some of the different ways students were thinking about the patterns. I checked with the children whose papers I chose to be sure it was OK if I shared them with the class. All agreed.

I began with Tony and Josh's work. Because they were both avid sports fans, their choice was predictable. They had picked "players on football teams" and had investigated the multiples of eleven. I told this to the class and was immediately corrected by Josh.

He said, "We did players on the offense team, or else it would be twenty-two."

I accepted his correction and showed the class Tony and Josh's table and 0–99 chart (see Figure 10–1). I had selected their work because it gave me the opportunity to reinforce the meaning of diagonal. They had written: *Our pattern goes by elevens. Our pattern goes diagonal.* I read this to the class.

"Who can explain what diagonal means?" I asked, holding up Tony and Josh's 0–99 chart. I waited a few moments to give the children a chance to collect their thoughts. I called on Maria.

"It goes in a slant," she said.

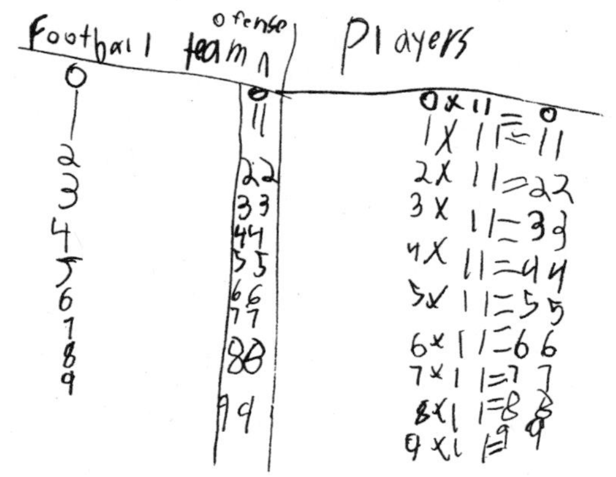

▲▲▲▲▲▲Figure 10–1 *Tony and Josh investigated the pattern of football players on the offense team.*

Brian had a different explanation. "It kind of goes over and down, over and down," he said.

I called on Lindsay next. "It's like a staircase," she offered, "and it can go up or down, either way."

I then talked with the class about Emily and Jenny's work. They had chosen "sides of triangles" and had listed the multiples of three. They had written: *The pattern of investagating triangle's is a diagonal pattern going down counting by three's and it starts at 0 and ends at 99.* I showed their 0–99 chart and asked the children to compare this pattern with Tony and Josh's.

Lisa raised her hand. "We're doing a threes pattern also," she said. "We're doing colors on traffic lights, the regular kind with three. We haven't finished yet." Other children raised their hands to tell what they were doing, but I refocused on my agenda.

"The reason I'm showing some samples of finished work is to give you ideas about different ways to look at patterns," I said. I posted a sheet of chart paper and continued. "I'm going to list some words that are useful for describing patterns," I said. "You can look at this list to get ideas or to check your spelling." I wrote *pattern* and *diagonal* on the list.

I then showed Alex and Maria's investigation of animals' feet. They had recorded the number of feet for one to twenty-five animals and colored in their chart. I showed their table and 0–99 chart.

I commented, "I noticed that Maria and Alex shared the work of writing about the patterns. Maria wrote about the multiples in their table, and Alex wrote about the patterns on the zero through ninety-nine chart. It's fine to share the work as they did, but be sure you talk with each other about what you're writing."

I then read their discoveries to the class. Maria had written: *The ones pattern is 4, 8, 2, 6, 0. In the tens, it goes 1, 1, 2, 2, 2, 3, 3, 4, 4, 4, 5, 5.* Alex had written: *The paterns I found are horisontel, parelel, and diagonle. The row with 1s, 3s, 5s, 7s, and 9s don't have any coler on them, like in 1s I mean 1, 11, 21, 31, ect.* I added *horizontal* and *parallel* to the vocabulary list and talked with the class about the meanings of these words. I also wrote vertical on the list to offer another option.

I then had the children continue working on the activity. James and Elena were working on multiples of twelve. "We're doing Coke cans in twelve-packs," James told me. (See Figure 10–2.)

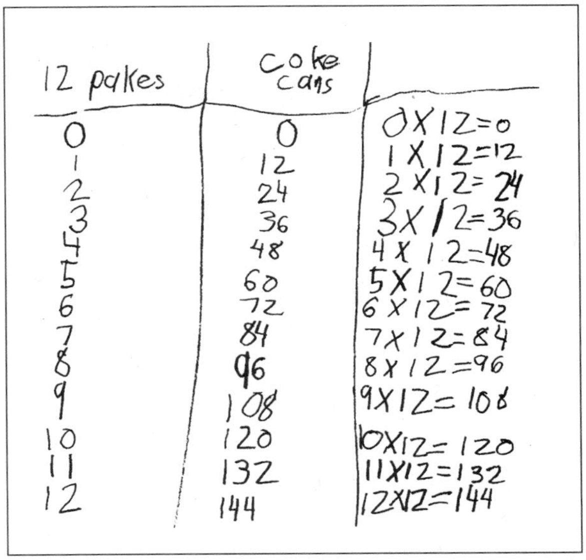

12 pakes	Coke cans	
0	0	0X12=0
1	12	1X12=12
2	24	2X12=24
3	36	3X12=36
4	48	4X12=48
5	60	5X12=60
6	72	6X12=72
7	84	7X12=84
8	96	8X12=96
9	108	9X12=108
10	120	10X12=120
11	132	11X12=132
12	144	12X12=144

▲▲▲▲▲**Figure 10–2** ***James and Elena investigated 12-packs of Coke.***

"Why did you choose that one?" I asked.

"So there won't be so many to do," he said. "We first started to do people and thumbs yesterday, but there were too many numbers to color so we switched."

Although it's apparent to adults that there are more multiples of two on the 0–99 chart than multiples of twelve, it's not obvious to children. When James shared his observation in a later class discussion, there was genuine surprise from others. As they colored the multiples on the 0–99 chart, James and Elena came upon the problem of what to do with the multiples larger than ninety-nine. They solved this by continuing the numbers on the chart (see Figure 10–3). I left them to work.

I went to talk with Tony and Josh about their spelling. They were working on other patterns. I pointed out the errors on the work they had done together and suggested they check the vocabulary list when doing more writing. Children respond differently to criticism. In this case, Tony blushed and Josh shrugged. I told the boys, "Your ideas are fine, but correct spelling would make them easier for others to read." I left them to make the changes.

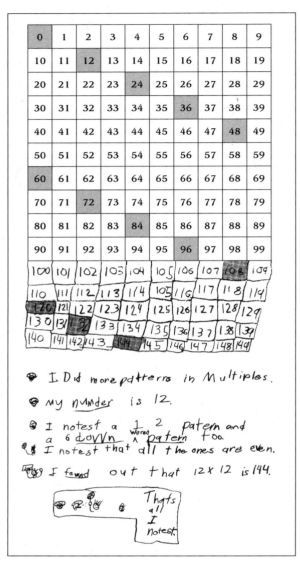

0	1	2	3	4	5	6	7	8	9
10	11	12	13	14	15	16	17	18	19
20	21	22	23	24	25	26	27	28	29
30	31	32	33	34	35	36	37	38	39
40	41	42	43	44	45	46	47	48	49
50	51	52	53	54	55	56	57	58	59
60	61	62	63	64	65	66	67	68	69
70	71	72	73	74	75	76	77	78	79
80	81	82	83	84	85	86	87	88	89
90	91	92	93	94	95	96	97	98	99
100	101	102	103	104	105	106	107	108	109
110	111	112	113	114	105 116		117	118	119
120	121	122	123	124	125	126	127	128	129
130	131	132	133	134	135	136	137	138	139
140	141	142	143	144	145	146	147	148	149

- I Did more patterns in Multiples.
- My number is 12.
- I notest a 1 2 patern and a 6 down woed [downward] patern too.
- I notest that all the ones are even.
- I fownd out that 12 X 12 is 144.
- Thats all I notest.

▲▲▲▲▲▲**Figure 10–3** *James and Elena added five more rows to their chart to accommodate the multiples up to 144. They wrote about what they noticed.*

I also talked with Alex about his spelling errors. He had already used the chart to make changes.

Lisa and Kim were finishing their investigation of the multiples of three from "colors in traffic lights." They wrote: *Diagonally starting from the top left corner, it goes one,*

skip two, one, skip two, ect. From the top right corner it goes diagonally all the way throgh. Going vertically, it goes skip two, one, skip two, one, ect. Going horizontally the pattern is skip two, one skip two one ect.

Koji and Sam had chosen "eggs in half a dozen." They wrote: *The paterrn in the numbers are 0, 6, 2, 8, 4, 0, 6, 2, 8, 4, 0, 6, and so on. We think it looks like steps with one step missing. The pattern is to skip five.*

I checked back to see how James and Elena were doing. James was just finishing his writing about the patterns, and Elena was rummaging through the bucket of markers at the supply table. (Elena often wandered, both physically and mentally.) I read what James had written: *I did more patterns in multiples. My numder is 12. I notest a 1 2 pattern and a 6 down wored [downward] patern too. I notest that all the ones are even. I fownd out that 12 × 12 is 144. Thats all I notest.* James had great difficulty with spelling but was an original and often profound thinker. I wrote in his personal dictionary the words he had misspelled and asked him to read what he had written to Elena. He nodded and went to get her.

DAY 3

The children continued work on the activity for the first fifteen minutes of Day 3. Then I gathered them for a class discussion. Before we talked as a class, however, I had children talk in groups about what they had discovered about the patterns of multiples for different numbers. While they did this, I posted a 0–99 chart with multiples colored in for each of the numbers from two to twelve. Then I called for the children's attention.

"Which numbers have only even multiples?" I asked. "Look at the charts I've posted or at your papers and raise your hand when you've found one." The children began to pore over their lists and charts. As I called on children, I recorded the numbers on the board.

"Twelve," James reported.

"Six," Koji added.

"Four," Brian said.

Soon I had listed all of them on the board.

12, 6, 4, 10, 2, 8

"Can someone help me write these numbers in order?" I asked. With Lisa's help, I rewrote them.

2, 4, 6, 8, 10, 12

"They're all even!" Tanya noticed.

"Yes, the multiples of the even numbers are all even," I said. "Are there any numbers with only odd multiples?"

Again the children examined their papers. After a few false starts, they decided that no numbers had only odd multiples.

"The rest all have even and odd ones," Elena said.

I paraphrased, "Odd numbers have both even and odd multiples."

"And they go odd, even, odd, even," Josh noticed.

"What about zero?" I said. "See if you colored in zero on your chart." Some children were surprised to find zero on all the charts. A few noticed that they had neglected to color in zero but agreed that it should have been colored in.

"Is any other number on every chart?" I asked. The children made some guesses, but disproved each one. They couldn't find any.

"What about numbers that aren't colored on any chart?" I asked. This called for another search, and they began to find some, all the prime numbers greater than

12—13, 17, 19, 23, 29, 31, 37, and so on. Although children don't formally study prime numbers in the third grade, this is a good way to introduce them to the concept.

I said, "The numbers that aren't colored on any of the zero through ninety-nine charts also have something else in common. In the *Candy Box Research* activity, these numbers have only one rectangle. These special numbers are called prime numbers."

I then focused on specific multiples. "The multiples of five are easy to remember," I said. We said them aloud together.

"Why are these so easy?" I asked.

"They end in fives or zeros," Rebecca said.

"The tens are easy, too," Sam said.

"The sevens are hard," Angie said.

"Not if you think about touchdowns," Josh said.

I then asked the children to look at the charts I had posted. I said, "I had to do a lot of coloring for the multiples of two, but not so much coloring for the numbers ten, eleven, and twelve. Why do you think this is so?"

Most of the children had no idea, but some had thoughts.

"The bigger numbers are farther apart," Brandon said.

"There's more of them for the twos and threes," Lisa said.

"For ten there is only one stripe, but five has two stripes," Josh noticed.

Time was up for the class, so I ended the discussion. Doing more *Patterns in Multiples* investigations was of interest to some of the children, and they did additional papers when there was choice time (see Figures 10–4 and 10–5).

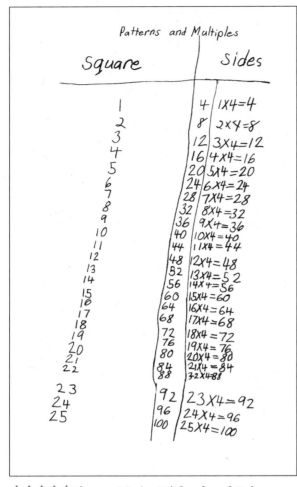

Patterns and Multiples

Square	Sides	
1	4	1X4=4
2	8	2X4=8
3	12	3X4=12
4	16	4X4=16
5	20	5X4=20
6	24	6X4=24
7	28	7X4=28
8	32	8X4=32
9	36	9X4=36
10	40	10X4=40
11	44	11X4=44
12	48	12X4=48
13	52	13X4=52
14	56	14X4=56
15	60	15X4=60
16	64	16X4=64
17	68	17X4=68
18	72	18X4=72
19	76	19X4=76
20	80	20X4=80
21	84	21X4=84
22	88	22X4=88
23	92	23X4=92
24	96	24X4=96
25	100	25X4=100

▲▲▲▲▲▲Figure 10–4 *Michael and Brian chose to investigate the sides of squares. Michael noticed that all of the mulitples were*

0	1	2	3	4	5	6	7	8	9
10	11	12	13	14	15	16	17	18	19
20	21	22	23	24	25	26	27	28	29
30	31	32	33	34	35	36	37	38	39
40	41	42	43	44	45	46	47	48	49
50	51	52	53	54	55	56	57	58	59
60	61	62	63	64	65	66	67	68	69
70	71	72	73	74	75	76	77	78	79
80	81	82	83	84	85	86	87	88	89
90	91	92	93	94	95	96	97	98	99

Patterns and Multiples

I can find 3 patterns on my Patterns and Multiples. One of them is one skip one one and so on. One of them moves in the way of a knight. One pattern is like this ▨▨ ▨. One of them goes diaggnally one and then sideways one.

▲▲▲▲▲▲Figure 10–5 *Michael and Brian colored the multiples of 4 and wrote about the patterns they found.*

Questions and Discussion

▲▲▲

▲ *I don't think that most of my students know what the word **multiples** means. Shouldn't I explain this first?*

Many of my students weren't familiar with the word *multiples.* However, rather than defining it, I chose to use it and allow the children to become familiar with the term in the context of the activity. Mathematical language is more easily learned when connected to children's firsthand experience.

▲ *What if the students don't have any ideas to write about the patterns?*

I haven't had this situation, although some children notice more patterns than others do. A colleague has found it helpful to give her students more direction for describing the patterns on the 0–99 chart. She asks the children to examine the chart for four types of patterns—vertical, horizontal, diagonal, and overall patterns. Figure 10–6 shows how one child described the multiples of eight.

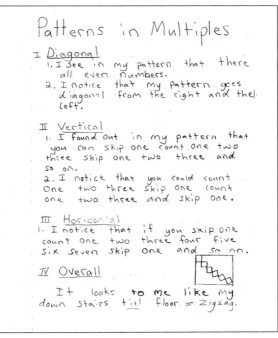

▲▲▲▲▲▲**Figure 10–6** *For the multiples of 8, Greta described the diagonal, vertical, horizontal, and overall patterns on the 0–99 chart.*

CHAPTER ELEVEN
CALCULATOR PATTERNS

Overview

In this lesson, children explore the multiples of various numbers. Similar to *Patterns in Multiples,* this activity reinforces the relationship between multiplication and addition. However, instead of using the charts from *Things That Come in Groups* to generate lists of multiples, the children use calculators. They choose a number and repeatedly add it, keeping track of the totals that are displayed. When they have a list of at least twelve multiples, they write about the patterns they notice. A children's book, *Ready or Not, Here I Come!,* by Teddy Slater, is used to introduce this activity.

Materials

▲ *Ready or Not, Here I Come!*, by Teddy Slater (Hello Math Reader series, New York: Scholastic, 1999)
▲ calculators, at least 1 per pair of students
▲ optional: directions for activity, 1 per student (see Blackline Masters)

Time

▲ two class periods

Teaching Directions

1. Read aloud the Hello Math Reader *Ready or Not, Here I Come!*, by Teddy Slater. In the story, children count to one hundred by ones, fives, tens, and twenties. Talk with the children about other numbers they could use to count to one hundred. List the numbers they identify.

2. Show the children how to use the calculator to count by a particular number. Demonstrate with five, a number with multiples that are familiar to most children. As you explain to the class what you are doing, press "5" on the calculator, then the

114

"+" key, and then the "=" key. Show the calculator to the children seated near you and ask them to read aloud the number displayed. (It should be 5, the same number you first entered.) Press the "=" key again and ask the same children to read the new number displayed. (It should be 10.) Continue to press the "=" key, having the children read the number each time. Repeat until the display shows 100. Record the multiples next to the 5 you've listed on the board.

3. Repeat the procedure for ten and twenty, again explaining to the children how to use the calculator and asking children to read the numbers. Record the multiples next to each of these numbers.

4. Next to the number 1 on the board, record 1, 2, 3, 4, 5, . . ., 100. Explain to the class that this is a shortcut way to record all of the numbers from one to one hundred, and that the three dots indicate the numbers that are missing.

5. Use the calculator to test the other numbers the children predicted would land on 100. Along with 1, 5, 10, and 20, the other numbers that work are 2, 4, 25, 50, and 100. It's OK if the children don't identify all of these. However, point out that the ones they identify are *factors* of one hundred because one hundred is a *multiple* of each of them.

6. Introduce the activity. You may wish to write directions on the board or an overhead transparency or distribute a copy to each child. Also, if you have a sufficient number of calculators, you may wish to have the children do the activity individually.

Calculator Patterns

You need: a calculator
             a partner

1. Clear your calculator.

2. Choose a number from 2 to 10, write it down, and then press it on the calculator.

3. Press the "+" key.

4. Press the "=" key. (You should see the same number you first entered.)

5. Keep pressing the "=" key, each time listing the number that comes up. Continue until you have written at least twelve numbers.

6. Write about the patterns you notice.

---

7. After children have investigated at least two patterns, initiate a class discussion. Begin by asking the following questions:

What patterns did you notice in the ones column?

What patterns did you notice in the tens column?

Continue the discussion with the following questions:

For which numbers did you list only even multiples?

For which numbers did you list only odd multiples?

Which numbers have both even and odd multiples?

The fives were easy to predict. Which other numbers were easy? Why?

8. Help children connect this activity to *Patterns in Multiples.* Choose a number and ask a child who investigated it using a calculator to report its multiples. Then, ask a child who investigated the same number for *Patterns in Multiples* to share the results. Ask the children: "Why do you think the numbers from the two different activities are the same?"

Teaching Notes

In the story *Ready or Not, Here I Come!,* Emma, Rose, and Lulu are playing hide-and-seek. Emma's little sister, Maggie, asks to play. Emma claims that Maggie is too young, but Maggie insists that she can count to one hundred and begs to be included. The older girls agree and let Maggie be "It." Maggie turns around and begins to count. But she counts very, very slowly, giving the older girls enough time to squeeze in two speed hide-and-seek games by themselves, counting to one hundred by fives and then tens. They start a third game of superspeed hide-and-seek, with Emma as "It" counting by twenties, but Maggie reaches one hundred just as Emma does. She opens her eyes, sees the older girls in the kitchen, and tags them all!

The story provides an entry for talking with the class about counting to one hundred in different ways and then introducing the activity of counting by other numbers. Also, the story provides a context for introducing or reinforcing for children the correct terminology of *multiple* and *factor.*

Calculator Patterns is similar to *Patterns in Multiples.* In both explorations, children list the multiples for different numbers and explore the patterns that emerge. While it's not essential, I think that it's a good idea to introduce this activity after the children have had experience with *Patterns in Multiples.* Using the contexts in *Patterns in Multiples* helps children see the connection between multiples of numbers and real-world situations, while the calculator exploration is more abstract.

Children don't always notice the similarity between the two activities or realize that the same numbers generate the same multiples. This may be because in *Patterns in Multiples,* children focus on the *Things That Come in Groups* class charts, while in *Calculator Patterns,* they focus on the numbers on the calculator display without a connection to any context. Also, children may not investigate the same numbers for both activities and, therefore, have no evidence of their own to compare. Even if children investigate the same numbers, however, don't be surprised if they don't notice that the patterns for the same number are the same.

After introducing the activity to the class, repeated experiences are appropriate and valuable. The activity is suitable for choice time.

The Lesson

▲▲

DAY 1

I showed the class the cover of *Ready or Not, Here I Come!* and asked the children what they thought the book was about.

"It's about hide-and-go-seek," Edna said.

"They're playing hide-and-seek, but I think the girl is peeking," Koji said.

"I think it's about counting," Kim said.

I read the story and stopped when Rose suggested that she, Emma, and Lulu play speed hide-and-seek. "How do you think they'll play speed hide-and-seek?" I asked.

"I think they'll count by tens," Brandon predicted.

I responded, "That would certainly speed up the game. Listen to what the girls do." I continued reading until the end of the book.

After children had a chance to report what they liked about the story, I shifted to a discussion of the mathematics. I said to the class, "The girls knew that they would land on one hundred if they counted by fives, tens, and twenties. What other numbers do you think they could count by to reach exactly one hundred?" I listed on the board *5, 10, 20,* and then the children's predictions—*50, 100, 2, 1,* and *15.*

"A calculator can help us check these numbers," I said. I chose the number five to demonstrate how to use the calculator to count by fives. Not only did it head the list on the board, but most children are familiar with its multiples.

I explained, "To count by fives, we have to add five over and over again, and we can use the calculator to do this." I modeled for the class how to enter "5" into the calculator, then press the "+" key, and then the "=" key.

"What number is on the display?" I asked the children at the front table.

"Five," they answered in unison.

I said, "I'm going to press the equals key again. What do you think the calculator will show?"

"Ten," they predicted. I pressed the "=" key and showed the calculator to the children up front.

"It's ten," Maria confirmed.

I then said, "I'm going to press the equals key one more time."

"It will be fifteen," Josh said. I pressed the key and the children verified that 15 was on the display. I continued pressing the "=" key until the display showed 100. I then asked the class to count aloud by fives as I recorded the multiples on the board.

"So it's pretty easy to count by fives," I commented.

Brian agreed. "They go five, zero, five, zero, five, zero, so it's easy to remember," he said.

"What goes five, zero, five, zero?" I asked Brian, pushing him to be more precise in what he said.

"The numbers on the end of each one," he responded.

"Oh, you mean the digits in the ones place," I said, putting his thought into proper mathematical language. He nodded his agreement.

"Let's use the calculator to count by tens," I then said. I gave the calculator to Libby and directed her to enter "10," then press the "+" sign, and then the "=" sign.

"What number is on the display?" I asked.

"Ten," Libby reported. I recorded 10 next to the *10* on the board.

"Before you press the equals sign again and again, I'd like the rest of the class to predict what number will come up next. Then you'll press equals and check, and I'll write the number on the board." As the class chanted, I recorded the multiples of ten on the board.

I repeated the process for twenty, giving Sam the calculator this time. Then I continued with the numbers the children suggested. For fifty and one hundred, it wasn't necessary to use the calculator for verification. However, we used the calculator to check as children counted by twos and fifteens. For the number one, I again didn't use the calculator and, instead, showed the children a shortcut way to record all of the numbers from one to one hundred. Most of the students were surprised that fifteen didn't land on one hundred.

5	5, 10, 15, 20, 25, 30, 35, 40, 45, 50, 55, 60, 65, 70, 75, 80, 85, 90, 95, 100
10	10, 20, 30, 40, 50, 60, 70, 80, 90, 100
20	20, 40, 60, 80, 100
50	50, 100
100	100
2	2, 4, 6, 8, 10, 12, 14, 16, 18, 20, 22, 24, 26, 28, 30, 32, 34, 36, 38, 40, 42, 44, 46, 48, 50, 52, 54, 56, 58, 60, 62, 64, 66, 68, 70, 72, 74, 76, 78, 80, 82, 84, 86, 88, 90, 92, 94, 96, 98, 100
1	1, 2, 3, 4, 5, . . . , 100
15	15, 30, 45, 60, 75, 90, 105

After we had investigated all of these numbers, I said, "One hundred isn't a multiple of fifteen, but it is a multiple of the other numbers on the board. Five, ten, twenty, fifty, one hundred, two, and one are all factors of one hundred, but fifteen isn't." As much as possible, I try to help students connect the correct mathematical terminology to what they are doing.

I then introduced the activity they were to do in pairs. "Who remembers what I did when I started using the calculator to count by fives?" I asked. I called on Alex.

He said, "You pushed 'five' and then 'equals' lots of times."

"Let me clear the calculator and try Alex's idea," I said. I showed the children how to use the key to clear the display. Then I pressed "5" and the "=" sign. I showed the calculator to Alex, and he verified that the display read 5. I pressed the "=" key and again showed the calculator to Alex.

"Hey!" he said. "It's still five."

I pressed the "=" key several more times to convince Alex and the others that we would continue to get 5 on the display.

"What were we hoping for after the five?" I asked.

"Ten," the children answered.

"And how do we get from five to ten?" I asked.

"You just count up five more," Libby answered.

"You add five," Brian said.

"Five and five makes ten," Josh added.

I said. "If I want the calculator to count by fives, then I have to press the addition key before the equals key so the calculator will *add* five each time. Alex, you were right to start by pressing 'five.'" I cleared the calculator and pressed "5."

I continued to explain, "Then, to tell the calculator to count by fives, I have to tell it to add, so I press the 'plus' key before I press 'equals.' Then, if I press the 'equals' key over and over again, the calculator will keep adding the first number I entered, the five." I demonstrated again for the children.

I then said, "The numbers that come up are the multiples of five. I got five from pressing 'equals' once, then ten after pressing 'equals' two times, then fifteen after pressing 'equals' three times, and so on."

I showed the children the directions I had duplicated. "For this activity, you and your partner will investigate the multiples of other numbers and see what patterns you notice. I think it's easier to see patterns in the ones and tens places if you write the multiples in a list vertically." I rewrote the multiples of five in a list, listing only twelve of them, to land on sixty.

"It's enough to list twelve numbers, but you can write more if you'd like," I said. "Then you write about the patterns you see. First I'll write what Brian reported." I wrote on the board:

The digits in the ones place go 5, 0, 5, 0, 5, 0, and so on.

"What else can I write?" I asked. "Talk about this for a moment in your groups, and then I'll ask you to report." When students have a chance to talk among themselves, their conversations often spark one another's thinking. After a few moments, I called the class to attention and asked for volunteers. Several raised their hands and I chose Alex.

"The other numbers go one, one, two, two, three, three, four, four," he said.

"Can you be more specific about which numbers you're referring to?" I asked him.

Angie helped out. "They're in the tens place," she said.

I wrote on the board:

The digits in the tens place go 1, 1, 2, 2, 3, 3, 4, 4, and so on.

"Anything else?" I asked.

"Josh had a good one," Emily said.

Josh was known in the class as a number whiz. He explained what he had noticed. "I added sideways," he said, "and got a funny pattern: five, one, six, two, seven, three, eight, four, nine, five, ten, six." It took me a moment to realize that Josh was adding the digits in each number.

"Repeat those numbers and I'll write them down," I said. I wrote each next to the corresponding number down to 60 to show more clearly that they were the sums of the digits. However, some of the children still didn't understand what Josh had done. Others didn't see the pattern in the number sequence he had reported.

5	5
10	1
15	6
20	2
25	7
30	3
35	8
40	4
45	9
50	5
55	10
60	6

"Tell a little more about the pattern, Josh," I said.

"See, it goes back and forth," he said. "You have to go every other one to see it—see, five, six, seven, eight, and the others go one, two, three, four." He came to the board and showed what he meant. More of the students caught on, and there was a buzz in the room as some explained to others at their tables. I gave them a moment to talk among themselves and then called them back to attention.

"See if what I write explains Josh's pattern," I said. I blended my language with Josh's words and wrote:

If you add the digits of each multiple, you get a back-and-forth pattern of numbers. There's one pattern in between another pattern.

"Raise your hand if you know what comes next in Josh's pattern," I said to the class. I waited a moment. More than half the students raised their hands.

"Let's say it together quietly," I said. "What comes next?"

"Eleven," the children chorused. I wrote *11* under the 6 and we continued Josh's pattern a little further. There was more conversation as children talked about what we were doing. "I see now." "I still don't get it." "See, you add the six and five and you get eleven." "Oh yeah." "Then the next one would be seventy and that would be seven." "Yeah." "I get it now."

I then returned to explaining the directions. As a model, I left on the board the list of the multiples of five and the sentences I had recorded. After I explained what they were to do, I gave one last direction. "When you've finished investigating the multiples for one number, repeat the activity for another number."

The children began working on the activity. I interrupted them at the end of the period and collected their papers. "We'll continue working on these tomorrow," I told them.

DAY 2

The children returned to work the next day. As I circulated, I noticed that some of the students were coloring their calculator patterns on 0–99 charts. I hadn't suggested this, but plenty of blank charts were available. I also noticed that none of the children used Josh's suggestion in the patterns they reported. Most focused on the number patterns in the ones column, the tens column, or both.

Roberto and Sara, for example, wrote the following for the multiples of three: *The pattern in the 1 collum is odd, even, odd, even.* For the multiples of six, they wrote: *The pattern in the 1 collum is all evens.*

Edna and Jason explored the number ten. They wrote: *The ones colum is always zero.*

I interrupted the children and brought their attention to the vocabulary list I had started during the *Patterns in Multiples* activity. I showed the children the correct spelling of *column* and added it to list. The spelling improved on some of their papers. Angie and Jennifer, for example, wrote about the multiples of eight: *The pattern in the ones column is decreasing by two from 8 to zero. They are all even numbers.* Figure 11–1 shows Lisa and Kim's work on this problem.

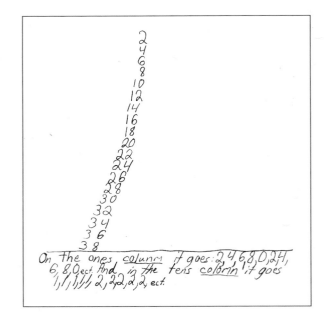

On the ones colunm it goes: 2,4,6,8,0,24, 6, 8,0 ect. And in the tens colorin it goes 1,1,1,1,1, 2,2,2,2,2, ect.

▲▲▲▲▲▲**Figure 11–1** *Lisa and Kim listed the multiples of 2 up to 38. This gave them enough information to identify the pattern in the tens column.*

When about half the period remained, and the children had investigated at least two numbers, I interrupted them for a class discussion. Several children reported about patterns they had noticed in the ones and tens columns in the multiples they had investigated. We talked about which multiples were easier to predict than others. I asked them to check to see if their lists contained only even, only odd, or both even and odd multiples. They were curious about why no lists had only odd numbers.

"No matter if the number is even or odd, two sets of that number will always be even," I said. "Whenever you combine two groups that are the same, you get an even amount, even if there is an odd number in each group."

I don't expect children necessarily to understand from this explanation why a number can't have all odd multiples, but it seems important to offer an explanation that some of them might find useful.

Josh had made a discovery. "I found out that the number four will get to one hundred," he said. Because I had told the children that it was sufficient to list only twelve multiples, others hadn't made this same discovery. But Josh had been curious and had continued the list.

"Did anyone find any other numbers that landed on one hundred?" I asked. No one had, but Elena had an idea.

"I think that eight will," she said.

"Why did you predict that multiples of eight will reach exactly one hundred?" I asked.

"Because it's double four," she answered.

"It won't work," Michael said. "It will go over." He had investigated eight, and ninety-six was on his list.

"Three won't work. It's one away," Jason said.

"What do you mean by 'one away'?" I asked.

"It will get to ninety-nine," he explained.

"So does nine," Kim added.

Josh's hand shot up. "I know another number that would get to one hundred," he said. The children and I looked at him with interest.

"Twenty-five," he said. "It's easy if you think of quarters." Money is a useful context for children to think about mathematical ideas. Some children agreed with Josh. A few reached for calculators to check his idea. Some weren't interested.

"Who investigated the number six?" I asked. Roberto and Sara raised their hands, and I asked them to come up with their paper.

"Who remembers if you investigated the patterns for six by using the *Things That Come in Sixes* chart when you did *Patterns in Multiples*?" Sam's hand went up. He remembered investigating the sides of a hexagon. He fished his work from his folder and came to the front of the room.

"Roberto, read the numbers in your list," I said.

Roberto read, "Six, twelve, eighteen, twenty-four," and so on up to seventy-two.

"They're the same as my numbers," Sam said.

"I knew they would be the same," I said. "How do you think I knew that?"

I asked the children to discuss this at their tables first and then asked for comments. It was obvious to some that both were lists of the multiples of six. Others were surprised and not quite sure why the numbers on the lists matched.

EXTENSIONS

Have children who are interested repeat *Calculator Patterns* for numbers they haven't yet investigated, especially larger numbers.

Questions and Discussion

▲▲

▲ *When I introduced the activity with multiples of five, the children didn't really need to use the calculator. Is it necessary for them to do so?*

The reason for choosing the number five when introducing the activity is that children are generally familiar with its multiples. Using the calculator verifies what they know. Also, it models for the class how to use the calculator to identify multiples with which they're not as familiar.

▲ *Because only a few children can see your calculator when you introduce the activity, wouldn't it be better if all of the students were following along with their own calculators?*

Either way would be fine. The goal is for children to understand how the constant addition feature on the calculator works and also to understand what they are to do in this activity. This can happen by them watching as you model or by them working along with you. You should do whichever you feel would work best in your class.

▲ *How can I help children who aren't as capable or confident as others in predicting multiples?*

Class discussions in which children explain how they arrive at the next multiple can help others think about possible strategies. Also, having children work in pairs gives them the support of a classmate when they're figuring. Finally, the focus on patterns is useful for helping students realize when a prediction doesn't make sense.

CHAPTER TWELVE
TOO MANY COOKS

Overview

The story *Too Many Cooks,* by Alicia Buckless, presents children with a rollicking, zany context for thinking about multiplication. The book is useful for reinforcing the concept that multiplication can be represented as repeated addition. Also, it's valuable for introducing multiplying by zero and helping children learn that when at least one of the factors in a multiplication problem is zero, the product is also zero.

Materials

▲ *Too Many Cooks,* by Alicia Buckless (Hello Math Reader series, New York: Scholastic, 2000)

Time

▲ one class period

Teaching Directions

1. Read aloud the Hello Math Reader title *Too Many Cooks* and give children the chance to express their opinions about the story.

2. Revisit the story, focusing on the ingredients used in the soup. For each ingredient, record on the board the related multiplication equation and how you might compute the answer. For example, the charaters put in two tomatoes for each of the six people. As children report the equation and how they figured, record on the board:

$6 \times 2 = 12$

2, 4, 6, 8, 10, 12

$2 + 2 + 2 + 2 + 2 + 2 = 12$

$6 + 6 = 12$

Continue in this way for the onions, the carrots, the beets, the beans, and the noodles.

3. Use the example of the beets to initiate a discussion about multiplying by zero. Ask: "Who can explain again why six times zero is zero?" Discuss for other numbers and then ask children to explain why multiplying any number times zero results in zero. Ask children to use the words *factor* and *product* in their explanations, introducing these words if you haven't yet done so.

4. To check on the children's understanding, reverse the order of factors and ask children to solve 0×6. As another check, ask the children to write about multiplying by zero and to include all the ideas they have.

Teaching Notes

Too Many Cooks takes place in the kitchen and tells how Cara and her two brothers, Marcos and Jay, try to make a pot of soup for their mother and grandparents. The cookbook gets soaked by a spilled glass of milk and the children have to work hard to make out the ingredients on the soggy page. Multiplication comes into the story as the children in the story figure out the quantities of ingredients needed to make soup for six people. Their effort is sincere and their mathematical reasoning for adjusting the recipe to feed all six of them is sound, but their cooking skills are humorously lacking. The story delights children as Jay, the youngest, "helps" by slipping into the pot some ingredients that aren't in the recipe—a red rubber ball along with the tomatoes, two orange cars along with the carrots, some yellow string along with the noodles, and more. The story relates multiplication to repeated addition and skip-counting and also reinforces correct mathematical representations

Discussing the story with the children, as suggested for the first part of the lesson, replicates their experience with *Amanda Bean's Amazing Dream*. This repetition is useful, I think, and it really doesn't matter in which order you use the books.

I've often been surprised to find that children haven't grasped a concept I had assumed they understood. This occurred during the class discussion about the story. One of the ingredients called for in the recipe is beets, but Cara, Marcos, and Jay take a strong "no beets" stand. This brought up the idea of multiplying by zero, and it's clear to the cooks that with zero beets for each person, six times zero is zero. The children in the class understood this idea in the context of the story, but when we talked about what happens in general when you multiply by zero, I learned that some of the students' understanding was fragile. This part of the lesson focuses on the idea of multiplication by zero and aims at helping children examine, verify, and justify their understanding.

The Lesson

▲▲

Before reading aloud *Too Many Cooks,* I showed the cover of the book to the children and asked them to predict what the story was about. After hearing their ideas, I read the story aloud. When I was done, most of the students raised their hands to offer an opinion.

"I liked how Jay was putting stuff in the soup," Jessica said.

"I liked how the grandfather looked into his soup and the green dinosaur looked back at him," Tomas said.

"I think it's a ten," Evan said, rating the story. "It was funny when the grandma put her spoon into her bowl and got a marble."

"I'd give it an eight," Kelly said. "I liked that they got pizza at the end."

"I think that I'd change the title of the book to *The Wrong Recipe,*" Ruthie said.

"It was really funny how Jay put in an orange car for carrots," Amelia said.

I then turned the conversation to the mathematics in the story. "Who remembers what Cara, Marcos, and Jay put into the pot first?" I asked.

"The tomatoes," Bo answered. "They put in two for each person."

"They put in twelve tomatoes," Aaron added.

"How many people were going to eat the soup?" I asked.

"Six," Lydia said, "the three children, their mother, and their grandma and grandpa."

"How did they figure out that they needed twelve tomatoes?" I asked. Even though this was not a difficult problem for most of the children, I decided to use their interest in the story to reinforce using multiplication to represent a real-world situation.

"It's six times two," Jay said.

"You can count by twos—two, four, six, eight, ten, twelve," Amelia said. I wrote on the board:

$6 \times 2 = 12$

$2, 4, 6, 8, 10, 12$

$2 + 2 + 2 + 2 + 2 + 2 = 12$

"You could add two sixes," Alicia said. I wrote on the board:

$6 + 6 = 12$

I said, "Yes, even though the problem is about six twos, you can do the figuring by switching the factors and adding two sixes. That's because multiplication is commutative, so the product stays the same." Whenever possible, I use correct vocabulary, such as *factor, product,* and *commutative.* I find that if I do so, the words work their way into becoming part of children's mathematical vocabulary.

"What went into the soup next?" I asked.

"Carrots, I think," Jessica said.

"It was onions," Kelly corrected.

We checked in the book and found out that onions came next, one per person. I read from the story, "'Okay,' said Cara. 'Three times one onions for us.'"

"But she forgot the others," Jay said, "it was really six times one."

"That's easy," Sally said, "it's six." I wrote on the board:

$6 \times 1 = 6$

$1 + 1 + 1 + 1 + 1 + 1 = 6$

"The carrots came next," I said. Hands shot up and I called on Peter.

"They put ten carrots in for each of them," he said.

"That's when Jay threw in the cars," Sergio said. The children giggled.

"How many carrots did they put in the pot and what multiplication sentence can I write?" I asked.

"It's ten times six equals sixty," Lydia said.

Hands shot up. "No, it's the other way around," Aaron said. "It's six tens, so that's six times ten."

"Oh yeah," Lydia said, "that's what I meant because I went ten, twenty, thirty, forty, fifty, sixty." I wrote on the board:

$6 \times 10 = 60$

10, 20, 30, 40, 50, 60

$10 + 10 + 10 + 10 + 10 + 10 = 60$

The beets were added next. "Six times zero is zero," Amelia said. I wrote on the board:

$6 \times 0 = 0$

$0 + 0 + 0 + 0 + 0 + 0 = 0$

"That's a really easy one," Aaron said, rolling his eyes.

"You can't count by zeros," Jessica said.

"Yes, you can," Jay said. "You just go zero, zero, zero, zero, zero, zero. It's *really* easy." A few children laughed.

I moved on to the next ingredient— beans. "Who remembers how they measured the beans?" I asked.

"They did two cups for each of them," Greta said. "It's six times two equals twelve."

I showed the class the page in the book where the cups of beans are pictured as six rows with two cups in each row. "Look at

Jay putting in the dinosaur," Sergio noticed on the spread.

"And the yellow bulldozer," Chuck added.

I then told the class, "I don't have to record the math for the cups of beans." I pointed to what I had recorded for the tomatoes. "The mathematics is the same for the beans and the tomatoes. Even though the ingredients in the soup aren't the same, the math we use to describe the problems and figure the answers is the same." I turned the page in the book. "The noodles come next," Amelia said. "They each got five." I showed the children the recording in the story and then copied it onto the board:

5, 10, 15, 20, 25, 30

$5 + 5 + 5 + 5 + 5 + 5 = 30$

$6 \times 5 = 30$

"That's when Jay put in the gummy worms," Kelly said.

"He thought they looked like noodles," Peter said.

MULTIPLYING BY ZERO

"Who can explain again why six times zero is zero?" I said.

Lydia explained, "It's six zeros, and if you add zero plus zero plus zero, like that, you'll still get zero." I wrote on the board:

$6 \times 0 = 0$

As I was writing on the board, Alicia said, "No matter how many zeros you add, you never get more than zero."

"So how much is eight times zero?" I asked her.

"Zero," she said without hesitation.

"And eleven times zero?" I asked. Hands shot up.

"Zero," Aaron said.

"And twenty-three times zero?" I continued.

"Zero," several children answered. I listed these problems on the board and added one more to the list:

$8 \times 0 = 0$

$11 \times 0 = 0$

$23 \times 0 = 0$

$436 \times 0 = ?$

Everyone had a hand raised. "Let's say the answer together," I said. As they chorused, "Zero," I recorded a zero for the question mark.

"What's so special about zero?" I said.

"If something is timesed by zero, it's nothing," Alicia said.

I nodded and said, "Who has another way to explain?"

"Whatever you do times zero, you get zero," Jay said.

"Zero times anything is zero," Aaron said.

"If you multiply by zero, the answer has to be zero," Kelly said.

I continued, giving each child who wanted to explain the chance to do so. "There are many different ways to express this mathematical idea," I said, "and all of yours are fine. Who would like to try to explain the idea using the words *factor* and *product*?" I wrote on the board:

factor

product

I waited until about six hands were raised. To try to engage more children in thinking about my questions, I asked them to talk with their neighbors about how to use the words *factor* and *product* to explain what happens when you multiply by zero. After a few moments of conversation, I brought the class back to attention and again asked the question. I called on Alicia.

"If the factors are zero, the products are zero," she said. I recorded her sentence on the board.

"I don't think that's exactly right," Peter said. "They both don't have to be zero, only one of them."

"That's what I meant," Alicia said.

I said, "What your sentence says is that zero times zero is zero." I wrote on the board:

$0 \times 0 = 0$

"This is true." I said, "But how could you change your sentence to mean that anything times zero is zero?" I asked her.

Alicia thought for a second and then said, "If one factor is zero, the product is zero." I corrected her first sentence on the board.

Next to one of the examples I had written on the board, I reversed the factors of the equation and wrote:

$0 \times 6 = ?$

"What's the answer to this problem?" I asked.

"It's six, I think," Tomas said. His answer surprised me, but I recorded it on the board:

$0 \times 6 = 6$

For a moment, the class was silent. Then hands went up.

"It has to be zero," Kelly said, "because multiplication is commutative." Kelly often answers a question by generalizing, which is not typical for most third graders, I've found. I recorded so the following was now on the board:

$0 \times 6 = 6$

$0 \times 6 = 0$

"So which is right?" I asked the class.

Evan said, "I think that it is zero because one times six is six and two times six is twelve, so it can't be six because one times six is six." I recorded:

$0 \times 6 = 0$

$1 \times 6 = 6$

$2 \times 6 = 12$

Jay added, "See, there's a pattern. You could add three times six equals eighteen and see how the answers go down. Or up. It's like *Patterns in Multiples*." I added Jay's idea:

$0 \times 6 = 0$

$1 \times 6 = 6$

$2 \times 6 = 12$

$3 \times 6 = 18$

"Zero groups of six has to be zero," Ruthie said.

Alicia said, "If you have zero groups of people, no matter how many in a group, it means you have zero people."

Tomas then raised a hand. "I think my answer can't be right," he said. "If one times six is six, then zero times six can't be six. You should cross out my idea."

"Are you sure?" I asked.

"Pretty sure," Tomas said.

"Can someone give Tomas another reason to help him be absolutely sure?" I asked.

Lydia said, "I go with Kelly's idea because it's commutative. Six times zero and zero times six have to be the same."

"Zero groups of anything is zero," Peter said.

I then gave the children a writing assignment. "I'm interested in how you think about multiplying by zero. Reading your papers will help me think about what other ideas I could ask you to think about. Write down all of the ideas you have. To help you, I'll list some words on the board that might be helpful." I listed on the board:

commutative

factor

product

groups

"Are there any other words that you might use that I should write on the board to help you?" I added their suggestions—*digit, multiply, equation, addition,* and *subtraction*.

Multiplying by Zero

If you use zero in a multiplication problem you always get zero because if you have 0 × a number it would be just like 0 groups of something and that 0 groups of something has to equal zero because if you have 0 groups you can't have anything in the groups because there are no groups. 0 × a number can't be the number because 1 × that number equals that number because it is that number one time which equals that number.

▲▲▲▲▲▲**Figure 12–1** *Kelly understood what happens when zero is a factor in a multiplication problem.*

Children expressed their ideas in different ways. Kelly, for example, wrote: *If you use zero in a multiplication problem you always get zero because if you have 0 × a number it would be just like 0 groups of something and 0 groups of something has to equal zero because if you have 0 groups you can't have anything in the groups because there are no groups.* (See Figure 12–1.)

Tomas wrote: *At frist I thaut that 0 × 6 = 6 but Evens idea was 0 × 6 = 0 because 1 × 6 = 6 and wen I thaut abaut Evens idea I thaut that one is more then zero witch proved Even was rite because one is more then zero so it coldint have the same anser as a number that is grater then it.* (See Figure 12–3.)

Jay wrote: *If one factor is zero then the product must be zero because 0 × 6 = 0 zero rows of six. There are no rows of six.*

Ruthie included in her paper: *Think of adding. 6 × 0 is the same as 0 + 0 + 0 + 0 + 0 + 0. It all equals zero.*

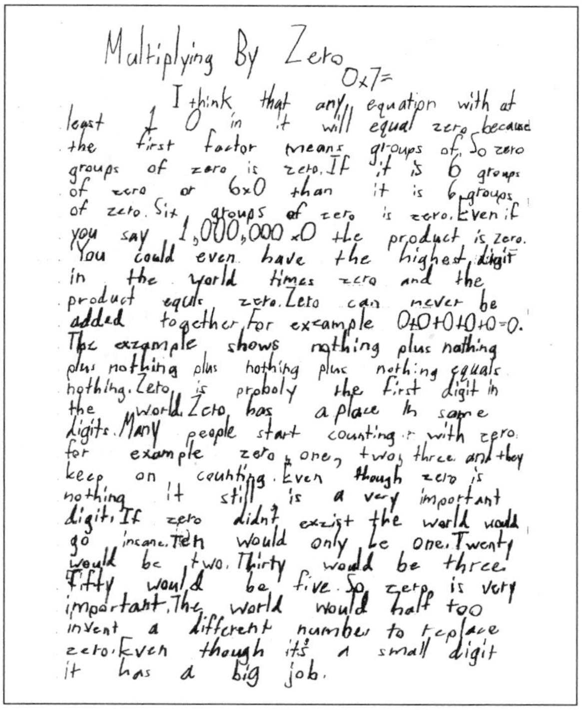

Multiplying By Zero 0×7=

I think that any equation with at least 1 0 in it will equal zero because the first factor means groups of. So zero groups of zero is zero. If it is 6 groups of zero or 6×0 than it is 6 groups of zero. Six groups of zero is zero. Even if you say 1,000,000 ×0 the product is zero. You could even have the highest digit in the world times zero and the product equals zero. Zero can never be added together for example 0+0+0+0=0. The example shows nothing plus nothing plus nothing plus nothing equals nothing. Zero is probaly the first digit in the world. Zero has a place in same digits. Many people start counting with zero. for example zero, one, two, three and they keep on counting. Even though zero is nothing it still is a very important digit. If zero didnt exist the world would go insane. Ten would only be one. Twenty would be two. Thirty would be three. Fifty would be five. So zero is very important. The world would half too invent a different number to replace zero. Even though its a small digit it has a big job.

▲▲▲▲▲▲Figure 12–2 **Figure 12–2** *Peter had quite a lot to say about zero, its place in multiplication, and its general importance.*

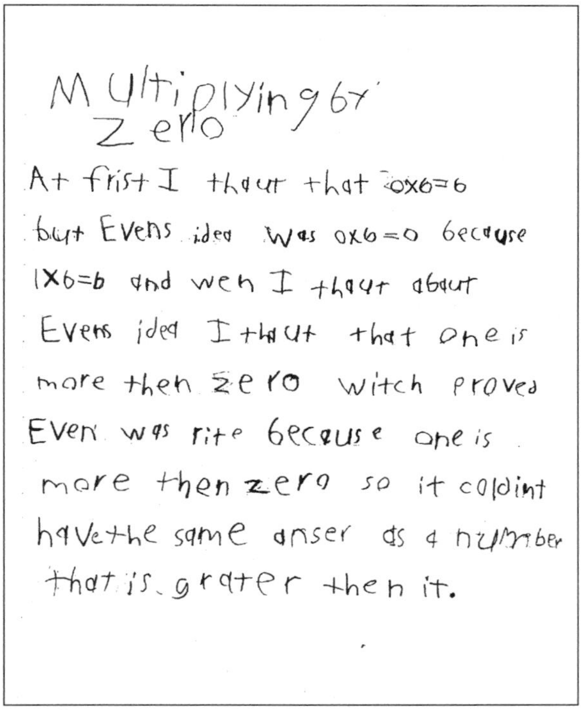

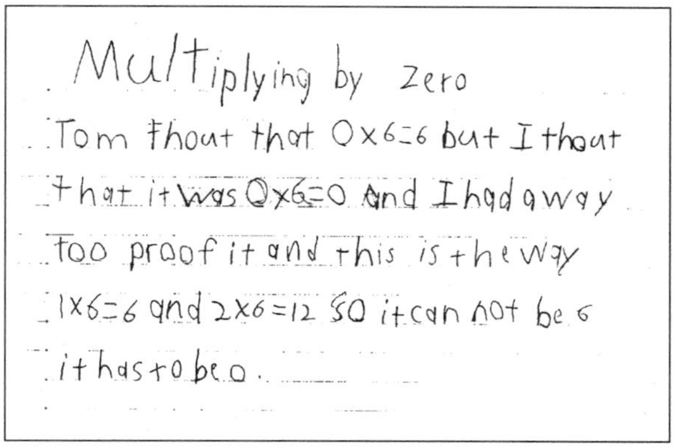

Multiplying by Zero

Tom thout that 0×6=6 but I thout that it was 0×6=0 and I had a way too proof it and this is the way 1×6=6 and 2×6=12 so it can not be 6 it has to be 0.

▲▲▲▲▲▲**Figure 12–4** *Evan wrote about why Tomas's thought couldn't be correct.*

Some children's papers showed that their understanding was still fragile. Marea, for example, included in her paper: *I didn't know that zeros can be so cunffuseing. 0 × 6 is really cunffuseing because the answer could be 0 or 6.* (See Figure 12–5.)

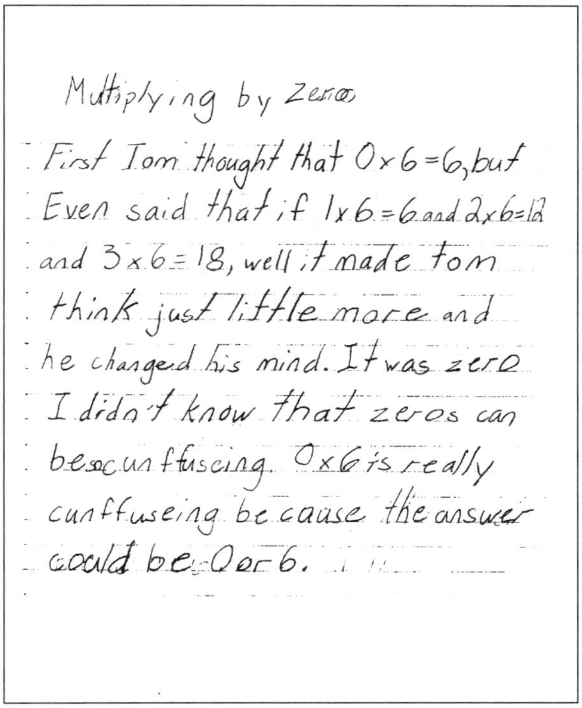

Multiplying by Zero

At frist I thout that 0×6=6 buyt Evens idea was 0×6=0 becayse 1×6=6 and weh I thout about Evens idea I thout that one is more then zero witch proved Even was rite because one is more then zero so it coldint have the same anser as a number that is grater then it.

▲▲▲▲▲▲**Figure 12–3** *Tomas wrote about how Evan's argument convinced him that 0 × 6 = 0.*

Multiplying by Zero

First Tom thought that 0×6=6, but Evan said that if 1×6=6 and 2×6=12 and 3×6=18, well it made tom think just little more and he changed his mind. It was zero. I didn't know that zeros can be so cunffuseing. 0×6 is really cunffuseing because the answer could be 0 or 6.

▲▲▲▲▲▲**Figure 12–5** *In her paper, Marea expressed her confusion about multiplying by zero.*

Questions and Discussion

▲▲▲

▲ *Is it important for third graders to learn vocabulary such as* **factor, product,** *and* **commutative?**

I think that it's valuable for third graders to learn the correct terminology for mathematical ideas. Whenever possible, I take the opportunity to connect correct terminology to the students' experiences. In this way, I introduce mathematics vocabulary in the context of their learning experiences, not as isolated lessons. I find that the more I use the correct vocabulary, the more easily children become familiar with new words and comfortable using them.

▲ *Why did you have all of the children explain why zero times a number is zero?*

I've come to realize that one child's explanation may not be the same way others are thinking. Also, not everyone may understand one child's explanation, even if the idea is correct. Giving children the chance to explain their thinking with their own words helps each of them cement his or her understanding. It's supportive of children's learning to give as many of them as possible the chance to voice their ideas, and it's certainly worth the time.

▲ *Why did you ask the children to write about multiplying by zero?*

I think that writing helps children revisit their thinking, extend their ideas, and cement their understanding. Also, because I had been surprised by Tomas's notion, I wondered how else I might be surprised by children's thinking. The children know that the purpose of their writing is to help me understand how each of them is thinking and, therefore, be more helpful to them. It was in that spirit that I asked the children to write at that time.

ADDITIONAL ACTIVITIES

The seven activities described in this section extend the lessons from the previous chapters and offer additional ideas for classroom instruction. Each activity presents an overview, the materials and time required, teaching directions, and samples of student work. Three of the activities—*How Many Were Eaten?*, *The Biggest Garden*, and *Tiles on the Countertop*—provide students experience with interpreting multiplication geometrically. *How Many Cubes?* uses a statistical investigation to present a multiplication problem. *Evens and Odds* and *Why Is It True?* engage students in making and investigating numerical conjectures. *Multiplication Bingo* gives children experience with probability as they practice basic facts.

How Many Were Eaten?

OVERVIEW

This activity is an appropriate follow-up to the children's candy box investigations (see Chapter 7) and provides children another experience interpreting multiplication geometrically. Preparing for this activity calls for collecting an assortment of boxes about the size of shoeboxes and putting seven 1-inch or 2-centimeter cubes in each. Working in pairs and using just the seven cubes in the box to represent candies, children figure out how many candies were eaten. This activity gives students an experience with measuring volume.

MATERIALS

▲ empty boxes (provided by you or the students), at least 1 per pair of students
▲ 1-inch or 2-centimeter cubes, seven for each box

TIME

▲ one class period

TEACHING DIRECTIONS

1. Show the children one of the boxes with seven cubes in it. Choose a box that would take more than one layer of cubes to fill. Explain: "This box was once full of these candies."

2. Present the problem to the children: *Figure out how many candies were eaten. Explain how you figured out the answer.*

3. After children have solved the problem, lead a class discussion for them to share their strategies.

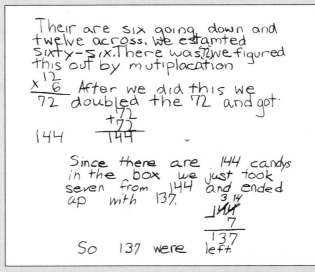

▲▲▲▲▲▲**Figure 1** *Angie and Jennifer solved the problem for a two-layer box. They recorded the estimate they made before they did the calculation.*

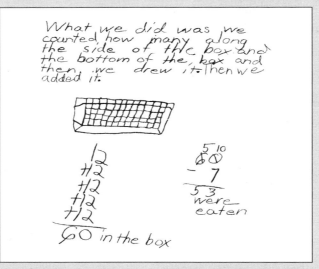

▲▲▲▲▲▲**Figure 2** *Sam and Koji drew a diagram, used addition to figure out the number of candies the box held, and then subtracted to find out how many were eaten.*

How Many Cubes?

OVERVIEW

For *How Many Cubes?*, each child takes a handful of cubes, reports for a class graph the number of cubes in his or her handful, and then puts the cubes in a large container. Students discuss the graph and then use the information to figure out the total number of cubes in the container. This activity provides children experience using multiplication to interpret statistical data. After students have solved the problem, they verify the solution by actually counting the cubes in the container.

MATERIALS

▲ interlocking cubes, enough for a handful per student
▲ container large enough to hold the cubes
▲ chart paper

TIME

▲ one to two class periods

TEACHING DIRECTIONS

1. Post the chart paper and title it *How Many Cubes?*

2. Tell the children that they're each going to take a handful of cubes, count how many they have, and report the information. Demonstrate the way to take a handful by picking up cubes in one hand and giving a shake or two to allow any loose cubes to drop.

3. Quickly go around the room and have each child take a handful. Then ask students to report the number of cubes they have one by one. When the first child reports, record by numbering from 1 to the number reported and mark the handful with a tally mark. Ask the child to put the cubes in the container.

> 1
> 2
> 3
> 4
> 5
> 6 /

4. Ask the next child to report. Record the number reported with a tally mark and ask the child to put the handful of cubes in the container. Continue until you've collected the information from all of the students, adding to the list of numbers as needed to accommodate larger handfuls.

5. Talk with the class about the information on the graph. Although third graders do not formally learn about averages or study mean, median, and mode, they can be introduced to these ideas informally. The following are suggestions for a class discussion:

What can you say about the information on the graph?

What does this tally mark represent? (Point to a tally mark. Repeat for several more.)

Which size handful was grabbed more often than any other? (Point out that mathematicians call this the mode.)

Looking at this information, what would you say is the typical handful in our class? Why do you think that?

6. Give the assignment. "Use the information on the class graph to figure out the total number of cubes in the container. Work with a partner and explain your reasoning in writing."

7. After children have solved the problem, lead a class discussion for them to share their strategies. Finally, count the cubes as a check on the solution, organizing the cubes into tens and, thus, reinforcing place value.

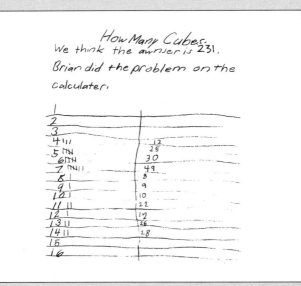

▲▲▲▲▲▲Figure 3 *Michael and Brian carefully copied the information from the graph and figured out the total number of cubes for each size handful.*

▲▲▲▲▲▲**Figure 4** *Roberto and Sara used multi-plication to represent the information about the total for each size handful.*

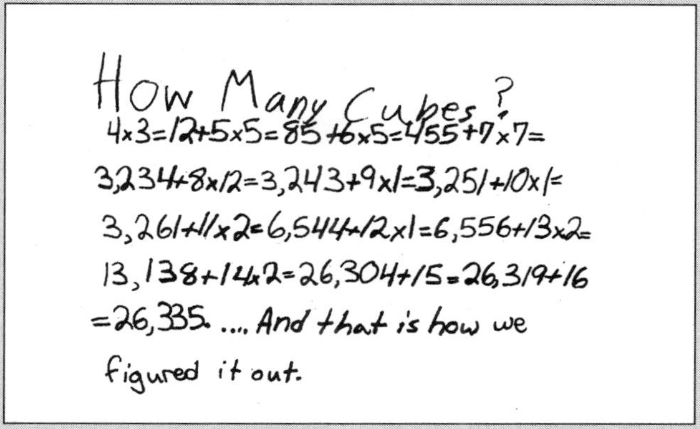

▲▲▲▲▲▲**Figure 5** *Although Kristina and Libby used the idea of multiplication correctly, their writing showed that they used the calculator incorrectly.*

Evens and Odds

OVERVIEW

Children in third grade typically know about even and odd numbers. This activity builds on the students' knowledge and asks them to think about whether the products will be even or odd when two factors are both even, both odd, or one of each. The children explore different examples to make conjectures and then look for ways to justify their conjectures. Along with providing multiplication practice, this activity provides students the challenge of creating convincing arguments for why a conjecture is or isn't true, giving them experience with creating mathematical proofs.

MATERIALS

▲ color tiles, at least 10 per student

TIME

▲ one class period

TEACHING DIRECTIONS

1. Discuss with the children how to tell whether numbers are even or odd. Typically children know about looking at the digit in the ones place. If no one offers another way, suggest some. Even numbers can be divided in half without a remainder. Even numbers can be represented as two times a number. You might model with tiles how an even number of tiles can be split into two equal groups, but with an odd number of tiles, you'll always have one extra. Or show how you can arrange any even number of tiles into rectangles that are 2 by something, but odd numbers of tiles will always have one left over.

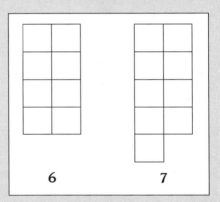

2. Ask: "What happens when we multiply two even numbers? Is the answer even or odd? Why is this so?" Typically, children will try some examples and conclude that the product will always be even. Discuss how they might be sure for all possible situations; for example, 24 × 32 and other problems with numbers too large for mental computation.

3. Ask: "What happens when we multiply two odd numbers? Is the answer even or odd? What about multiplying an even times an odd number?" Discuss.

4. Ask children to record their ideas in writing. Write the following on the board to represent the conjectures:

Even × Even = Even

Odd × Odd = Odd

Even × Odd = Even

Explain why these are true.

Even And Odd

① ExE=E ExE=E because 2x2=4,
② OxO=O 6×6=36, 4×4=16, 8×8=
③ ExO=? 64, 10×10=100 and 8×10=
④ OxE=? 80 so I think you know
what I meen. From all the
equagins I have done with ExE=
E, I found out that no matter
what, it equals even.

② OxO=O because all the
equagins on the board and
the equagins that I know
that are OxO=O and OxO
will always have a O for
a answer.

③ ExO=E because I have
tried all the equagins
with ExO and all of them
eqqaled E. So no matter
what, it equals even.

④ OxE=E because I looked
on the board and I looked
at the OxEs and all of
them equaled E and I tried
some others and they all
equaled E.

Even and Odd

② 1×1=1   all of these equal
3×3=9   odd numbers
5×5=25
7×7=49
9×9=81
1×3=3
3×5=15
5×7=35
7×9=63
9×11=99

③ 4×3=12   all of these equal
5×4=20   even number
6×5=30
7×6=42
8×7=56
9×8=72
10×9=90
12×11=132

④ 3×4=12   all of these equal
4×5=20   even numbers
5×8=30
6×7=60
7×8=56
8×9=72
9×10=90

▲▲▲▲▲▲**Figure 6** *Marea relied on trying examples. This method doesn't offer a convincing proof, but it is a typical approach for young children.*

Even x Even=Even Odd x Odd=Odd Even x Odd=?
Odd x Even=?

I think that Odd times Even and
Even times odd can equal on odd number
or an even number because: 7×4=28 equals on
even number and 10×9=90 and that is an odd
number

7 × 4 = 2   10 × 9 = 90

E

I think that EvenxEven
= Even because if
you use tiles or sheets
of centimeter squares there is an equal amount of
squares in the area and on the sides.
I think that OddxOdd=Odd
for the same reason why
EvenxEven=Even except that
it is odd.

8 × 6 = 48

▲▲▲▲▲▲**Figure 7** *Bo showed his partial understanding and confusion by stating that even × odd can be odd or even. He mistakenly identified 90 as an odd number.*

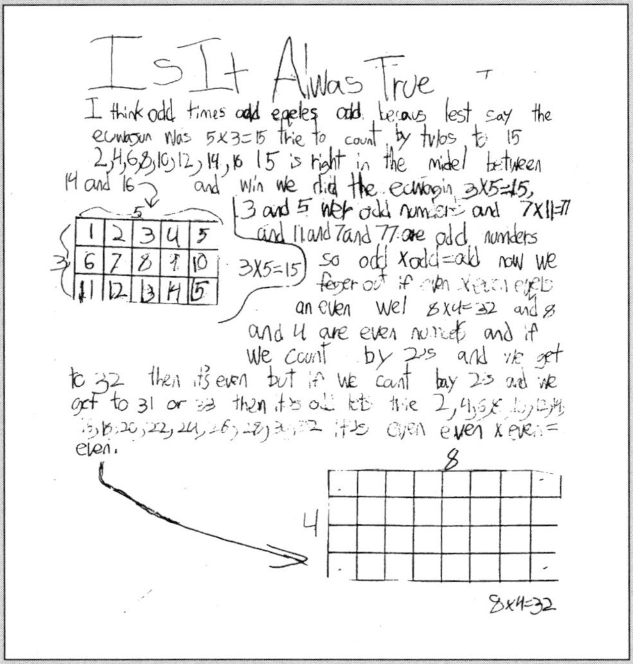

Is It Alwas True
I think odd times odd eqeles odd becaus lest say the ecwasun was 5x3=15 trie to count by twos to 15
2,4,6,8,10,12,14,16 15 is right in the midel between 14 and 16 and win we did the ecwasin 3x5=15,
3 and 5 wer odd numbers and 7x11=77 and 11 and 7 and 77 are odd numbers so odd xodd=odd now we fegor out if even x even egels an even wel 8x4=32 and 8 and 4 are even numbers and if we count by 2's and we get to 32 then it's even but if we count bay 2's and we get to 31 or 33 then it's odd lets trie 2,4,6,8,10,12,14, 16,18,20,22,24,26,28,30,32 it's even even x even = even.
5
1 2 3 4 5
6 7 8 9 10
11 12 13 14 15
3
3X5=15
8
4
8x4=32

Figure 8 *Sergio relied on examples and also incorporated the idea of counting by twos.*

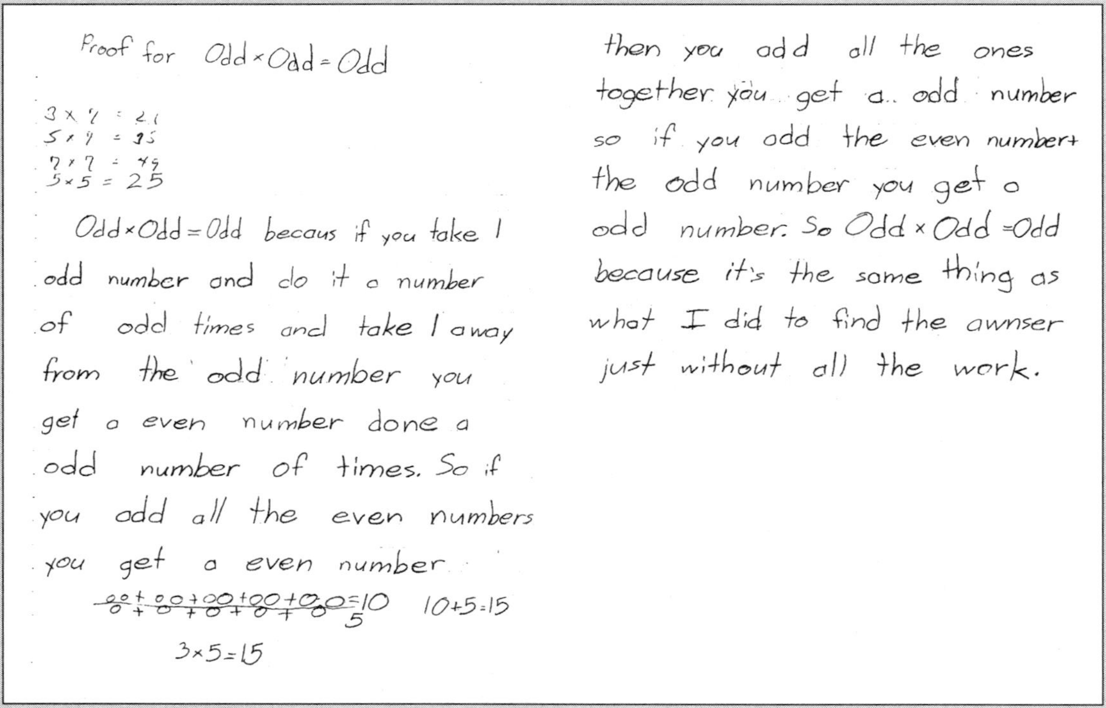

Proof for Odd × Odd = Odd
3 × 7 = 21
5 × 7 = 35
7 × 7 = 49
5 × 5 = 25
Odd × Odd = Odd becaus if you take 1 odd number and do it a number of odd times and take 1 away from the odd number you get a even number done a odd number of times. So if you add all the even numbers you get a even number
00+00+00+00+00=10 10+5=15
0+0+0+0+0=5
3×5=15
then you add all the ones together you get a odd number so if you add the even number+ the odd number you get a odd number. So Odd × Odd = Odd because it's the same thing as what I did to find the awnser just without all the work.

Figure 9 *For a third grader, Kelly wrote a remarkable proof about why odd × odd = odd.*

The Biggest Garden

OVERVIEW

This activity provides children experience interpreting multiplication geometrically in a context that is similar to the candy box investigations (see Chapter 7). For *The Biggest Garden,* students compare the sizes of rectangular gardens, all of which require 24 feet of fencing. The activity provides experience with the ideas of area and perimeter. Children (and adults) often incorrectly think that shapes that have longer perimeters must have more area, and this activity gives another perspective on that idea.

MATERIALS

▲ one-half-inch squares, at least 1 sheet per student (see Blackline Masters)

TIME

▲ one class period

TEACHING DIRECTIONS

1. Tell the children that you are planting a rectangular garden and have 24 feet of fence. Draw a square on the board and label each side: 6'. (This is a good opportunity to introduce the symbol for feet.) Ask the children to verify that you'd need 24 feet of fence to enclose a garden this size.

2. Then draw a rectangle with one side half as long as the side of the square and the other side one and a half times as long; label the sides 3' and 9'. Ask the children to verify that you'd need 24 feet of fence to enclose this garden, too.

3. Then sketch three other rectangles that are 2' by 10', 4' by 8', and 5' by 7'. Label them and verify that 24 feet of fencing is needed to enclose each.

4. Present the problem: *Which of these gardens has the most area? Predict first and then figure it out.* Give children grid paper for drawing the rectangles.

5. After children have solved the problem, lead a class discussion for them to share their strategies.

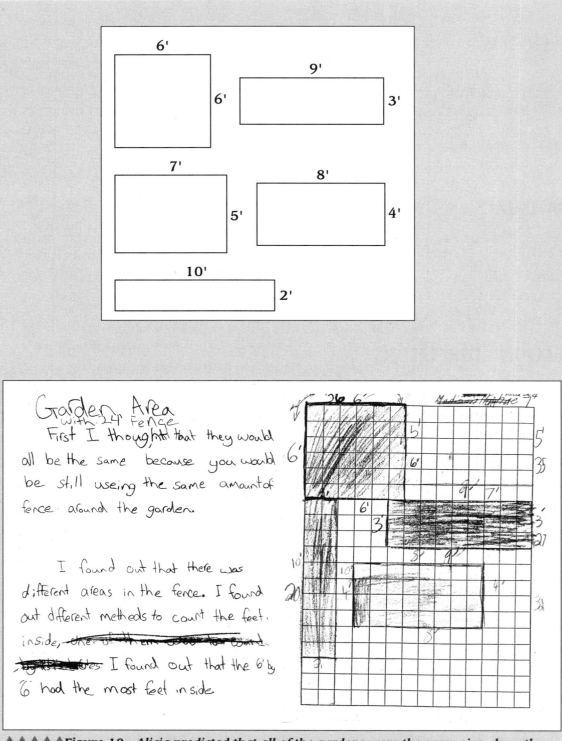

▲▲▲▲▲▲**Figure 10** *Alicia predicted that all of the gardens were the same size, drew the gardens on squared paper, and then wrote about what she found out.*

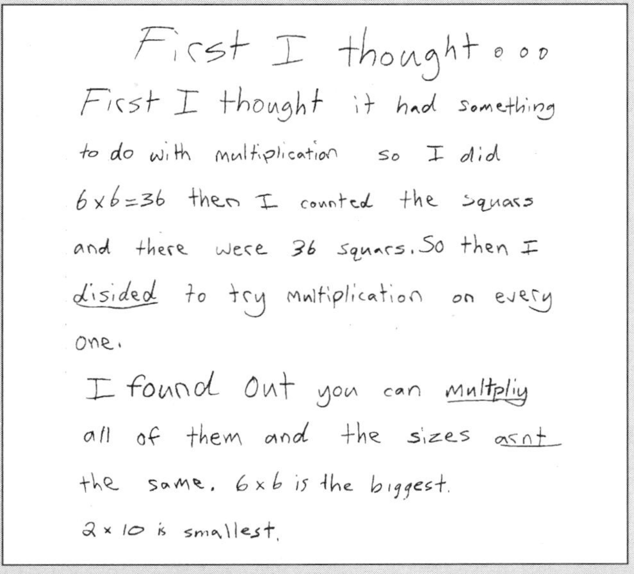

First I thought... o o o

First I thought it had something
to do with multiplication so I did
6x6=36 then I counted the squars
and there were 36 squars. So then I
disided to try multiplication on every
one.

I found out you can multpliy
all of them and the sizes asnt
the same. 6x6 is the biggest.
2x10 is smallest.

▲▲▲▲▲▲**Figure 11**   *Greta explained that she used
multiplication to solve the problem.*

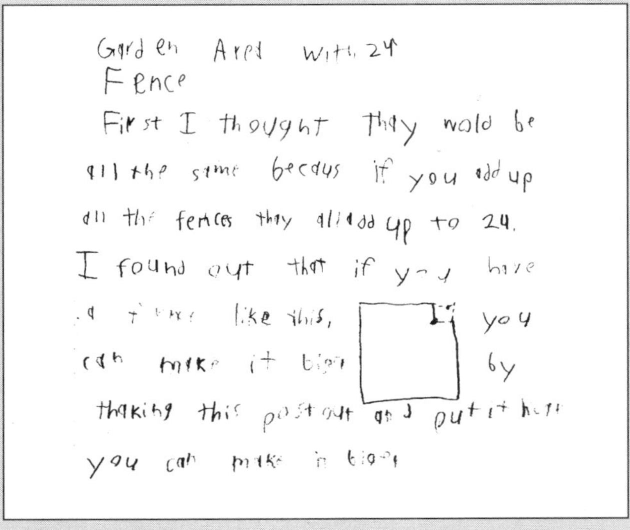

Garden Area with 24
Fence

First I thought thay wold be
all the same becaus if you add up
all the fences thay all add up to 24.
I found out that if you have
a fence like this, 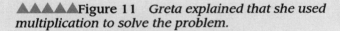 if you
can make it bigr   by
thaking this post out and put it her
you can make it bigr

▲▲▲▲▲▲**Figure 12**   *Tomas made a discovery that
convinced him that you could use the same length
fence and increase the area in a garden.*

Tiles on the Countertop

OVERVIEW

This activity provides children additional experience connecting multiplication and a rectangular array, in this case a square array. Children figure out the number of tiles there are on a 12-by-12 countertop. Showing the children how to divide the countertop into smaller sections and combine the number of tiles in them demonstrates how to use the distributive property.

MATERIALS

▲ optional: *Amanda Bean's Amazing Dream*, by Cindy Neushwander (New York: Scholastic, 1998)
▲ optional: centimeter squares, 1 sheet per student

TIME

▲ one class period

TEACHING DIRECTIONS

1. Show the class the illustration from *Amanda Bean's Amazing Dream* that shows the 12-by-12 kitchen countertop. Sketch the countertop on the board. (If you choose not to use the book, just sketch a 12-by-12 countertop for the class.)

2. Ask the class: "How can we figure out how many tiles are on the countertop?" The difficulty of this question will depend on the students' prior experiences. Record their suggestions and verify in several ways that the answer is 144. You may wish to show the class how to facilitate counting the squares by dividing the countertop into smaller sections and adding the number of squares in each to find the total, a visual way to demonstrate how to use the distributive property. The following is one example.

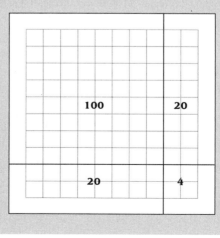

3. When I taught this lesson, the children had counted to find out that there were twelve tiles across and twelve tiles down, then multiplied to get 144. Present the idea that Jay suggested: "Jay thought that you couldn't find the number of tiles from multiplying twelve times twelve because then you counted a corner tile twice." Ask your students what they think about Jay's idea. I've typically found that some children agree and some don't.

4. After the students have discussed this, ask them to think about Jay's idea with a smaller problem. Sketch a 2-by-3 rectangle on the board. The children can verify easily that there are six tiles, and they also typically know that 2 × 3 or 3 × 2 equals 6. This may help resolve Jay's error for some, but others may still be confused.

5. Give children a writing assignment: *Some children think you can't multiply 12 × 12 to figure out the number of tiles in a 12-by-12 countertop because that means you counted the corner tile twice. What do you think? Explain your reasoning.* Putting their thoughts in writing is a way for children to clarify their thinking, extend it, or raise questions.

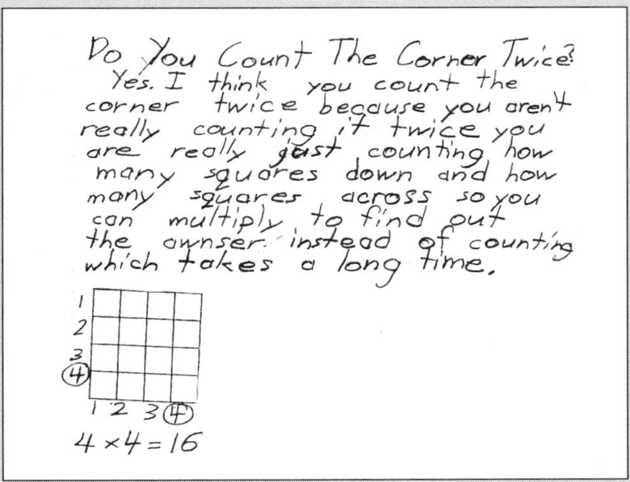

▲▲▲▲▲▲**Figure 13** *Kelly was clear that you were counting squares to figure the dimensions so you would know what to multiply.*

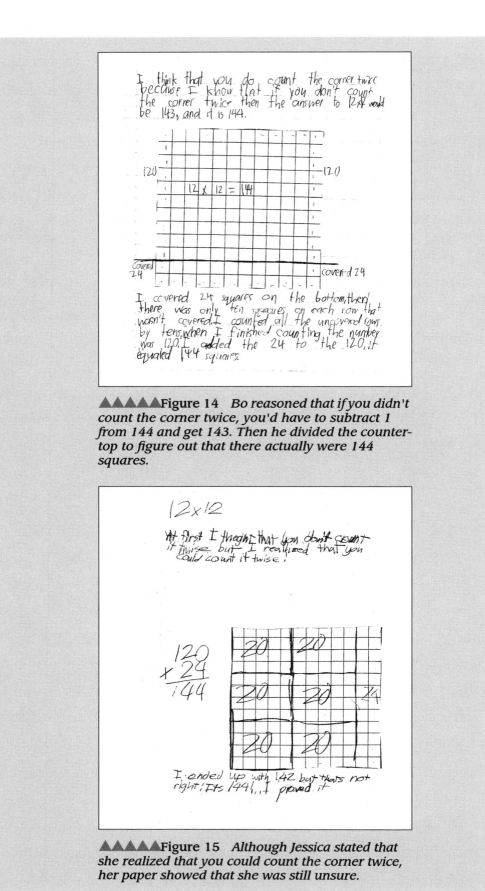

I think that you do count the corner twice because I know that if you don't count the corner twice then the answer to 12×f would be 143, and it is 144.

120   120

12 × 12 = 144

Covered 24   covered 24

I covered 24 squares on the bottom, then there was only ten squares on each row that wasn't covered. I counted all the uncovered rows by tens, when I finished counting the number was 120. I added the 24 to the 120, it equaled 144 squares.

▲▲▲▲▲▲**Figure 14**   *Bo reasoned that if you didn't count the corner twice, you'd have to subtract 1 from 144 and get 143. Then he divided the countertop to figure out that there actually were 144 squares.*

12 × 12

At first I thought that you don't count it twise but I realized that you could count it twise!

120
× 24
144

20   20

20   20   24

20   20

I ended up with 142 but thats not right. Its 144. I proved it

▲▲▲▲▲▲**Figure 15**   *Although Jessica stated that she realized that you could count the corner twice, her paper showed that she was still unsure.*

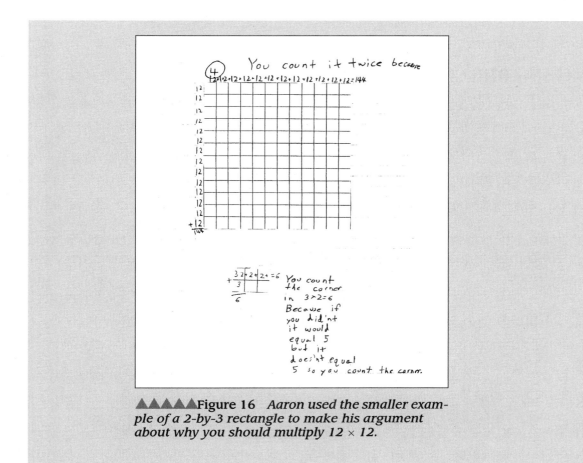

You count it twice because

$12+12+12+12+12+12+12+12+12+12+12+12=144$

You count the corner in $3 \times 2 = 6$ Because if you did'nt it would equal 5 but it does'nt equal 5 so you count the corner.

▲▲▲▲▲▲**Figure 16** *Aaron used the smaller example of a 2-by-3 rectangle to make his argument about why you should multiply 12 × 12.*

Why Is It True?

OVERVIEW

While reinforcing basic multiplication facts, this activity gives children experience looking for patterns, making conjectures, and explaining their reasoning. The activity also introduces children to square numbers, reinforcing how numbers and geometry connect. For an individual assignment, children analyze why 5 × 5 is one more than 4 × 6.

MATERIALS

▲ optional: color tiles, about 50 per student
▲ optional: centimeter squares, 1 sheet per student

TIME

▲ one class period

TEACHING DIRECTIONS

1. Write on the board two multiplication problems: *4 × 4* and *3 × 5*. (Notice that the factors in the second problem are one less and one more than the factors in the first problem, but don't reveal this to the class.) Tell the students that you used the first problem to write the second problem, and they are to be math detectives and figure out what you did.

2. Write another problem on the board: *5 × 5*. Ask: "What problem do you think I would write next to this one?" If a child answers incorrectly, respond that that isn't what you were thinking, that you had a particular pattern in mind and they were to figure it out. Continue having children guess until someone answers correctly—4 × 6 (or 6 × 4).

3. Continue with another example: *3 × 3*. Again have children guess the second problem until someone guesses correctly. Continue until your list goes from 1 × 1 to 10 × 10. Ask the children to provide answers for each.

1 × 1 = 1	*0 × 2 = 0*
2 × 2 = 4	*1 × 3 = 3*
3 × 3 = 9	*2 × 4 = 8*
4 × 4 = 16	*3 × 5 = 15*
5 × 5 = 25	*4 × 6 = 24*
6 × 6 = 36	*5 × 7 = 35*
7 × 7 = 49	*6 × 8 = 48*
8 × 8 = 64	*7 × 9 = 63*
9 × 9 = 81	*8 × 10 = 80*
10 × 10 = 100	*9 × 11 = 99*

4. Ask the children to look for patterns in the information. Accept all of their discoveries. If no one notices, point out the answers in each pair of problems differ by one; for example, 5 × 5 is one more than 4 × 6.

5. Represent a few problems from each column as rectangles (see next page). Discuss with the class why the rectangles that represent the problems in the left column are squares, and the rectangles from the right column aren't squares. Tell the children that numbers that can be represented as squares are called square numbers.

6. Ask children to think about why the answers to the pairs of problems differ by one. Encourage them to use color tiles or squared paper. After they have had time to explore, have a class discussion for them to share ideas. Finally, ask them to write about their reasoning.

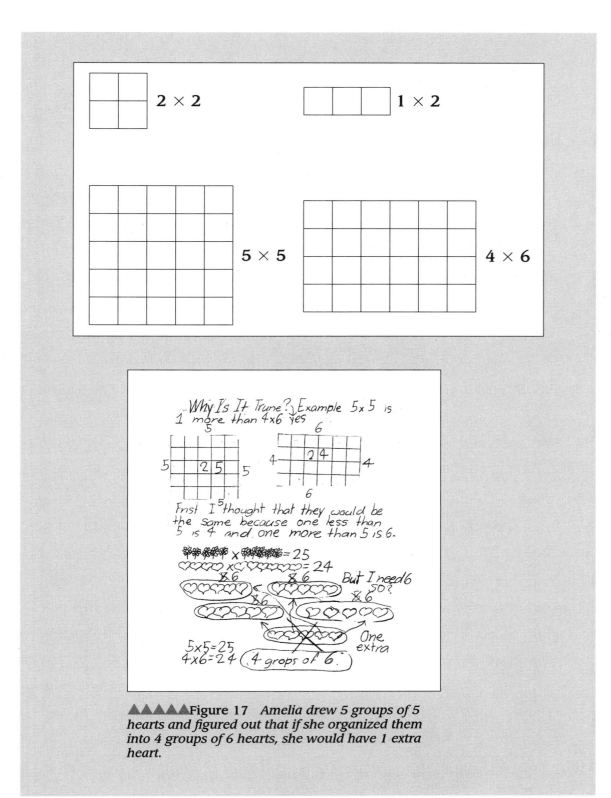

▲▲▲▲▲▲Figure 17   Amelia drew 5 groups of 5 hearts and figured out that if she organized them into 4 groups of 6 hearts, she would have 1 extra heart.

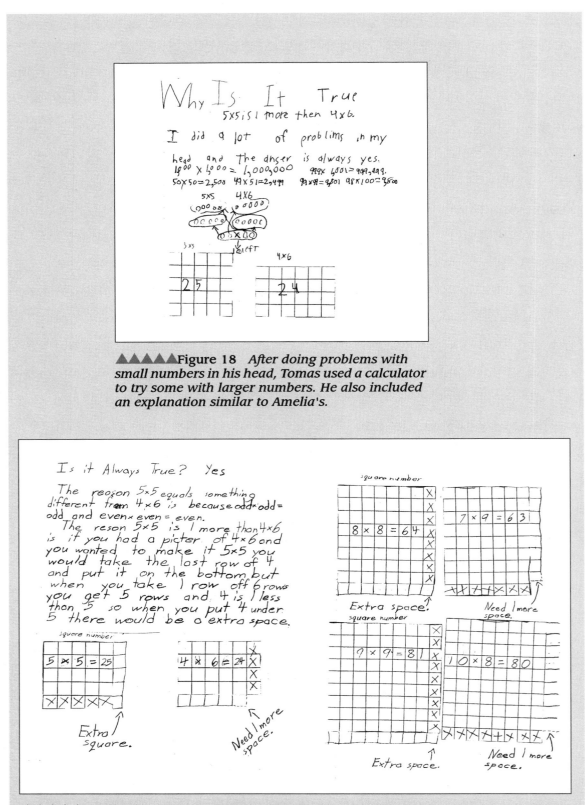

▲▲▲▲▲▲**Figure 18** *After doing problems with small numbers in his head, Tomas used a calculator to try some with larger numbers. He also included an explanation similar to Amelia's.*

▲▲▲▲▲▲**Figure 19** *Kelly incorporated odds and evens into her reasoning. After explaining why 5 × 5 is one more than 4 × 6, she explored 8 × 8 and 9 × 9.*

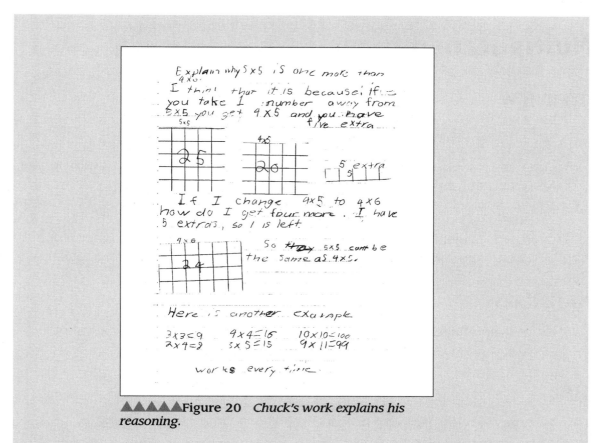

Explain why 5×5 is one more than 4×6.

I think that it is because if you take 1 number away from 5×5 you get 4×5 and you have five extra.

5×5

[25]

4×5

[20]

5 extra

If I change 4×5 to 4×6 how do I get four more. I have 5 extra's, so 1 is left.

4×6

[24]

So 5×5 can't be the same as 4×6.

Here is another example

3×3 = 9   9×4 = 16   10×10 = 100
2×4 = 8   3×5 = 15   9×11 = 99

works every time.

▲▲▲▲▲▲**Figure 20**   *Chuck's work explains his reasoning.*

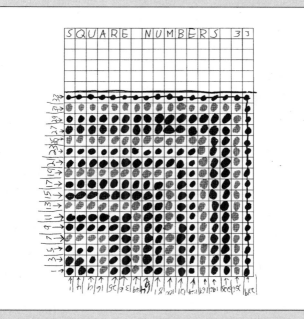

▲▲▲▲▲▲**Figure 21**   *Sam was delighted to discover a geometric way to show the pattern that square numbers increase by consecutive odd numbers.*

Multiplication Bingo

OVERVIEW

These two variations of Bingo provide a way to link instruction about probability and practice with basic multiplication facts. One version is played on a 5-by-5 grid with the center square free for everyone; the other is played on a 3-by-3 grid with no free space. Students make their own Bingo cards by filling in numbers. To play, roll two dice and have the children multiply the numbers that come up. Students who have that product on their Bingo cards mark it with an X. If the product appears more than once, they mark only one of them. The winner on the larger grid is the first to get a Bingo. For *Baby Bingo Blackout,* the version on the smaller grid, the winner is the first to mark all nine squares.

MATERIALS

▲ one-half-inch squares, at least 1 sheet per student
▲ 2 dice

TIME

▲ one class period to introduce; additional time for repeat games

TEACHING DIRECTIONS

1. Ask the children what they know about playing Bingo, and then explain to them how playing *Multiplication Bingo* is different. Explain that after you roll two dice, they multiply the two numbers that come up and then mark the product if it's on their Bingo cards. Also explain that they will make their own Bingo cards by outlining a 5-by-5 grid on squared paper and writing in twenty-four numbers of their choice. It's OK for them to write a particular number more than once.

2. Discuss the smallest and largest numbers that could come up from rolling two dice and multiplying. After you've established that the smallest possible product is one (1 × 1) and the largest is thirty-six (6 × 6), ask if all of the numbers in between are possible. Initially, children may think that this is so. You can either have them fill in numbers and play, giving them the opportunity from playing to realize that not all of the numbers are possible products, or take the time to discuss the possible products before they play.

3. Before you start rolling the dice, list the numbers from 1 to 36 on the board. As you roll each time, mark the product that comes up with a tally mark. Keep adding to this list as you play so that over time, children will have evidence about products that come up more often than others.

4. After the children are familiar with the game, lead a discussion about how products can be made. Use the list of numbers, and to the left of each, write the possible multiplication problem. Remember that you can use factors only from 1 to 6. Establish that there are eighteen possible products: 1, 2, 3, 4, 5, 6, 8, 9, 10, 12, 15, 16, 18, 20, 24, 25, 30, and 36. There is only one way to get some of them (1, 9, 16, 25, and 36). (Remember, only the numbers from 1 to 6 are possible factors.) Some numbers have two different ways to come up; for example, a product of 2 comes up if you have a 1 on one die and a 2 on the other or a 2 on the first die and a 1 on the other. (Thinking about the dice as being two different colors can help you understand this.) The number 4, however, has three possible ways to come up—1 × 4, 4 × 1, and 2 × 2—and 12 has four ways—2 × 6, 6 × 2, 3 × 4, and 4 × 3.

5. Introduce the rules for *Baby Bingo Blackout.* Children write numbers in all nine squares on a 3-by-3 grid. (There isn't a free space.) They may write numbers more than once. The first student who marks all nine numbers on his or her card wins. Again, keep track of the products with tally marks on the 1–36 chart.

6. These games are suitable to play at home. Ask children to write the rules for playing the games. Also, ask them to write about the strategies they use for choosing numbers for their cards.

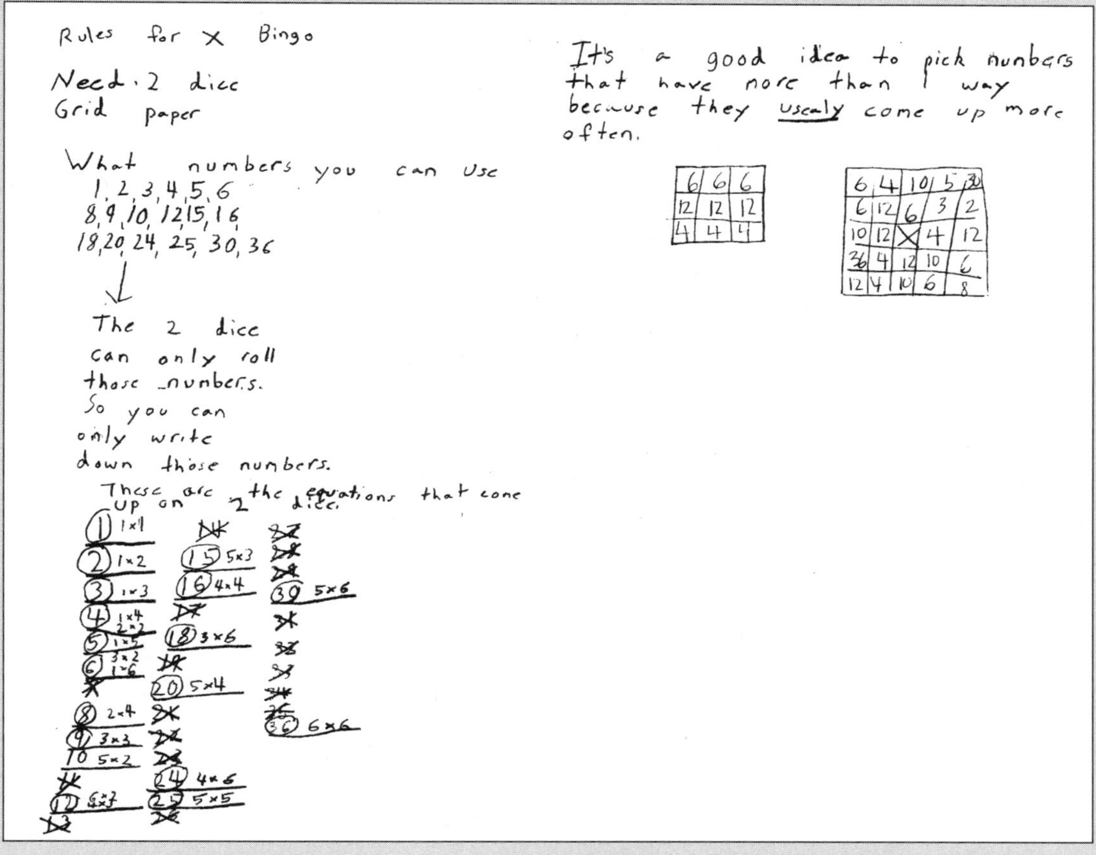

▲▲▲▲▲**Figure 22** *Aaron understood that some products come up more often than others, but he omitted some of the possible ways to make some products. See Ruthie's paper for a correct analysis.*

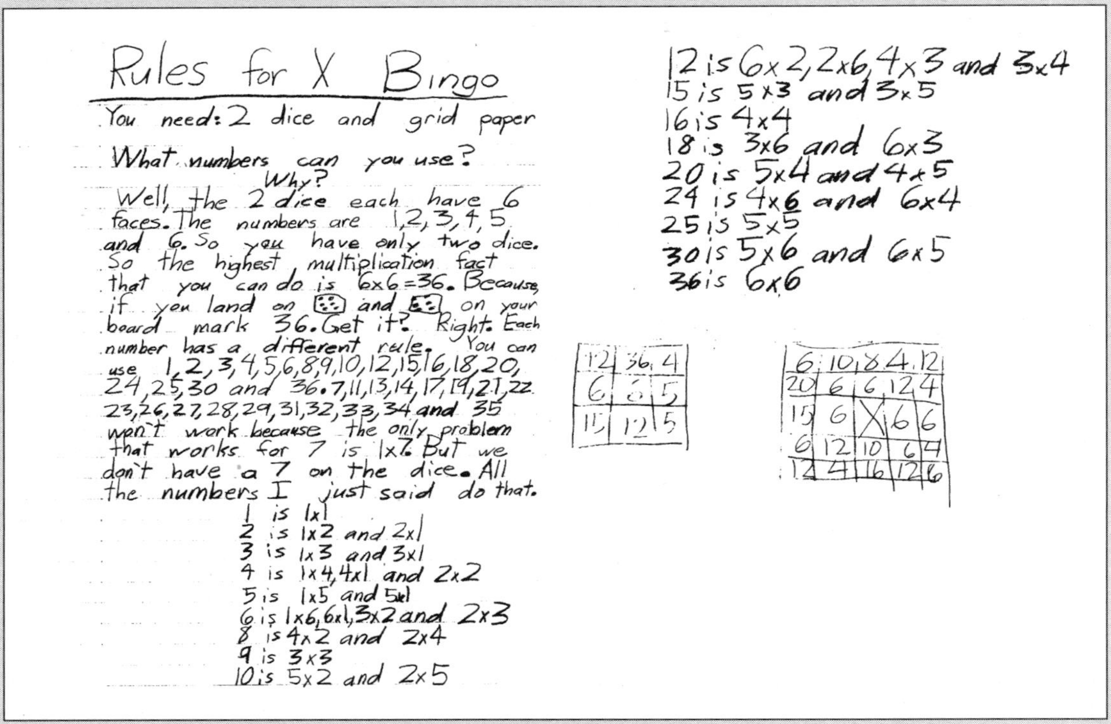

Rules for X Bingo

You need: 2 dice and grid paper

What numbers can you use?

Why?
Well, the 2 dice each have 6 faces. The numbers are 1,2,3,4,5 and 6. So you have only two dice. So the highest multiplication fact that you can do is 6x6=36. Because if you land on 🎲 and 🎲 on your board mark 36. Get it? Right! Each number has a different rule. You can use 1,2,3,4,5,6,8,9,10,12,15,16,18,20, 24,25,30 and 36. 7,11,13,14,17,19,21,22 23,26,27,28,29,31,32,33,34 and 35 won't work because the only problem that works for 7 is 1x7. But we don't have a 7 on the dice. All the numbers I just said do that.

1 is 1x1
2 is 1x2 and 2x1
3 is 1x3 and 3x1
4 is 1x4, 4x1 and 2x2
5 is 1x5 and 5x1
6 is 1x6, 6x1, 3x2 and 2x3
8 is 4x2 and 2x4
9 is 3x3
10 is 5x2 and 2x5

12 is 6x2, 2x6, 4x3 and 3x4
15 is 5x3 and 3x5
16 is 4x4
18 is 3x6 and 6x3
20 is 5x4 and 4x5
24 is 4x6 and 6x4
25 is 5x5
30 is 5x6 and 6x5
36 is 6x6

12	36	4
6	8	5
15	12	5

6	10	8	4	12
20	6	6	12	4
15	6	X	6	6
6	12	10	6	4
24	16	12	6	

▲▲▲▲▲▲**Figure 23** *Ruthie analyzed the products correctly, but she decided afterward that she used too many 6s for 5-by-5 Bingo.*

Rules for X Bingo

Frist you get cranos and 2 dice, grid paper. Then you make a 5 by 5 on the paper.

nambers on dice:
1,2,3,4,5,6, so whan you roll the dice it has to be one of the nambers on the dice x anouth namber on the dice.

nambers that could:
1,2,3,4,5,6,8,9,10,12, 15,16,18, 20,24,25,30, 36. You can't use 7 and up becase then the product of this nambers.

My striatry was to use the nambers that more likly to show up on my scunt one. I mostly used 6 and 12 becuse on the frist those mostly showed up. My stratrgy did work becaus I was thinking adout the nambers if they shoved up much on the frist game maybe they show up as much on the frist game and they did.

▲▲▲▲▲**Figure 24** *Sally explained that her strategy came from noticing which products came up more often.*

ASSESSMENTS

This section contains eight assessments that are useful for evaluating what students are learning as they study multiplication. The first assessment, *What Is Multiplication?*, is useful before beginning multiplication instruction as a way to collect information about children's prior knowledge. The other assessments are appropriate after students have experienced introductory lessons such as those presented by the first three chapters in this book. *Interpreting 6 × 5* provides information about children's understanding of the standard symbolism of multiplication. *A Multiplication Story Problem* reveals if children can connect multiplication to a real-world situation. *Why Does 3 × 5 = 5 × 3?* provides insights into students' understanding of the commutative property of multiplication. *Which Box Holds More?* measures students' ability to relate multiplication to rectangles. *Solving Brandon's Problem* and *Ways to Solve 7 × 6* are opportunities to assess children's strategies for computing. Finally, *What Is Multiplication? (Revisited)* provides a comparison with what children wrote when beginning to study multiplication.

Teaching Notes

Assessing what children are learning is a continual process. Teachers learn about what students understand from listening to what they say during class discussions, from observing and listening to them as they work on independent activities, and from reading their written work. But not all children contribute regularly in class discussions and, therefore, whole-class discussions don't necessarily provide sufficient information about every student. Also, when students work on activities, they often work with partners or in small groups and, therefore, a child's knowledge or lack of knowledge can be masked. For these reasons, it's useful and important to assess children periodically with assignments that they complete individually and in writing.

The assessments presented in this section are similar to the instructional activities in this book in that they are opportunities for children to continue their learning about multiplication. Writing requires thinking, and any opportunity to focus on a topic can enhance learning. Not only do such papers provide valuable information about individual students, but class sets of responses provide useful information about the overall effectiveness of the instruction provided.

It's important, however, to realize that these particular assessments won't provide all the information necessary for a complete and comprehensive picture of each child's understanding. The work that students do on all of the activities in the book is also useful for tracking their strengths, weaknesses, and growth. One way that I've found particularly helpful to facilitate assessment is to set up file folders for the students and keep in them copies of all work they do that provides insights into their thinking. This sometimes requires making copies of papers they've worked on collaboratively or would like to take home to share, but creating a chronological record of each child's progress is well worth the effort.

What Is Multiplication?

PROMPT

Write everything you know about multiplication. Include ideas you think may be right but you aren't sure about and also things others have told you about multiplication.

Many children have some familiarity with multiplication before formal instruction begins in third grade. They may have learned about multiplication in second grade or at home from parents or older brothers and sisters. Even with prior experience, however, most children do not have a comprehensive understanding of what multiplication is or how it's used.

It's helpful to precede this assignment with a class discussion. Tell the children that they'll be studying multiplication and that you're interested in learning about what they already know. Hear from all volunteers and accept their thoughts without judgment or correction. You may want to ask children to clarify their ideas, but don't push too hard. This is not a time to teach but, rather, to collect information about the range of understanding and experience in the class.

After all interested children have responded aloud, give the directions for the assignment. The students' writing will give you information about those who didn't vol-

What is multiplication?

Multiplacation is like addition but it's diffrent for example: Ten plus ten is diffrent from ten times ten, because ten times ten is ten tens, and ten plus ten is two tens. Do you understand? If you don't understand, I'll try to explain.

▲▲▲▲▲▲**Figure 1** *Tanya explained how multiplication relates to addition.*

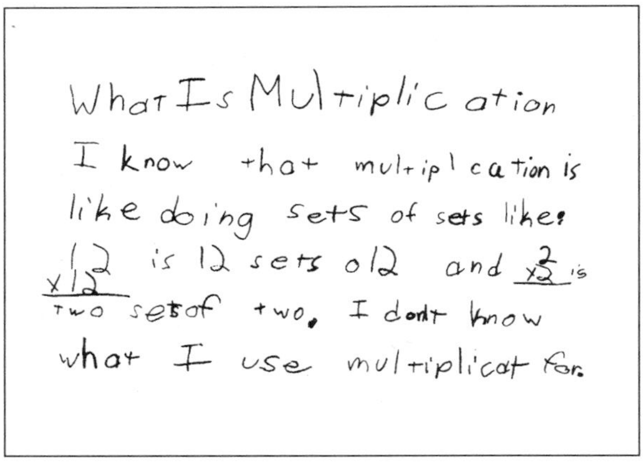

What Is MUltiplication
I know that multiplication is like doing sets of sets like: 12 is 12 sets of 2 and 2 x 2 is two set of two. I don't know what I use multiplicat for.

▲▲▲▲▲▲**Figure 2** *Sam's paper told what he did and didn't understand about multiplication.*

unteer their thoughts and will clarify the general perceptions you got from the class discussion. Tell the children that they'll have a chance to write again after they've studied about multiplication and will then have a chance to see what they've learned.

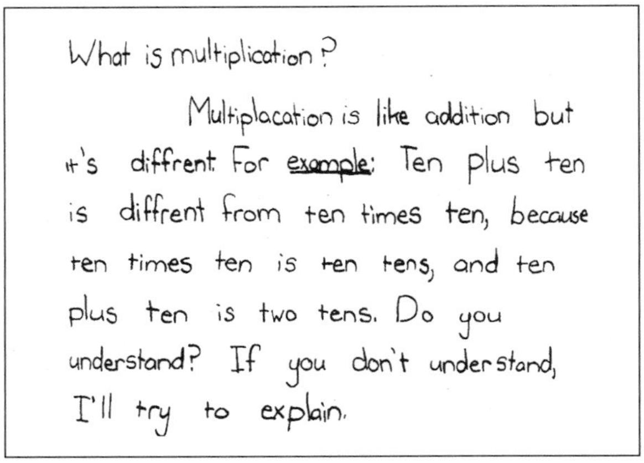

Interpreting 6 × 5

PROMPT

Write about what you think of when you see 6 × 5. Include all the different ways you can think of to interpret this multiplication fact. Also, explain how you could find the answer if you couldn't remember it.

This assignment helps convey the message to children that it's important for them to learn to think and reason, not merely to memorize. When you begin teaching multiplication, your instruction should not emphasize memorization but instead should focus on helping children develop understanding. They should learn to interpret the meaning of multiplication and develop strategies for computing answers. Therefore, instead of testing students' knowledge of the times tables, this assessment asks them to explain the meaning of one particular fact: 6 × 5.

Because most children learned the multiples of five as a childhood chant, they find the fives times table fairly easy to learn and may already know the answer to 6 × 5. It's for that reason that this particular problem makes sense. Then the assessment won't present a numerical hardship for most students and can reveal their current perceptions of multiplication.

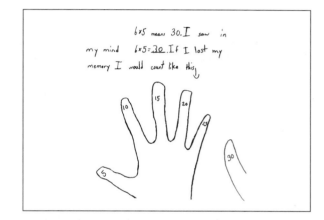

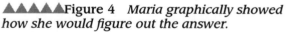Figure 3   *Brandon showed he understood the idea that multiplication is commutative.*

▲▲▲▲▲▲Figure 4   *Maria graphically showed how she would figure out the answer.*

A Multiplication Story Problem

PROMPT

Write a multiplication story problem.

   1. Your story must end with a question.

   2. You should be able to answer the question by multiplying.

After writing your story problem, solve it in at least two ways.

Use this assessment a week or so after the students have had experience relating multiplication to real-world contexts (see Chapters 4, 5, and 6). Students' story problems reveal if they are able to create a situation from the world around them that relates to multiplication. A key element to look for when assessing children's problems is that they involve combining equal groups of some sort and, therefore, present a problem that can be represented by and solved with multiplication. When examining children's solutions, keep in mind that it's typical for children, when solving multiplication problems in more than one way, to include a solution that uses addition. This is appropriate and tells you that the child sees how multiplication and addition are related.

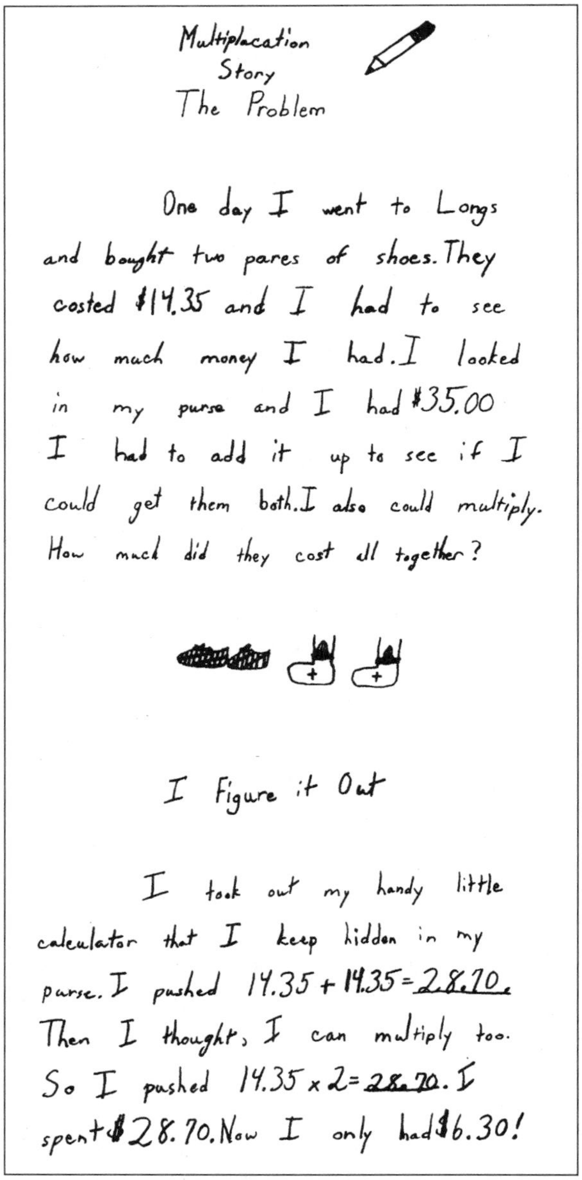

Multiplacation
Story
The Problem

One day I went to Longs and bought two pares of shoes. They costed $14.35 and I had to see how much money I had. I looked in my purse and I had $35.00 I had to add it up to see if I could get them both. I also could multiply. How much did they cost all together?

I Figure it Out

I took out my handy little calculator that I keep hidden in my purse. I pushed 14.35 + 14.35 = 28.70. Then I thought, I can multiply too. So I pushed 14.35 x 2 = 28.70. I spent $28.70. Now I only had $6.30!

▲▲▲▲▲▲**Figure 5** *Maria's work showed that she understood how mulitplication and addition are related. The calculator gave her the ability to work with numbers that might have been too difficult otherwise.*

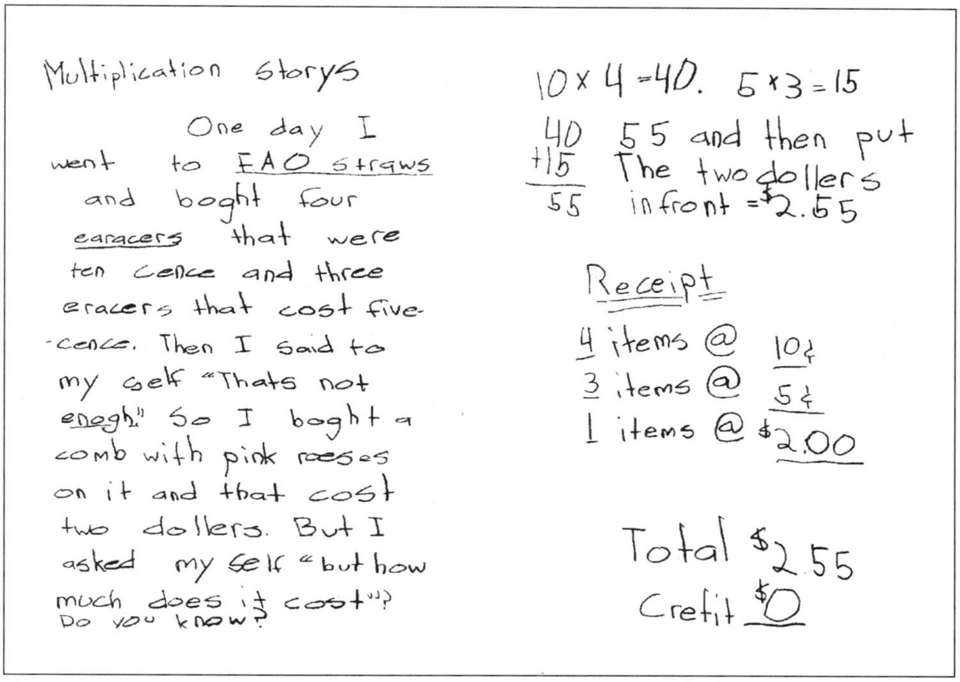

Multiplication storys

One day I
went to FAO straws
and boght four
earacers that were
ten cence and three
eracers that cost five-
cence. Then I said to
my self "Thats not
enogh." So I boght a
comb with pink roeses
on it and that cost
two dollers. But I
asked my self "but how
much does it cost"?
Do you know?

10 × 4 = 40.   5 × 3 = 15

  40   55 and then put
 +15   The two dollers
 ___   infront = $2.55
  55

Receipt

4 items @ 10¢
3 items @ 5¢
1 items @ $2.00

Total $2.55
Crefit $0

▲▲▲▲▲▲Figure 6   *Emily wrote a story, solved it, and made a receipt to show a second solution, as she had done when working on* Billy Wins a Shopping Spree *(see Chapter 6).*

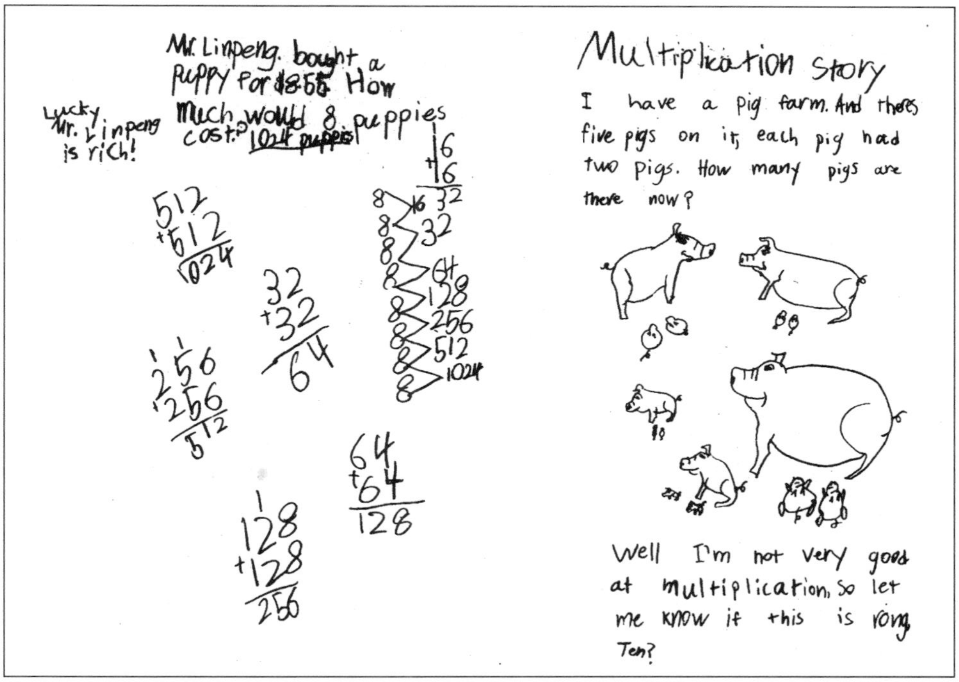

Mr. Linpeng. bought a
puppy for $8.00 How
much would 8 puppies
cost? 1024 puppies

Lucky
Mr. Linpeng
is rich!

512
+512
1024

 256
+256
 512

  1
 128
+128
 256

 32
+32
 64

 8
 8
 8
 8
 8
 8
 8

16
+16
32

32

64
128
256
512
1024

 64
+64
 128

Multiplication story

I have a pig farm. And thers
five pigs on it, each pig had
two pigs. How many pigs are
there now?

Well I'm not very good
at multiplication, so let
me know if this is rong
Ten?

▲▲▲▲▲▲Figure 7   *Karin wrote two problems, and although they correctly related to multiplication, her solutions revealed her confusion.*

Why Does $3 \times 5 = 5 \times 3$?

PROMPT

Explain why $3 \times 5 = 5 \times 3$. Use words, numbers, and pictures.

Commutativity is an important property of multiplication. From the lessons in this book, children have experience using the commutative property when solving problems, and this assessment provides information about their understanding of why reversing the order of factors doesn't affect products. Notice that the prompt does not include the mathematical terminology of *commutative, factor,* or *product.* The emphasis here is on the children's understanding of the concept without the interference of interpreting terminology. However, if your students are comfortable with the terminology, then you might want to reword the prompt. Also, you might want to make an addition to the prompt, asking children to include a reference to rectangles in their explanations so you can see how they connect multiplication to the geometric interpretation of rectangular arrays.

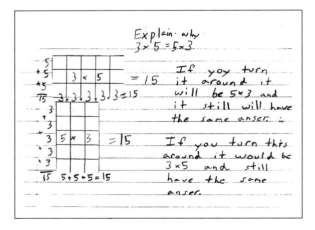

▲▲▲▲▲▲**Figure 8** *Aaron cut out rectangles and also used repeated addition to explain why $3 \times 5 = 5 \times 3$.*

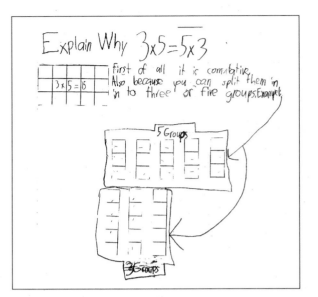

▲▲▲▲▲▲**Figure 9** *Bo split a 3–by–5 rectangle two ways to show 3 groups of 5 and 5 groups of 3.*

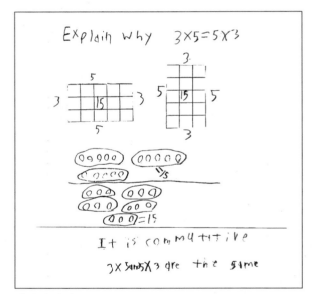

▲▲▲▲▲▲**Figure 10** *Tomas explained the commutative property in two ways.*

Which Box Holds More?

PROMPT

One box measures 8" by 6" and another box measures 9" by 5". They are the same height. Which box holds more?

This assessment presents a problem situation that relates to the candy box research the children did (see Chapter 7). The children compare two boxes that have the same height. The student work is useful for assessing whether children relate multiplication to rectangles and the approaches they use for computing.

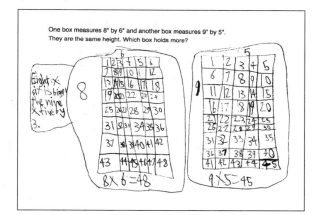

▲▲▲▲▲▲**Figure 11** *After drawing the boxes, Brian numbered the squares to figure out the area of each. He included in his solution that the 8"–by–6" box was larger by 3.*

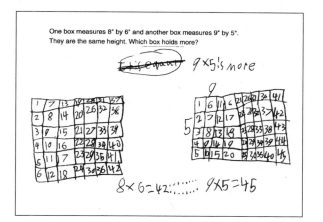

▲▲▲▲▲▲**Figure 12** *As Brian did, James drew boxes and numbered the squares. However, he drew a 7"-by-6" box instead of an 8"-by-6" box and thus arrived at the wrong conclusion.*

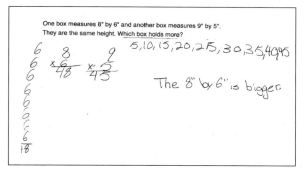

▲▲▲▲▲▲**Figure 13** *Rebecca didn't draw rectangles but figured the answers numerically.*

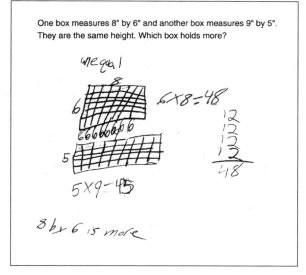

▲▲▲▲▲▲**Figure 14** *Kim drew rectangles. She knew the answer for 5 × 9 and added to figure out 8 × 6.*

Solving Brandon's Problem

PROMPT

Brandon, a third grader, wrote the following multiplication story problem. Figure out the answer and explain your reasoning.

> *Once I went up to my uncle's farm. He had 13 hens and they each laid 8 eggs. And he had 4 chickens and they each laid 2 eggs. How many eggs were there altogether?*

This problem is one that Brandon actually had written for *A Multiplication Story Problem,* the assessment described on page 158. I planned to use these children's stories for choice time, having children solve one another's problems. I introduced Brandon's problem not only to assess the students but also as a way to introduce this choice time option.

I selected Brandon's problem for this assessment for several reasons. First of all, it's a two-step problem, representative of the more complicated story problems children should learn to solve. Also, the numbers were large enough to be interesting for the more confident students while still being accessible to the others. Finally, it was a way to acknowledge Brandon, a boy who needed encouragement. Of course, you can change the problem, either selecting one written by one of your students or choosing any other problem you think would be more appropriate for your class. Emphasize to the students that they should explain their reasoning and display their calculations.

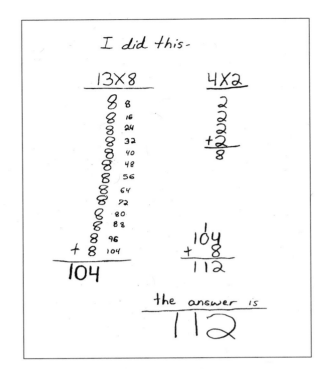

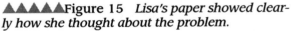

▲▲▲▲▲▲Figure 15 *Lisa's paper showed clearly how she thought about the problem.*

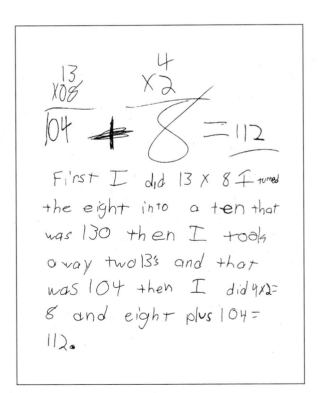

▲▲▲▲▲▲Figure 16 *Although the children hadn't been formally introduced to the distributive property, Sam explained how he used the principle in his solution.*

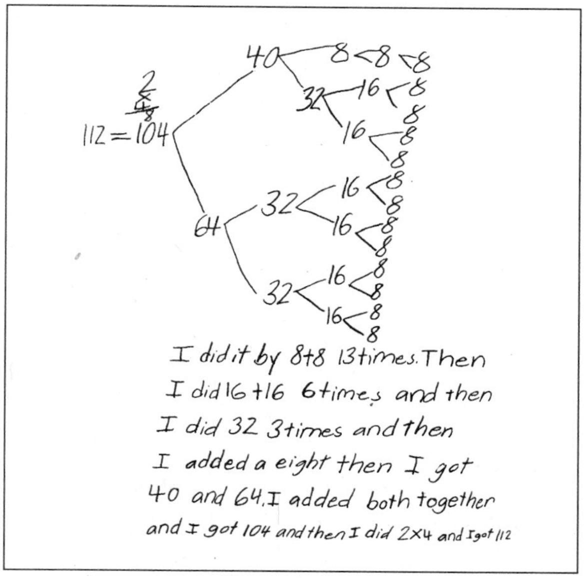

I did it by 8+8 13times. Then
I did 16 +16 6times and then
I did 32 3times and then
I added a eight then I got
40 and 64. I added both together
and I got 104 and then I did 2X4 and I got 112

▲▲▲▲▲▲Figure 17 *Michael organized the numbers from the problem in a visual way that made sense to him. His approach was not standard, but it was effective.*

Ways to Solve 7 × 6

PROMPT

Solve 7 × 6 in at least two ways. Explain your reasoning.

While an earlier assessment suggests that children interpret 6 × 5, this assessment asks children to figure out the answer to a fact with which they may not be as familiar. Giving this assessment some time later than *Interpreting 6 × 5* gives you a way to assess children's progress. When you examine both sets of papers, look to see if children used the same way to figure answers in both instances or how their approaches changed.

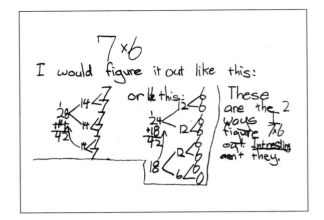

▲▲▲▲▲▲**Figure 19** *Tanya wasn't able to recall the answer for this fact as she had for 6 × 5. She showed two ways that she could figure out the solution.*

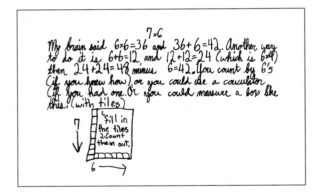

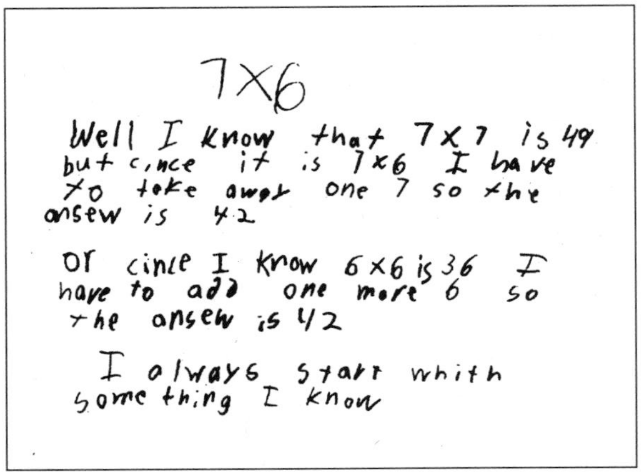

▲▲▲▲▲▲**Figure 18** *Emma included several numerical approaches to figuring the answer and also provided a geometric interpretation.*

▲▲▲▲▲▲**Figure 20** *Josh's strategy was to start with what he knew—a friendly number, he called it.*

What Is Multiplication? (Revisited)

PROMPT

What does multiplication have to do with addition? Geometry? Real-life situations? What methods do you use to multiply?

The primary focus of this assessment is not children's numerical proficiency, but their overall understanding of multiplication. What do children now understand about multiplication? What misconceptions do they have? How do these differ from their perceptions before the instruction unit began? Ask the children to write all that they know about multiplication, as they did previously. Before students get to work on this assignment, I've found it to be helpful to list on the board and review with them the lessons they experienced while studying multiplication.

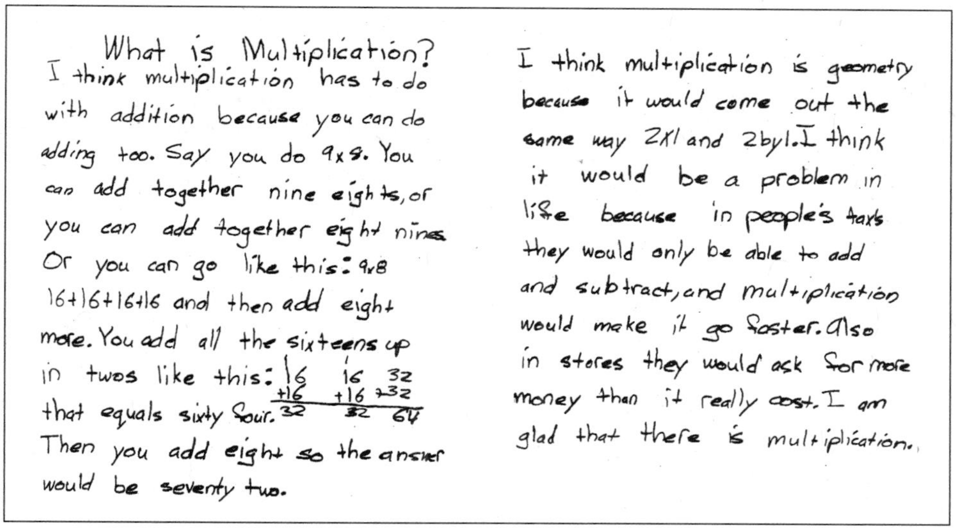

What is Multiplication?
I think multiplication has to do with addition because you can do adding too. Say you do 9x8. You can add together nine eights, or you can add together eight nines Or you can go like this: 9x8 16+16+16+16 and then add eight more. You add all the sixteens up in twos like this: 16 16 32 / +16 +16 +32 / that equals sixty four. 32 32 64 Then you add eight so the answer would be seventy two.

I think multiplication is geometry because it would come out the same way 2x1 and 2by1. I think it would be a problem in life because in people's taxs they would only be able to add and subtract, and multiplication would make it go foster. Also in stores they would ask for more money than it really cost. I am glad that there is multiplication.

▲▲▲▲▲▲**Figure 21** *Rebecca included specific information about how she related addition and multiplication.*

What is Multiplacation?
I think what multiplacation has to do with addition is this: the sign is all most the same x + see? But the way they are used is the way they're really the same, because the sum gets larger not smaller like division & subtraction, in them, they both get smaller

I think what X has to do with geometry is this: 5 $\overset{by}{\underset{\wedge}{4}}$ is the same as 5 times 4.

I think what X has to do with real life is this: when you buy 3 cans of beans that each cost 3 dollars you need to know what 3×3 is, I know it the answer is 9.

This is how you do X: If it's 5 you count by 5's if it's 3 you count by 3's ect.

▲▲▲▲▲▲Figure 22 *Tanya clearly addressed each of the questions posed in the directions.*

What is multiplucation?
Multiplucation has to do with math because when you have the problem 2×10 you can just go 10+10 and you will get the same anser wich is 20. Multiplucation has to do with geometry because if you have a rectangle that's a 6×5 you can just do the problem and you will know there are 30 squares. Multiplucation has to do with real life because if you are at a store and you have 35 dollars and you want to buy three things and each of them costs ten dollars and you want to know if you have enough money you do 3×10 and you will have 5 dollars extra.

▲▲▲▲▲▲Figure 23 *Michael's paper demonstrated his understanding.*

BLACKLINE MASTERS

Circles and Stars Class Chart

1	19
2	20
3	21
4	22
5	23
6	24
7	25
8	26
9	27
10	28
11	29
12	30
13	31
14	32
15	33
16	34
17	35
18	36

From *Lessons for Introducing Multiplication, Grade 3* by Marilyn Burns. © 2001 Math Solutions Publications

Multiplication Stories

Estimate   Equation   _____

10

20

30   Problem   _____

40   _____

50   _____

60   _____

70   _____

80   _____

90   _____

100   _____

>100

Figuring

From *Lessons for Introducing Multiplication, Grade 3* by Marilyn Burns. © 2001 Math Solutions Publications

Which Has More Cookies?

___ rows with ___ cookies in each row

or ___ rows with ___ cookies in each row

_____

From *Lessons for Introducing Multiplication, Grade 3* by Marilyn Burns. © 2001 Math Solutions Publications

Which Has More Windowpanes?

a window with ___ rows of panes with ___ panes in each

or   a window with ___ rows of panes with ___ panes in each

_____

From *Lessons for Introducing Multiplication, Grade 3* by Marilyn Burns. © 2001 Math Solutions Publications

Which Has More Wheels?

_____ bicycles

or _____ tricycles

_____

Science Museum Store Price List

$3.00	$4.00	$5.00
1. Origami paper	1. Kaleidoscope	1. Koosh ball
2. Crystal and gem magnets	2. Large magnifying bug box	2. Glow-in-the-dark solar system stickers
3. Furry stuffed seal pups	3. Sunprint kit	3. Inflatable world globe
4. Prism	4. Inflatable shark	4. Wooden dinosaur model kit

Candy Box Research

You need: color tiles

one-half-inch squares

scissors

tape

1. Use color tiles to build all the rectangular boxes possible for 6, 12, and 24 candies.

2. Cut out each box from one-half-inch squares and label its dimensions.

3. Write a memo to the president explaining what you've learned about possible boxes and what shape box you recommend. Include your cutout boxes with your memo.

From *Lessons for Introducing Multiplication, Grade 3* by Marilyn Burns. © 2001 Math Solutions Publications

More Candy Box Research

You need: color tiles

one-half-inch squares

scissors

tape

bag with numbers

1. Pick a number from the bag.

2. Use the tiles to find all possible rectangles for that number.

3. Cut each rectangle you build out of one-half-inch squares and label.

4. Tape the rectangles on the class chart.

5. Repeat for another number from the bag.

One-Half-Inch Squares

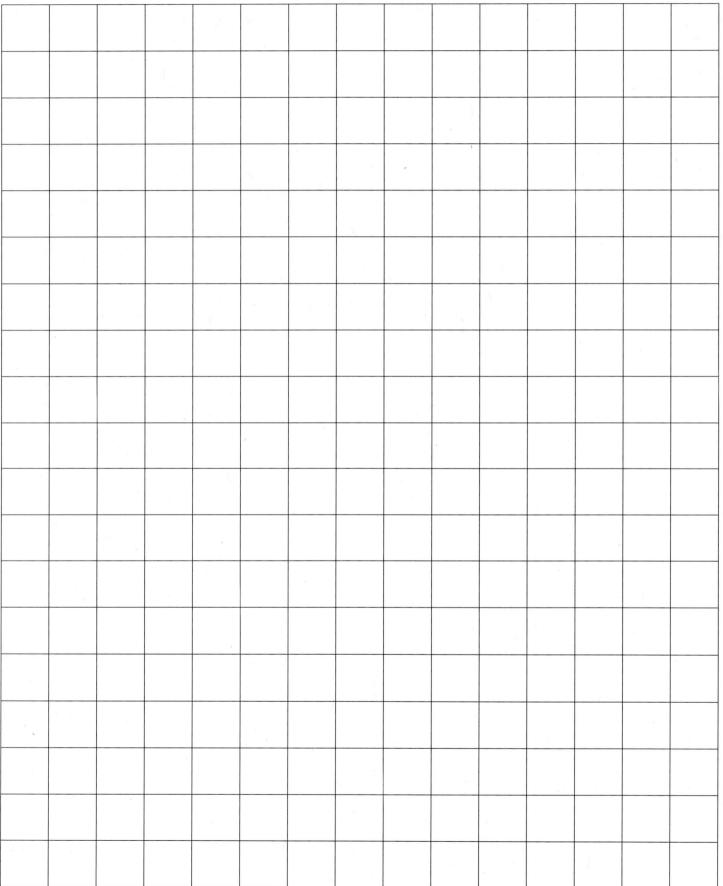

From *Lessons for Introducing Multiplication, Grade 3* by Marilyn Burns. © 2001 Math Solutions Publications

How Long? How Many?

You need: Cuisenaire rods

a die

How Long? How Many? record sheet

a partner

1. Each partner uses a different record sheet.

2. On your turn, roll the die twice. The first roll tells how long a Cuisenaire rod to use. The second roll tells how many rods to take.

3. Arrange the rods into a rectangle. Trace it on your grid. Write the multiplication equation inside.

4. When one person is blocked and can't place a rectangle because there's no room on the grid, you both stop.

5. Figure out how many squares on your grid are covered and how many are uncovered. Check each other's answers.

How Long? How Many? Record Sheet

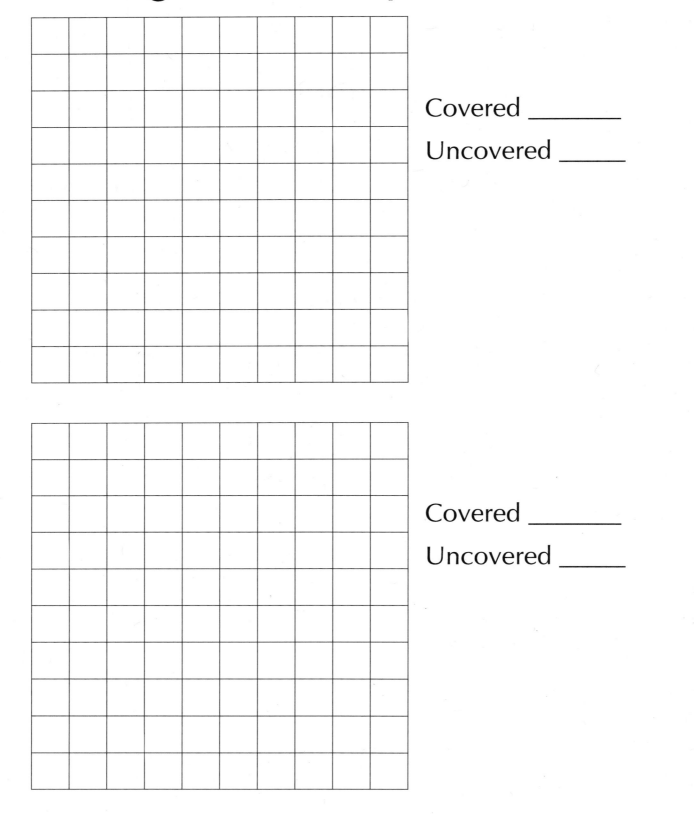

Covered _____

Uncovered _____

Covered _____

Uncovered _____

Centimeter Squares

Patterns in Multiples

You need: *Things That Come in Groups* charts

0–99 chart

1. Choose an item from one of the *Things That Come in Groups* charts.

2. List at least 12 multiples, and write a multiplication equation for each.

people	eyes	
1	2	$1 \times 2 = 2$
2	4	$2 \times 2 = 4$
3	6	$3 \times 2 = 6$
.	.	
.	.	
.	.	

3. Color the multiples on a 0–99 chart. Then continue the coloring pattern to the end of the chart.

4. Write about the patterns you see in the numbers on your list and on the 0–99 chart.

0–99 Chart

0	1	2	3	4	5	6	7	8	9
10	11	12	13	14	15	16	17	18	19
20	21	22	23	24	25	26	27	28	29
30	31	32	33	34	35	36	37	38	39
40	41	42	43	44	45	46	47	48	49
50	51	52	53	54	55	56	57	58	59
60	61	62	63	64	65	66	67	68	69
70	71	72	73	74	75	76	77	78	79
80	81	82	83	84	85	86	87	88	89
90	91	92	93	94	95	96	97	98	99

Calculator Patterns

You need: a calculator

                a partner

1. Clear your calculator.

2. Choose a number from 2 to 10, write it down, and then press it on the calculator.

3. Press the "+" key.

4. Press the "=" key. (You should see the same number you first entered.)

5. Keep pressing the "=" key, each time listing the number that comes up. Continue until you have written at least twelve numbers.

6. Write about the patterns you notice.

From *Lessons for Introducing Multiplication, Grade 3* by Marilyn Burns. © 2001 Math Solutions Publications

INDEX

critical thinking. *See* reasoning
cubes
    creating statistical data with, 133–35
    measuring volume with, 131–32
Cuisenaire rods
    arranging in rectangles, 79–80
    for *How Many? How Long?* lesson, 77–87

diagonal patterns, 107, 108, 113
dice
    alternatives to, 21
    for Circles and Stars, 11, 16
    for *How Many? How Long?* lesson, 77, 79
    with numbers from 1–10, 86
distributive property, 44
    assessment, 164
dozen, 70

ellipses (...), 115
equal groups, 24, 27
    in 12, 92–93
    in 100, 89, 90–92
    relating rectangles to, 69
    in student story problems, 156
    student understanding of, 37
errors
    learning from, 47
    in receipts, 65
    recording, 58
    in rectangles, 87
    spelling, 109–10
estimating
    from multiples of 10, 35, 36–37, 40
    student understanding of, 36–37
even numbers
    adding, 55
    factors, 135–38
    as multiples even numbers, 111
    as multiples of two, 74, 101
    multiplying, 56, 111, 135–38
    patterns, 120
    products of, 135–38
    zero as, 101
Evens and Odds, 131, 135–38
extensions, xiii

factors
    of 100, 88, 118
    combining, 57
    correct order of, 25, 29, 34
    even, 135–38
    finding, with rectangles, 70–73, 74
    introducing, 116
    in *Multiplication Bingo,* 150–51
    multiplication by zero and, 127
    odd, 135–38

for one, 105
    order of, 23–25, 29, 34, 44–45, 160
    for prime numbers, 105
    using term with children, 125, 130, 160
five
    counting by, 33
    counting to 100 by, 114, 117
"friendly numbers," 164

geometric representation, 77, 79, 131–32
    area, 139–41
    perimeter, 139–41
grouping objects, 1–10
    brainstorming, 6
    commutative property and, 23–27
    in equal groups, 24, 27, 37
    parent letter, 9
    student disagreement about, 6–7
    by twos, 2, 3–5
    value of, 1
    by various numbers, 5–6, 6–8
    writing solutions to, 2, 6, 10
"groups of," multiplication as, xiv

half-dozen, 70
homework
    Billy Wins a Shopping Spree lesson, 61
    Circles and Stars, 21
    Things That Come in Groups lesson, 8–9
horizontal patterns, 107, 109, 113
How Long? How Many? lesson, 77–87
    challenge problems, 86
    directions, Blackline Master, 177
    extension, 86
    lesson, 79–86
    materials, 77
    overview, 77
    questions and discussion, 87
    record sheet, 79, 80
    record sheet, Blackline Master, 178
    teaching directions, 77–79
    teaching notes, 79
    time required for, 77
How Many Cubes?, 131, 133–35
How Many Were Eaten?, 131–32

incorrect answers. *See* errors
Interpreting 6 × 5, 157

lessons
    purpose of, xiii
    structure of, xiii
    using, xiv–xv

materials
    exploring, 76

materials (continued)
    for lessons, xiii
Math By All Means: Multiplication, Grade 3 (Burns),
    xi
mathematical ability
    partner work and, 122
    range of, 22, 51, 117
mathematical language
    introducing to children, 113
    using terms with children, 125, 130, 160
mean, 134
median, 134
memo writing, for candy box research problem,
    70–71
mental calculation, 17
Mode, 134
money, as reference for numbers, 121
More Candy Box Research
    directions, 66
    directions, Blackline Master, 175
    research problem, 68, 73–75
multiples
    adding digits of, 119
    coloring in 0-to-99 charts, 100–101, 102
    creating table of, 108
    defining for students, 113
    even, 111
    finding with calculators, 114, 115, 117–18
    introducing, 116
    odd, 111
    patterns in, 99–113
    of ten, estimating from, 35, 36–37, 40
    of two, 74, 101
multiplication
    addition of even and odd numbers and,
        55–56
    addition vs., 49, 50, 57
    area measurement and, 66, 69
    assessing student understanding of, xi–xii,
        156, 165–66
    checking with addition, 26
    commutative property, xiv, 14, 23–27, 29, 33,
        34, 45, 125, 127, 128, 130, 157, 158
    comparing products, 48–58
    counting and, 10, 24, 25, 29, 30, 33, 38, 74, 87,
        106
    defined, 4
    distributive property, 44, 164
    figuring with addition, 28, 32–33
    geometric representation of, 77, 79, 131–32,
        139–41
    as "groups of," xiv
    instruction goals, xii
    pictorial representation of, 14, 38
    reasoning vs. memorization of facts, 157
    rectangles and, 66, 69–76, 142–45
    as repeated addition, 11, 56–57, 114, 115,
        117, 123

strategies, 32–33, 38–40
    writing equations, 23–24, 28, 29–30
    by zero, 100, 124, 126–29, 130
Multiplication Bingo, 131, 150–53
multiplication sentences
    for factors of 100, 89
    order of factors in, 23–25, 29, 34, 44–45
    reading aloud, 14, 106–07
    for rectangles, 80
    teaching students to write, 12, 18, 106–07
    understanding the meaning of, 34
    value of, 14
    writing, 24, 27–28, 38
Multiplication Stories lesson, 35–47
    Blackline Master, 169
    lesson, 37–46
    materials, 35
    observing students, 41–43
    overview, 35
    questions and discussion, 47
    teaching directions, 35–36
    teaching notes, 36–37
    time required for, 35
    worksheet, 35
Multiplication Story Problem, A, 158–59
multiplication strategies
    assessment, 164
    testing, 55–57
multiplication symbolism, xiv, 18
multiplication tables, xii, 15

Neushwander, Cindy, 23
nonparticipating students, 58
numerical patterns, 105

observation
    Circles and Stars lesson, 18
    Multiplication Stories lesson, 41–43
    value of, 18
odd numbers
    adding, 55–56
    factors, 135–38
    as multiples, 111
    multiplying, 56
    patterns, 120
    as products, 20–21
    products of, 135–38
one
    counting to 100 by, 114
    factors for, 105
    prime numbers and, 105
one-half-inch squares
    Blackline Masters, 176
    for *Candy Boxes* lesson, 66
    for *Multiplication Bingo*, 150
one hundred (100)
    adding to, 81
    arrays of 100 items, 90–98